NEVER STAY DOWN

NEVER STAY DOWN

MIKE BURTON

AN AUTOBIOGRAPHY

MIKE BURTON
AND
STEVE JONES

Queen Anne Press
Macdonald and Co London and Sydney

First published in 1982 by Queen Anne Press,
a division of Macdonald & Co (Publishers) Ltd,
Holywell House, Worship Street, London EC2A 2EN

ISBN 0356 08565 1

Photoset by Cylinder Typesetting Ltd, London

Printed in Great Britain by Hazell, Watson & Viney
Aylesbury, Bucks

CONTENTS

1
DIGGER

A large and almost oval face was looking down at me, framed by the sort of cauliflower ears which can only belong to old rugby forwards. The general impression was that of the FA Cup tilting over and peering down. I was concussed and bleeding and the only one of my senses in full working order was that of taste. I could taste my own blood as it slid down the back of my throat – and it didn't taste good. I was fifteen, and making my first appearance for Longlevens rugby club. For weeks after I had joined the club, they had made me reserve. I had never taken the field. I had bought a pair of shorts for 22s 6d, a pair of socks for 8s 6d from Hudson's of Gloucester and I was bursting to wear them. But I was always reserve.

One Saturday I was boarding the coach for a third XV match against Cairnscross, to act as reserve once again. Then came the glad, thrilling tidings. Someone had withdrawn from the team and I was in. I didn't care if the player who had dropped out had done so because he was injured, stricken with plague, or been shot by a jealous husband. At last I was going to play for Longlevens and get some mud on those gleaming shorts.

I put on my sparkling kit and went out on to the field and the game started. Then, not for the first time in my career, someone hit me. A cracking good effort it was too, and down I went in a heap. Eventually I came round and tried to focus my eyes on those great cauliflower shapes. They belonged to Digger Morris, a notorious Gloucester forward of the 1940s, a balding giant of a man with a gravelly, West Country accent. From somewhere between the cauliflowers came a voice. 'Come on son, never stay down', it said.

Digger reached down and took my arm. I tried to spring up and made the next scrummage the goal of my whole life. I wanted to wipe the blood away and bury my head. So I rose unsteadily. In fact, I didn't stay too long in this position due to the combined effects of concussion and the erroneous nature of Digger's prognosis. I collapsed and stayed down, reasoning that at least I deserved a flourish of the magic sponge and a few moments recuperation. The incident was then closed, because I did recover well enough. Digger left the field and took up his position on the touchline, from where he used to give both sides – and the referee – the benefit of his opinions.

That little episode had significant repercussions. Digger's words, 'never stay down', rang through my head. They were still ringing seventeen years later when I played my last match for England, against Wales at Twickenham. They were a persistent reminder for me wherever I played rugby and they shaped my whole rugby philosophy. They came to mean not only never stay down in the event of injury, but also never stand back from the confrontation; never let the opposition tower over you psychologically; never leave undone something in a game which would have benefited your team, no matter how distasteful or dangerous. Ultimately, this philosophy developed into a monster, and one a good deal too warlike and vigorous for my own good or for the image of the game. But my mental approach became steeled to take on all comers: nasties and quiet players, players bigger than I was, players who just dwarfed me; people out for trouble and those intent on the psychological domination that all leading representative sides seek in some form. I learnt also to take punishment, never to squeal, and to bide my time to retaliate. I played most of my rugby under the laws of the jungle and I admit that a fight was often appealing to me as a means of standing out, which was a thoroughly misguided way of carrying on. And it all began at Cairnscross, with Digger Morris peering down disdainfully at a heap of humanity cluttering up the rugby pitch! He went on to play a large, even a vital part in developing my philosophy of the game and my ability. He became a second father in many ways and a Svengali.

I was also deeply affected by my environment. I lived in the West Country, not far from the River Severn, which divides England from Wales. A rugby upbringing in the Forest of Dean and the little Welsh towns and villages was character-building, to put it mildly.

So on one hand I acquired the mental toughness to add to my ability, and to become an international sportsman. I was never a brilliant footballer in the sidestepping sense, as one or two people may just have noticed, but I reached the top as a hard, scrummaging prop. Therefore, I had the opportunity to dig myself out of my grindingly hard early days and become, in my own little way, a celebrity. I saw the world, never gave an inch to anyone on the field, never stood aside from any sort of confrontation, always did my duty even though it often hurt badly. I enjoyed it tremendously and found humour and genuine satisfaction in my life.

On the other hand, I won a reputation as the bad boy of rugby, the West Country wild man. I became the first Englishman to be sent off in an international in history, and I was ashamed and thunderstruck – not proud, as some people who half know me might think. I was sent from the field four times, which was exactly four times as often as Paul Ringer was dismissed. (Ringer was the former Llanelli player sent off in the 1980 England-Wales match, whom approximately threequarters of the population regard as a cross between Frankenstein and a child-molester.) I was involved in some shameful incidents, often as the protagonist. On the Ringer scale of contempt I should have been every public enemy from number one to number ten.

When I sunk back to earth at Cairnscross, it was the first and last time I ever did stay down on the field. I got up and carried on with a broken jaw, with a variety of other ailments, with my senses swirling, all over the world. Only once did I fail to finish a game apart from those four occasions when I was sent off, and that was in a match between Northern Transvaal and Gloucestershire when I just couldn't walk. My almost fanatical determination to carry on seemed the thing to do at the time and, as I say, it did my reputation as a prop no harm. Such behaviour seems rather ludicrous to the Burton of today and I would be angry if my son Andrew, a budding forward himself, ever showed that he had picked up one or two of my bad habits.

Modern day sports medicine does not agree with the battling-on view either. In the old days, the magic sponge was the cure for all ills and, anyway, it was your own fault for playing these rough games. I remember once taking a high ball in a club match between Gloucester and Bristol – more or less the equivalent in terms of danger of standing up at a Hitler youth rally and proclaiming yourself a communist. The Bristol pack ran straight over me as a body. It felt as if I had been mown down by a stagecoach and six horses, followed by Dick Turpin on Black Bess for good measure. I was hurt, but there was absolutely no way that I was going to have the trainer on in a Gloucester-Bristol match. A scrum began to form up and somehow I got up. Bob Clewes, the Gloucester wing, came over and examined the tattered remains of my jersey and my torso as I tottered around.

'Take a minute, You're injured', he said.

'I'm not bloody injured against Bristol', I replied. I interpreted the look on Clewes's face as being one of admiration for my fortitude. Actually he must have thought I was raving mad. To me, 'never stay down' even meant never have treatment. I really took Digger's philosophies to heart.

I came under his influence even more when my stepfather died of leukaemia. At the age of sixteen, I moved into lodgings two doors away from him on a council estate in Gloucester called Coney Hill, which has rather little in common with Beverly Hills. I had first met him in schools rugby. His son, Roy, later to become a Longlevens and Gloucester player too, went to Hatherley School, an establishment at the Tredworth end of Gloucester. I remember seeing Digger on the touchline when I was playing for Longlevens Secondary Modern against Hatherley. He was encouraging Roy. He seemed huge, and those flapping cauliflower ears indicated a hard career. After that match I was plodding away across the field on my way home, there being a distinct absence of any sort of luxury in the way of showers or changing rooms, when Digger came over. 'Hey son. You did well today', he said. I had taken some knocks and scrummaged against a much bigger boy. Those knocks hurt, too. At that age, I was unaware that I was accomplishing anything more than anyone else, but Digger had seen something which appealed to him. His encouragement was important, since at that time I was not in any way committed to playing rugby as a means of furthering myself during my free time.

Several years later, I played in a county colts trial at Lydney, and Digger was as usual stationed on the touchline to encourage Roy, who was playing in the centre. I wasn't chosen for the colts side, because I played against a lad much bigger than I was. His name was Barry Peacey and he made the side, yet Digger again singled me out. Then I came to join Longlevens, I was knocked out at Cairnscross, moved in next to Digger, and his influence grew even more. Since Roy and I both played for Longlevens, he would come along and support us both. He taught me the traditions of rugby in Gloucester, which do not have a great deal in common with twinkling half-back and dazzling play, and he taught me all the little tricks of the trade.

Among these was the animal instinct for survival. For example, when I sensed that a few punches were about to arrive in my immediate vicinity in a scrum, with my hands bound and rendered helpless, I would bend my head, so that when the punches came they would bounce off the hardest part of my whole body. I'm sure the punches sometimes hurt the throwers twice as much as they hurt me. Once Digger realised that I would make some sort of player, he took stock of the kind of knowledge which he felt was essential to my survival. His advice was useful even though it was not the kind one might give to young Rodney as he set out to play for his Old Boys club in Kent.

The reason for this relationship between the young player and the old man was probably because Digger saw something of himself in me. I was a little firebrand and there was probably even more material in me which Digger felt he could work on than in Roy. After all, Roy was a threequarter, one of that breed who are given the ball in Gloucestershire rugby only when the forwards have become absolutely bored and fed up to the back teeth with it.

Digger and I would cycle off down to the betting shop together, or sit in his front room in Coney Hill, the walls hung with team photographs, and talk about rugby and its villains and traditions and legends. I was grateful to him, despite the mess his advice sometimes got me into, despite my nasty habit of not finishing matches. After all, top of my list of skills for an international prop is 'bottle'. You can have a perfect body, perfect propping technique, iron strength and the skills of a French forward, but if you haven't added bottle to your repertoire, you may as well join Rodney in Kent. Of course, many people have come up to me and said: 'That Digger Morris, he ruined you. You were a good straight player till he got hold of you.' But Digger did give me bottle.

He is still a regular sight at Kingsholm, home of Gloucester. He served on the club's committee and still appears on his 1938 bike at my home near the ground every Sunday morning for his cup of tea. His own career was sometimes as controversial as mine but he was a very fine forward. He played for Gloucestershire and his original club in the area was Gloucester Wagonworks, now long defunct. His reputation as a villain on the field did not stop him leading the county. In fact, with all due respect, it probably made him an outstanding candidate for the captaincy! He led Gloucestershire to the final of the County Championship in 1947, where he had the sadness of holding Lancashire to an 8-8 draw at Blundellsands, only to go down at Kingsholm in the replay, 14-3. He played in several England trials as a lock but the famous Wheatley brothers from Coventry kept him out of the side. Then when he was reserve and the player nominated withdrew, he was passed over, and the selectors, in Digger's words, brought in a 'fellow from 'Arlequins who wore a white scrum cap'. Perhaps the selection of some rugby sides hasn't changed all that much. Poor Digger even had to share a room with the Harlequin before the match!

Life was a slog for Digger after the loss of his wife and it was hard for a big man to be domesticated and look after two sons. But he would metaphorically don his apron and bash the spuds diligently. With that reverence accorded to all villains who are generally recognised to be all right behind it all, he is fêted at Gloucester by dozens of people clapping him across the shoulders and taking his order for the bar. He would have to be fairly large to be larger than life, and he almost makes it. My caps and my controversies are partly due to him, the man with the cauliflower ears.

As I have mentioned before, it was Digger who gave me the encouragement to take up rugby, otherwise I might never have done so. Years before at Longlevens Secondary Modern, I was the original fat prop. I had a lot less in common with W. Beaumont than with W. Bunter. I didn't actually ever win a regular place in the school side. I was called upon when others were injured to add my particular brand of immobility to the front row. Nick Healey, of the Longlevens club, was a regular talent spotter at the school but he didn't pay a great deal of attention to me. However, he was interested in my best friend, Warren Fortey, and as Warren came up to school leaving age, Healey asked him to Longlevens for a trial. Warren accepted, but, loyally, laid down a condition. He would only go if his mate Mike could go along too. Warren Fortey and Mike Burton therefore became playing members. I survived my buffeting at Cairnscross and actually worked my way up to play for Longlevens first team when I was fifteen – against Whitehall Old Boys in Bristol. Nick Healey gave me the sort of selfless encouragement which helped me and therefore helped the club. The club coach at the time was Bumper Humphries, an old Gloucester scrum-half, and he, too, paid attention to my career, making me realise that if I trained hard and worked at it, I could do something.

Bumper was in charge of a Longlevens junior side in a sevens tournament in 1962 for which I was selected. Sevens was never my strong point but in this tournament, the North Gloucestershire Combination Sevens, there was a factor which drove me to play and which absolutely forced me to make the club's junior seven: the tournament took place at the end of April, 1962, and it took place at Kingsholm! For weeks before, I savoured the prospect of my short, fat, hairy legs carrying me on to the home field of Gloucester. It was consecrated turf to me, as to any young rugby fan in the area. Warren Fortey and Roy Morris were also in the team, savouring the thrill. Bumper Humphries came up to us before the tournament and offered to buy us a tie each if we won. To us, this was a tremendous incentive, but if we had thought more carefully, we would have realised that Bumper knew something we didn't. Shelling out on seven ties at 12s 6d each would have been rather an extravagance. Bumper knew he wouldn't have to, of course; he knew that the school team from Sir Thomas Riches was a superb combination and far too fast and slick for Longlevens. They had already won the Oxford School Sevens. Nevertheless, we ran on to Kingsholm with seven small chests bursting out of seven large jerseys.

Bumper's knowledge that he would not be visiting the gents' outfitters on our behalf was soon confirmed. The school side were superb. They seemed to be all even timers and they had a blisteringly fast wing, Alan Pontin. They won 40-0 and almost broke our hearts as we chased them around. The local paper reported that Pontin made 'even the nippy Longlevens team appear as carthorses'. I vividly remember one Pontin breakaway. With all the speed I could muster, I set off in a vain and valiant attempt to cut him off at the corner flag. He scored in a canter. But as I walked off, Bumper came up to me. 'If a big lad like you can chase like that at the end of a game, then you might make something of yourself', he said. What is more, I enjoyed the aura of Kingsholm despite the defeat. It was the beginning of a love affair with the place.

I returned to Longlevens in the meantime to lick my wounds and to carry on my education amongst the hard school of the area. Digger would be on the touchline with his comments. 'If you can't take it, don't dish it out', he would shout. I was, I freely admit, a wild man in those days. I became rather notorious in the district and fancied myself as a trouble-maker. Then, in February 1964, I received recognition that Longlevens thought so too. I had a letter from the club, signed by Nick Healey, who was then secretary.

'Dear Mick, You will notice that you have not been selected for any of the club's XVs on Saturday next. The selection committee feel that you should be rested re recent incidents in games and would also like you to be at the Fleece at 11am on Sunday morning, when the committee can have a chat with you.' The Fleece was the pub headquarters of the club. I was being disciplined for the first time. I dutifully arrived at the Fleece as requested. The committee were friendly and frank. They felt I had the ability to become a good player, they said. But I was too wild for my own good and there was a danger that my ability was going to be hidden behind the violent exterior.

While under that cloud at Longlevens, I decided to leave and make the giant step forward: to go to Kingsholm and join Gloucester. But though the timing was hardly subtle, the committee's warning had absolutely nothing to do with my decision. Even though I was not a regular in the Longlevens first team, I decided to make a real effort to cross the great divide between first-class rugby and the rest. I had nothing but gratitude for Longlevens and for Nick Healey, and Bumper Humphries, but I left. I told Nick Healey the news. 'I'm going to Gloucester.' 'You're too young', Healey replied. I was eighteen. I played the season out for Longlevens and bade them farewell.

It is a big step to join Gloucester from one of the dozens of smaller clubs in the area. The close rugby community provides a bush telegraph of movements, and the decision to try your luck with Gloucester implies a certain amount of conceit. It is noted in the local press that you are making your bid, and for every player who joins there are probably a dozen others who have played against him and say that if he can go to Gloucester then so can they. A lot of people fail to make the grade – after all, even a club as great as Gloucester can only field fifteen players at once in their first team.

I strode off down to Kingsholm for the trials and, in rugby terms, to seek my fortune. If I didn't have my worldly goods tied in a knapsack on the end of a stick, I did have my boots in a paper carrier-bag as I arrived at the ground. Even though I began life as a prop, Longlevens frequently played me in the second row, yet I was slotted into the trial teams as a number eight. The pace was murder. I remember staggering up to a line-out, blowing badly, and looking forward to the end of the match when I could put my boots back into the bag and go back to Longlevens, where the place wasn't filled with supermen.

I thought that I was never going to adapt to that sort of pace – never! For the first game, I was chosen as reserve for Gloucester United, so a good few other people felt the same way. In any case, the selectors were far more interested in the display of another player, Don Rutherford, already an international and later to become the first technical administrator to the Rugby Football Union. Incidentally, his job title was undoubtedly dreamed up by those sort of people who call dustmen 'waste disposal operatives'. Rutherford is, basically, the coaching organiser.

The following week, glory! I was chosen to play for the United against Cwmbran away in the second row, and I became accepted into the club as a regular United lock, which at the age of eighteen was quite a feat. One of the early season games was in Newport, that part of Wales which is sometimes called England by people wanting to offend inhabitants of the place. 'Course it isn't in bloody England!'

The opposition were Newport High School Old Boys, one of approximately five hundred clubs in Wales who play next to a river. Each time the ball is kicked into the muddy waters, an old chap with a long pole appears and fishes it out, provided the thing hasn't dissolved in the poisonous waters. When we reached their ground we were missing a prop, so I volunteered to pick up the threads of my front row career. I remember giving my opposite number a pasting, and shining as a frisky young lad in the loose. My standing went up another notch after that. I was developing as a Gloucester forward. The help of Digger and my other mentors was paying off and I was flexing my muscles as an increasingly dedicated Gloucester man. I was sixteen stone at the age of seventeen, so I was well-equipped both mentally and physically for what was to come. Too well-equipped mentally, it might be said.

The next hurdle was the big one – the *puissance,* if you like. The one which establishes you if you cross it, and dooms you if you don't. The first XV beckoned. It was now conceivable that I would wear that famous cherry and white first XV jersey: and I had thought that they were reserved for demi-gods.

Many young players get their first chance of first team action on a county day – that is, when Gloucestershire have a County Championship match and as many as threequarters of the Gloucester side are needed for county duty. On 14 November, 1964, the county did have a match. I did some mental selection and realised that I had a definite chance of being chosen for the weakened side. The prospect really thrilled me. People who play for Moseley or Waterloo, for Rosslyn Park or Richmond, even for Leicester or Cardiff, might not realise exactly what it means to play for Gloucester. They are all cosmopolitan clubs to some extent, and many regions and even several countries are represented in their first XVs. Gloucester is a club which fields, for the most part, Gloucester men; not Blues down from Cambridge, or players flitting from one first class club to another. Gloucester is a real town club and is a major part of the community for miles around. It is also one of the largest cities in England which doesn't have a football league club with which to compete for attention. Gloucester people think every bit as much of their rugby club as Liverpudlians think of their soccer team.

That was why I cycled down to training at Kingsholm on the night that the side was going to be selected for the match against Moseley on 14 November. I waited outside the club after the session. I must have pumped up my tyres at least ten times. In fact, there was so much air in them that I could probably have floated home. As the selection committee deliberated, I prayed. Then the clubhouse door swung open, and the great men walked towards me: and straight past. They ignored me completely. As I cycled home I convinced myself that I hadn't made it. Next day, in the *Gloucester Citizen,* was a headline proclaiming the fact that Roy Morris, son of the legendary former Gloucester forward Digger Morris, was to play his first game for the first XV at Moseley on the following Saturday. There was a sub-heading. 'And Burton plays too.' I was in!

My immediate opponent at Moseley was Mike Coulman, who won nine caps for England in 1967 and 1968 before joining the rugby league. His main talents lay outside the scrum but he was, as understating Gloucester people say, a handy boy. I remember trying a trick in that very first game which I felt made me a hard and clever chap but which seemed either provocative or ludicrous to the opposition. I slipped my left arm off the Gloucester hooker, Ken Taylor, and put my hand over the eyes of Lane, the Moseley hooker. Lane was not particularly taken with this sort of thing and it needed all my Digger philosophy to keep me on my feet and pointing at the next scrummage, in the face of some fairly forceful dissuasion. Even worse, I tried my brilliant trick right in the middle of the field. At least I could have tried it near one of the goal-lines. However, I kept my head above water against Coulman and, despite a Gloucester defeat, I was delighted. I had tested the deep water and found that I could stay afloat.

Before I reached nineteen, I met a number of other leading props around the country and came off quite well. I took all the knocks and proved a handful for some of the opposition. Not even Nick Drake-Lee, then the England prop, caused me much discomfort in the scrums and my confidence grew. I had had a hard apprenticeship, and now I was winning respect around the country. M.A. Burton was preparing to take the unsuspecting world of rugby by storm. But just before I leave my formative years and the influences, both bad and good, with which I came into contact, I would like to relate two stories of the different ways in which my abrasiveness and determination to keep going in the face of hardship both helped and greatly hindered my career.

The first incident reveals either outstanding bravery or rank stupidity on my part. It had its origins in my natural desire in the 1970s to cap my rugby career by making a Lions tour. At the start of the International Championship in January 1974, I was a stalwart of the Gloucester side and of the county team. I had played five times for England and was all too aware that the Lions were due to tour South Africa in May 1974. It was going to be a gladiatorial contest on the grand scale, a crusade for rugby in both countries, and I was by no means alone among international rugby players in the four home countries in desperately wanting to be a British Lion.

The first item on the agenda for those hopefuls was to stand out at international level during the Championship, for it is rare for Lions selectors to choose players not selected for their own national sides – although the 1980 South African tour did include several players, particularly Welshmen, who were not fixtures in their individual country's side. The 1974 Championship was therefore doubly important for me. I wanted to dazzle the selectors and I also wanted to regain the England place I had held throughout 1972 but was unable to bid for in 1973 due to the slight inconvenience of a broken leg. For the first match of the season, against Scotland, the selectors stuck by Fran Cotton as tight head. After all, he had played throughout the 1973 season. They also resisted any temptation to move him to the loose head side of the scrum to make room for me. They chose the dependable, likeable and thoroughly competent Cornishman, Claude Brian Stevens, at loose head. With a name like that, of course, Claude had to have a nickname. So everyone called him 'Stack'. Stevens and Cotton propped the England scrum as the side lost at Murrayfield. David Duckham made a horrendous mistake by running offside in the final minutes and Andy Irvine obliged with the winning penalty goal. The same props were retained for the next game, which was a home match against Ireland, with Burton in residence on the replacements' bench.

Prior to that match, there was one between Gloucester and Bristol to enjoy, so on to Kingsholm we all trooped one Sunday for the twice-yearly ritual of knocking the seven bells of hell out of each other in front of a crowd baying like the hounds of Dracula. That season had been a good one for Gloucester and we badly wanted to seal things with a win over the old enemy.

John Spalding was at scrum-half for Gloucester that day, and a good one he was. He played in the shadow of Mickey Booth and so only occasionally shared in club and county glory. But he was highly-rated and popular amongst the Gloucester players, especially for a dry sense of humour. Other dry regions when Spalding was around tended to include the beer glasses of those who thought they were supposed to be in a round and that it was

Spalding's turn to pay up. During the course of the match, Spalding received quite a roughing up at the hands of Dave Rollitt, the Bristol flanker. Rollitt was a good, hard player, a magnificent forward, and whenever we played Bristol we always had to legislate for his ability in our pre-match planning. We respected him. However, this respect did not extend to us allowing him to knock John Spalding about. In fact, another facet of my playing code was never to allow a player to rough up any member of my side. Tony Bodley, of the *Daily Express,* once wrote: 'I know Burton as one of the most delightful travelling companions. He is a born comedian, but there is little doubt that he regards a foul against any of his pack as a personal attack against himself.' That comment hit the nail squarely on the head – which is just what I did to Dave Rollitt, now I come to mention it.

Down went Rollitt, and I leaned in his direction to inform him that there was plenty more from the same source available should he care to harass Spalding again. But Rollitt's team mate, Dave Watt, had seen the incident. He was a 6ft 6in giant and he punched his weight. He swung a haymaker from behind and I was told afterwards that the punch had competition only from 'Enry's 'Ammer, which put Cassius Clay on the floor, as the punch of the century. I joined Rollitt on the ground.

The cheap side stands started to rock and I fought to remain in the land of the conscious. In fact, my jaw was badly broken, but Digger's motto boomed through my head just as loudly as if the man himself had been standing above me. I sprang up, and walked towards the position where a scrum was forming. This took longer than expected, because thirty yards is a long distance to cover when you are taking two steps sideways for every one forward and looking like a performer in the world solo Viennese waltz championships. I had no idea my jaw was broken. Eventually I reached the scrum and clung on gratefully to Mike Nicholls, the Gloucester hooker and captain. The referee had obviously not seen anything but he blew a long blast on his whistle. In fact, he was beckoning the trainer on. I felt the panic rising. There was no way I was going to receive treatment in a Gloucester-Bristol match. Call me pig-headed, but I didn't want someone waving smelling salts under my nose, or holding up his fingers so that I could estimate the number, give or take a few for the double vision. I wanted to be left alone to absorb the after-effects of the punch.

The trainer approached. Thankfully, though, he had come on to administer to Rollitt, who was still on the floor. Now the aforesaid Mike Nicholls was the best captain I ever played under. He was a hard and competitive hooker, and a no-nonsense captain. He stared at David Watt. The big Bristol man kept the buck passing along. He nodded in my direction, indicating that I had started it. Eventually, the scrum went down, with no one aware that I had sustained lasting damage. I packed down against the Bristol prop, Mike Fry. I describe my battles with Fry later, but I will say here that although he was not a big man, he was a fierce and unbending opponent.

As I went down against Fry I realised that my jaw was hurting unbearably and I knew that Watt's punch had done more than damage my pride. Still, there were ten more minutes to go before half-time and I had no intention of giving Bristol the satisfaction of seeing the back of me. Nor could I let on to Fry that I was injured, so my broken jaw became a private matter between me and my maker. For scrum after scrum we came thumping together, with me moving to one side as we bound. His head rammed into my jaw time and again and I remember trying to tense it against the pain. I could have gritted my teeth as well, except that when I closed my mouth, my teeth did not fit together any more. As the game wore on, I was in agony, and the pain was only partly relieved by the fact that we won, 8-6. Fry came over with his pint pot after the game, to shake hands. 'What was wrong with you today?' he asked. I smiled and didn't reply. For once in my life, I was unable to speak.

I went off quietly for an X-ray, which proved the break – it showed up clearly on the plates. 'Of course, now you'll have a long lay off', said the doctor, a splendid Indian gentleman of the Gloucester accident unit.

No, I decided, I wouldn't have a long lay off. England were due to play Ireland and I was on the bench: and then the Lions were going to go to South Africa. I desperately needed to stay on the England scene and not to fade out of the limelight. I had enough trouble staying in the England squad when I was fully fit during my career, and I just couldn't affort to give the selectors an obvious reason to leave me out. Just under two weeks after Dave Watt's punch had landed, I sat on the replacements' bench at Twickenham. Just before the match, John Elders came up to me. He had heard rumours. He tapped me on the jaw and asked me about it. I assumed a puzzled air, feigned complete fitness, and took my place.

In my moment of madness, I was really banking on the indestructibility of Fran Cotton. In that Irish match, he was taking on Ray McLoughlin, the finest prop I ever met. McLoughlin and Cotton were having a tremendous battle, but I didn't have to take the field.

Yet again, England lost. We trailed 26-9 at one stage but eventually pulled back to lose 26-21. The forwards were comfortable, but behind the scrum Ireland for once had a monopoly on attacking flair. I was still in the England squad, with my unsuspected broken jaw.

There were two weeks before the match against France at the new Parc des Princes stadium, and if ever there was a place for the fully fit, it was out there against the French. However, Cotton finished the Irish game with a bad ankle injury so with me and my jaw only half on the mend, I was chosen instead. A good performance against a tough prop named Jean Iraçabal could put me halfway into the Lions squad, I decided. I played a decent part in an England draw, and the pain I almost forgot in the general mayhem of a typical day out in Paris.

My gamble paid off even more handsomely. Cotton was still unavailable for England's last match of the season, against Wales at Twickenham. Nothing can bolster the rating of an England team more these days than if it beats Wales, so it did my Lions' chances no harm at all that I was on the tight head of the English scrum in a 16-12 win. Wales claimed, and they still claim now, that J.J. Williams was robbed of a try when the referee disallowed his touchdown after a race with Dave Duckham. But we were worthy winners, and my jaw, mercifully, suffered no further damage. I played myself into the ground in that England win, which had been secured with tries by Andy Ripley and Geoff Evans. Afterwards, I was chosen to climb that summit: I went to South Africa with the 1974 Lions. I have always regarded the trip as the pinnacle of my career.

My 'never stay down' philosophy could have done me a lot of harm to add to the pain; it was not a clever move to plough on with my jawbone in pieces, yet in the end, it helped me and assisted my career. Had I let the injury get on top of me, I could almost certainly have spent the 1974 summer on my front lawn rather than on the dry fields of the high veldt with Willie-John McBride.

Finally – in this description of the rise of an international sportsman or the demise of a lunatic, depending on your point of view – an incident which prevented me making a Lions tour. Having tasted the joys of victory in South Africa and continued my England career between 1974 and 1977, I began to set my heart on going to New Zealand to take on their assorted meanies on behalf of British rugby. The Lions tour to New Zealand in 1977 became a goal. With the precept that when in Rome you do as the Romans do, I felt my style of play would be successful. I also thought that I had an outstanding chance of making the tour due to one or two whispers.

During the months before selection, Gloucester had an important John Player Cup match. The opposition was Gosforth, who had won the trophy in 1976, when their cup run had included a bitter 3-3 draw at Gloucester, which they won by virtue of being the away side. The showdown was keenly awaited, as we travelled to the north-east to take on their aggressive and powerful side.

Gosforth fielded two large line-out forwards, Terry Roberts and John Hedley, so it was a tremendous blow to our chances when John Fidler, our own line-out champion, had to withdraw through injury. We thought of the grizzled and likeable Fidler as something of a veteran then, so it may be useful to point out that this was indeed the same John Fidler who won two caps for England at the end of the 1980-81 season in Argentina. We brought in Phil Winnel, a lively and courageous forward, but he has lived in Fidler's shadow as a purveyor of that vital line-out ball.

The early exchanges were harsh, but Winnel did surprisingly well. He rose above the giant John Hedley and brought the ball down on our side of the line-out. One of my tasks as a supporter at the line-out was to make sure no one came through the line and prevented our jumpers transferring the ball to the scrum-half, so I was not pleased when, several times, a Gosforth prop came round our side and prevented Winnel feeding the ball. His name was Andy Cutter, currently going strong in the south with Rosslyn Park. Cutter would move across as the ball was being thrown. He was a heavy and strong man and he was invalidating Winnel's efforts. I felt that the referee was allowing him to get away with it and also that, even worse, I was letting Winnel down terribly.

I could not let that state of affairs continue. I gave Cutter a few nudges and verbal encouragement to stop it. But he persisted, and, finally, came through the Gloucester line once too often. I hit him hard and he wobbled at the knees. Like any good fighter sensing the 'kill', I followed up with a left and a right cross and Cutter went down in a going, going, gone sequence. The referee was Norman Sanson, and what a good one he was. But Norman had been stationed on the other side of the line-out and saw nothing.

The crowd went berserk, and there was some movement towards the pitch from the terraces. I was unrepentant. I was not going to allow Gloucester players to be dictated to, and I was not going to stand back and watch Cutter gain a psychological and very practical advantage. As the crowd bayed, I took a few steps towards them, gesturing an invitation to them to join me on the field. The baying became a few decibels louder. But one person in the stand was not joining in the noise. He was watching in disgust. The crowd that day, I found out afterwards, contained George Burrell, the manager-elect of the 1977 Lions. I was crossed off the list of Lions possibles on Burrell's insistence after he watched that incident. I was judged and convicted by him, and I was not selected.

Looking back, I regret the extent of my actions, though I would in every case have dissuaded Cutter. I also had no chance if a puritanical Scot was deciding the team, a man who was a failure as a Lions manager. I felt, too, that if the Lions had chosen only those forwards who had not been seen in acts of skulduggery on the field, then a New Zealand Schoolboys XV would have had an excellent chance of winning that 1977 series. Yes, the abrasive way I played rugby union affected my career at every turn. I made a Lions tour because of it, but I also missed one because of it.

2

THE BOTTOM RUNG

WHEN people who have become well-known set down the stories of their lives, a good many of them seem to start with an account of the difficult conditions of their early days of hardship and poverty; the whole story becomes a 'rags to riches' effort. Even some of the leading names in rugby have produced books with this theme, where typically it is recorded that the subject found his first pair of boots on a rubbish dump, spent all his time kicking a rolled-up newspaper up a coal tip, and lived in a derelict hut with his grandmother and twelve brothers. He always tried to emulate his rugby hero and dreamed of playing at Twickenham or Cardiff or Murrayfield. Dave Duckham's hero could have been Peter Jackson, Barry John's could have been Carwyn James, Charlie Faulkner's could have been W. G. Grace.

My own story is not quite on the same lines – because I can outdo all the others. I may not have soared as high as some of them, but I beat them hollow at the other end. None have come from such a tangled wreck of an upbringing and from early years filled with such fear and confusion as I! When I arrived into the grim world of the post-war depression in 1945 I barely had a surname. I was christened Michael Alan Harrop, using my mother's maiden name, and I spent my first few screaming days and years in my grandmother's house in Maidenhead. The popular image of good old Mike Burton, a born and bred Gloucestershire man, is all wrong. I came from Maidenhead and, what is more, I wasn't even Mike Burton! I hate to admit it but I originally came from the home counties, where Rodney goes off to play for his Old Boys' club and doesn't really mind if he loses. However, to keep my dignity I should reveal that the current popular image of Maidenhead had little in common with our area in 1945. We lived on the wrong side of the tracks.

My mother was sixteen when I arrived, so it was easy to imagine the struggle which she faced in Britain at that time with the stigma of being an unmarried mother. There were no organisations for one-parent families and the like in those days. Yet my mother refused to dispose of me by putting me into a home, and decided to do her very best for me despite her tender age.

Her own mother had lost her husband in a car crash and then remarried, to a volatile Irishman called Jack Doherty. He came from Waterford and had served in REME. He had been married before but, eventually, his first wife had left him – and when I came to know Jack Doherty better I realised what a shrewd woman she must have been. So in Victoria Street, Maidenhead, Jack Doherty set up home with my grandmother, the former Mrs Harrop. Mrs Harrop's daughter, at the age of sixteen, bore a son and we all lived unhappily together. My mother's brother moved in with us too but after a very short time could take it no more, and joined the Royal Marines so that he could get out of the way. (All those still with me, please award yourself five points.)

Our living rooms in Victoria Street were actually in the basement of the place and our poverty was tangible. With rationing and the lack of funds a bag of stale cakes or broken biscuits prized from a shopkeeper represented a considerable luxury and a delight.

Jack Doherty was an unstable man and a drinker. It was certainly no fun growing up in his company, especially when the last thing he needed was his wife's daughter and her small son in the house. To make matters worse for us, he and my grandmother then produced two girls themselves, step-sisters for my mother. The eldest was just a year younger than me. They obviously became the apples of their parents' eyes and relegated my mother and me even further away from Doherty's affections, although my grandmother was never anything but kind to me and she tried to ensure that I got the same treatment as her daughters. However, her husband came to look upon my mother and myself as intruders in his home, even though he hadn't contributed anything to the house himself. To say the very least, he was unkind to my mother.

Doherty's rages were terrifying and frequent. He would spend all his money by the weekend, and then be desperate for two shillings for a packet of cigarettes. He would scratch together a few pennies and sit down, moodily drumming his fingers on the table, until someone cracked and provided him with the rest of the amount. His bad moods would always be taken out on the rest of the family.

As I grew up in Maidenhead, things did not improve. I remember vividly sitting at the breakfast-table one day, pouring milk slowly on to my cereal from our heavy glass milk jug. 'That's enough', said Jack. When I continued pouring, he reacted like a wild man – which he was. He jumped up, lashing out at the jug and sending it spinning down on to the floor where it smashed into hundreds of tiny pieces. Fortunately for me he was diverted from his proposed course of doing me considerable damage, because he had done himself considerable damage. He had cut his hand badly. He wrapped a blue flannel round the wound, charged out of the house, and ran a full mile to the nearest hospital, cursing loudly all the way. Apart from the cut, he had split some of the sinews in his hand and, even now, as he lives out his days in Maidenhead, he still lacks full movement in it as a legacy of me and the milk jug.

On another occasion, he came in from his usual Sunday lunchtime outing to the Greyhound pub in Maidenhead in his customary drunk, excited, belligerent mood. His dinner had been ready for a long time and his wife, my grandmother, tried a few words of reproval. Doherty picked up the plate with his dried lunch on it and flung it across the room, where it smashed into the Welsh dresser. And that became a familiar sight – every Sunday, without fail, along with the *Billy Cotton Band Show* on the radio, we would be 'entertained' by the sight of dinner plates flying across the room and homing in on various targets. 'Wakey Wa-key!' Billy would shout, crash would go the plates.

Matters came to a head when I was seven – seven unstable years for me, and difficult ones for my mother. The clashes between her and Doherty became more frequent and more upsetting. I remember him screaming at her once in the kitchen, and telling her to get out of the house, to leave completely. She curled herself into a ball, protecting herself by holding up her hands, and refused to go. Yet, finally, the pressure became too much. My mother went, leaving me behind with Doherty and his wife and two daughters, Betty and Margaret. Eventually I became used to calling my grandmother 'mum' like the two girls did.

My mother took a live-in job at a transport café. She used to come back as often as possible to visit me, and gave her mother money towards my keep. In time I became used to this arrangement, and accepted it. That was why in the end I couldn't understand the floods of tears which always ensued when my mother left me every week to return to her lodgings. I never felt she had deserted me – she just had no choice. Every week, on every visit, she would give me sixpence, which was a sizeable proportion of her wages. The coin would be pressed into my hand whether times were hard, or harder still.

Sometimes, she even took me out to the pictures, which cost ninepence. Doherty would point out that this was unfair to Betty and Margaret, so my mother would take them along as well which would really take care of the remainder of her money. It was a good arrangement for me, though, because I always got on well with Betty and Margaret, and still do today. But I could never understand the tears of my mother when we parted, the distress because she couldn't take her own son with her.

Her struggle to bring me up was nowhere better demonstrated than by an incident which occurred near our home when I was about six or seven and she was on a visit. It was a lovely warm day and I was out and about in my best urchin's suit. I was walking past Mr Steane's shop when I saw a magnificent pram – one of those giant, old-fashioned contraptions – parked outside. I leaned over the pram to see the baby; I was being curious, but certainly wasn't doing it any harm.

Suddenly, a tough-looking woman – she had far more in common with Desperate Dan than Sophia Loren – ran out of the shop. She grabbed my braces as I tried to run away: they stretched and then snapped, causing me to be hurled back by the contracting elastic. She gave me a good hiding and I ran screaming all the way home. My mother heard my sobbing story grimly and, as usual, prepared to stand up for me. We marched back to the shop. She asked Mr Steane to identify my departed attacker and we withdrew.

About a week later came high noon at Maidenhead, Berkshire's very own OK Corral. I saw the woman across the road and pointed her out to my mother, who parked me at the side of the road and told me to wait. She crossed over and gave the other woman a real beating. The woman sank lower and lower under the attack until finally she sat down heavily on the ground; she was counted out. The whole affair ended in court, where my mother was convicted and had to pay a stiff fine. Everyone kept calling her 'Miss Harrop', emphasising the Miss and drawing sneering attention to the fact that she was an unmarried mother. I remember my mother having to speak for herself, while the other lady, who after all had struck the first violent blow, was represented by a smooth-talking man with a wig and a black cloak.

In junior school I showed promise as a boxer, and my heroes were Sugar Ray Robinson and Randolph Turpin. By this time, my mother's brother had left the Royal Marines and he used to take me to watch my favourite team, Arsenal. We used to travel from Maidenhead to Highbury together. This was an early way in which sport helped me leave behind my troubles. Yet I had no interest in rugby, which in Maidenhead at the time was an upper-class sport and not a dazzling television spectacular either.

Finally, I left Victoria Street, Maidenhead, and Jack Doherty for good. My mother met and married a man called Dennis Burton from Gloucester and took me with her, so we were reunited. Despite the unhappiness of life in Maidenhead, the move westwards was an upheaval because all my friends and the school I had become used to were left behind. I now had to join a new school, find new friends, and learn to call my mother 'mum' instead of my grandmother. I had to leave Betty and Margaret, with whom I had been brought up, and of course my grandmother, who had been so kind to me. I even had to get used to a completely new surname – I took Dennis Burton's name and became Mike Burton of Gloucestershire for the very first time.

I was legally adopted by my mother and her husband.

Dennis lived in a caravan close to Longlevens rugby club, so we didn't immediately jump from poverty to great prosperity. But soon we moved into a house, a small semi-detached, where I anticipated a whole new future. Dennis Burton was a good man and was extremely kind to me. We even went on a holiday, to Blackpool in a borrowed car. That was the lap of luxury and high living, though we were not quite in the Rothschild class! We once walked into a café and sat down to examine the menu: egg and chips was highly priced, at 4s 6d. We rose simultaneously on seeing that, no words or glances being exchanged; we just walked out. Four shillings and sixpence for egg and chips!

Dennis Burton had no sporting inclinations at all – at least Jack Doherty read the racing pages of the newspapers – but he certainly was kind to me. I played for the England Boys clubs against Welsh Boys clubs at Neath and, although he knew nothing of rugby, Dennis drove from Gloucester deep into west Wales for the match, just to watch me play and give me some support. The M4 was non-existent then, even in the dreams of the motorway planners, and he chugged down to Neath in his little mini-van.

I began to go to school on a bike for the first time, and at last felt like just another one of the kids. Yet if I thought for one moment that all my troubles were over, then I was jumping the gun. Dennis was a long-distance lorry driver and he had to work long hours and nights to pay for the mortgage and support the family. So the marriage was under strain, and, sure enough, my mother left home. Divorce followed not so long after.

I felt at home with Dennis and stayed with him. He was still kind to me even when he began drinking to make up for the upheavals in his own life. I think I did him some good as well. But, once again, the picture changed for the worse. He contracted leukaemia, and the first real father that I had had, the man who gave me his name and encouraged me, died and left me on my own. I had lived with him for two years since moving from Maidenhead.

My mother had a new love in her life by that time. She went to live with Neville Blake, a Gloucester man; they are still happily married today, and run a transport café. She went without me to where her heart dictated and I was left to find digs on my own. I moved into a house on the Coney Hill estate in Gloucester and lodged with a Welsh couple, Jack and Violet Evans. More significantly from the rugby point of view, the house was two doors from that of Digger Morris, the fierce and formidable old Gloucester forward who, for better or worse, was to take me under his wing and give me a stern rugby education, as I described in the last chapter. He was such a strong influence on me that if he had been a poet, then I would have become one too. If he had been a murderer, I might even have killed people!

After my parents' divorce I spent every Sunday afternoon with Frank and Mabel Fortey, my friend Warren's parents, and they treated me almost as their own son. I would stay for tea and, every week, I would gobble up a statutory chocolate éclair and talk to Mr Fortey and to Warren about rugby and the past Gloucester 'greats'. In this way I obtained a historical perspective of the game and passed many happy Sunday afternoons in the process.

Gradually, rugby became the focal point of my life. I began to stand out as a player and the game opened doors for me, both socially and in business. From somewhere, and surprisingly perhaps after my troubled early life, I developed a sense of humour which has appealed, it seems, to every team I have played for and to every group of people I have joined. 'I had him worried', I used to say of a prop who had given me a hard time on the field. 'Why did you have him worried?' the doubters would ask. 'He thought he'd bloody killed me' I would answer.

When I was nineteen, I met a girl from Churchtown, the next village along from Longlevens. She was eighteen, and after a straightforward courtship of two years we married. I began to play for Gloucester and Pat used to come down to Kingsholm to watch, even though she wasn't a particular rugby fan. If you think this part of the story deserves a happy ending, then so did I – and it has one. Three lovely children, Nicholas, Andrew and Claire, arrived, and at the time of writing they have reached the ages of thirteen, twelve and eight. The turmoil of Maidenhead and Jack Doherty, the struggle and the strife, now recede into the background and remain only as a particularly vivid nightmare in my memory.

Running parallel to some of this story of my early life is the story of how I went about winning enough bread to stay alive. I held some posts during my career breathtaking in their boring and unprofitable nature. In fact, for half my working life I was averaging three jobs per year.

When I left Longlevens School at the age of fifteen my mother decided that I should have a trade to set me up for the future, and I duly signed on to begin work at the body shop of Taylors, Gloucester's main Ford dealer, as an apprentice panel-beater. The glittering career ahead of me in this field soon disappeared. I found that as my rugby career progressed it took up more and more of my time. For example, I could never work on Saturdays because I was playing for Longlevens. The man in charge of the apprentices, far from being a sports-mad employer willing to let his employees off for fixtures, gave no indication that he had ever heard of rugby union.

All the apprentices used to have a £1 share of the scrap metal which the plant collected and sold, and the boss would line us up for the hand-out. When he came to me he gave me only ten shillings, saying that I could have the rest if I started putting in the same hours as the others. After a very short career and very few beaten panels, I decided that the job wasn't for me.

That was my second job over, in fact, because while I was waiting to reach sixteen, the youngest age for apprentices to be signed on, I spent six months at Victor Healey, a coach builders and car repairers. That was in 1960, and they paid me the sum of £1 19s 0d per week. Even paying those sort of rates, the firm went bankrupt and I moved on to Taylors.

My next major career boost came when I got a job advertised as a representative for a firm selling vacuum cleaners. Of course, it turned out to involve hawking the cleaners door to door around the estates of Gloucester. The Gloucester fan who had noticed a new forward turning out for the United side might have been surprised to find that same forward's foot in his door the day after; there I was, vacuum cleaner in hand, purveying my line of patter. To earn commission I had to sell four cleaners per week and I actually became quite successful – but the man running the whole operation was not quite as successful at paying my commission, so at eighteen I resigned from my third job.

After several spells as a building works construction operative (labourer!) on various building sites and a short period spent falling off ladders for Wallaces, a local window-cleaning firm, I finally hit the big time: relief milkman for the Co-Op. My team-mates at Gloucester immediately christened me 'milk-top Burton'. My first day on the milk was inauspicious. The day before, I had played in a special match between Ron Pitt's XV and John Thorne's XV at Thorne's club, Cleve. After a riotous night the coach arrived back at Gloucester on a freezing morning at four o'clock. Half drunk, I stumbled straight from the bus into the milk depot to report for duty. The foreman gave me an overall to exchange for my old games raincoat, pointed out my electric float, and off went the slowest and least sober milkman in the west.

The main drawback of the job was that after a heavy night's celebration of my steadily progressing Gloucester career, I often had to take my headache and hangover to work with me in the early hours. I was twenty and, even if I was improving on the field, my off-the-field capabilities were yet to be realised. My work was often finished by eleven o'clock though and then I had the rest of the day to recover. Eventually I graduated to a much-coveted post – roundsman with the newly-arrived Gloucester Model Dairy.

The next stop on my particular course came as a bread delivery salesman with a local bakery, and, as you can see, in spite of a lot of effort I was still fairly unlikely to become a member of the Institute of Directors or the Stock Exchange. The low point of that particular job came when I was driving round the town in a tearing hurry to finish my deliveries, as I had to leave with Gloucester for an away match. I took a roundabout too quickly and a huge, five-tier cake intended for a wedding that day toppled over and flew out of the back door of the van, before rolling at speed down the A40. Apparently it was patched up just in time.

By the time I was twenty-one, I was employed by British Relay TV as a relief rent collector and electrical sales representative, really hitting the heights. However the job did give me confidence that I could sell things, and also it was my first experience of arriving for work in a collar and tie. I was quite successful and the job brought in a few extra pounds to help my early married life.

It was at this stage that I first experienced rugby's freemasonry at work; I first realised what being a successful rugby player could mean in terms of prestige and hard cash. Roy Long, a Gloucester stalwart, was an estate agent in Cheltenham and I became a junior negotiator in his office. I began to develop more confidence in dealing with people and now I graduated to a full suit as working clothes. After so many backwards and sideways steps among milk bottles, vacuum cleaners and rolling wedding cakes, at last I was progressing. I spent six years with the company and not only enjoyed myself, but also became an established white-collar worker.

The freemasonry really opened doors in 1974. I had returned from South Africa in the summer of 1974 a successful British Lion and a relatively well-known figure. I was appointed by a large oil company to a post covering Gloucester and Cheltenham. They never withheld my salary if I wasn't there half the time due to rugby commitments, paying me continuously even when I was away on long tours. In return for such great generosity, they used my name to help their own business in the area, which was a fine arrangement.

The job also convinced me that I had a future as a businessman. I proved that even if my name had given me the initial opening, then I had the ability to justify my position in my own right. Otherwise, I'd still be selling my gold-tops and beating off the amorous housewives to this day.

I stayed happily with the company until I retired from rugby in 1978. That year was a double turning point in my life, because as well as finishing active rugby service, I first began to pay attention to a tall lock at Gloucester, a Jon Voight-like figure called John Hall. He was the son of a Northumberland farmer, and he had a thick northern accent to match. He had played for Northumberland and the North of England in England trials, and against the 1972-73 All Blacks. Hall had moved south because he wanted to keep the farming business in the family – he enrolled at the Royal Agricultural College, Cirencester. As he took in the farming knowledge, however, the entrepreneur in him emerged. He began to sell contraceptives and other useful items to his fellow students; he organised dinners, fêtes, and catering; he even began to organise overseas trips. Farming was quickly forgotten.

Hall's rugby career progressed too, from Cheltenham to Gloucester, where he really infuriated me. He had great ability but he'd be available one week and disappear on business the next. Had he concentrated on rugby, I believe he could have reached the top. He had other things on his mind, though. He spotted the vast potential in a firm organising rugby travel. Thousands of individual supporters wanted trips organised to watch their favourite sides all over the world, while clubs arranging tours were broadening their horizons and needed specialist help and advice. He travelled the world making connections with rugby unions, groups, and individuals, and founded 'Gullivers Travels' who have become the most famous name in rugby travel. Now, Hall and his company send thousands and thousands of people round the world on superb tours. The firm took over a thousand Welsh fans to Paris in 1981 to watch the France-Wales game; they took a huge and happy party to South Africa to support the 1980 Lions; they send about seventy clubs to North America for tours each season. They even send a small family to Benidorm now and again. The rugby travel industry is rocketing in importance and turnover, and John Hall was there at the beginning of the rush. He helped create the boom all by himself, and he made his firm a market leader.

Returning to 1978, Hall approached me and offered me a post as tour consultant. He wanted to take advantage of my experience of rugby travel. I knew where rugby people wanted to go, what they could expect when they got there; I knew how they thought and acted. I could take advantage of the hundreds of contacts I had made all over the world to help Hall and his firm, so I spent four happy years doing just that. I arranged and led trips to all parts, including the South African adventure; I went abroad with thousands of English fans and Welsh fans and looked after them. I had my heart in my mouth many times when, for example, a group of irate Welshmen approached, having just handed Gullivers Travels their life savings. 'Mike, we've all been thrown out of the hotel, all five hundred of us. What can we do now?' I somehow survived and I am now a director of the company.

I was also able to help Hall and his company supply many of their clients with match tickets, which are desperately hard to come by for the man in the street. As well as my directorship with Gullivers Travels, I am presently a director of Severn Sound, the Gloucester independent radio station. I enjoy my involvement in the running of the station immensely, especially in the sports coverage. I also have my own firm, Mike Burton (Sports Management) Limited, in which I represent the interests of various sportsmen and arrange first-class outings to major sporting encounters of all types, not just rugby.

My own brand of street humour seems to have found a market-place, because I seem to have become a sought-after speaker at all kinds of dinners.

Invitations come from all over the place, and a week never goes by without a letter from a club secretary asking whether I would be available to project my line of chatter and jokes at their particular audience. The biggest compliment and the biggest surprise in this area came last year, when Diggers Rugby Club of Zambia invited me out to their dinner. They paid for first-class return air travel and all the extras just for me to say a few words at their dinner. They even seemed to think it was worth it when I left for home.

My present income is therefore able to provide a considerably better life for my family than ever appeared likely on some of the wages I brought home over the years. With the help of one or two people, and in particular with the boost from becoming a well-known rugby union player, I have been able to rise far above the complete wreck of my early life and the humdrum existence of an odd-job man!

Mike Harrop of Maidenhead? Who was he?

3

HELLO MUM

THE Welsh and English teams were lined up side by side in the tunnel at Twickenham ready to take the field. The noise from that vast arena outside was thunderous. I remember my eyes smarting from the preparation which the Welsh teams had used to tone up their muscles. I looked across and saw Mervyn Davies and Dai Morris, J. P. R. Williams and John Dawes. All the greats. But the preparation for the match in the England camp had been so thorough, and my adrenalin was running so swiftly, that despite the knotting in the stomach and the fear of failure and ridicule which must accompany a first cap, I felt that they were not unbeatable.

The Welsh crocodile started to move forward and the roars from their fans made Twickenham like a giant Angel Hotel. Then I noticed Gareth Edwards and Barry John, last in the line. They didn't bother to run out, to dash on to the pitch in a blaze of glory and excitement and bravado: they strolled towards the exit, chatting, as if about the weather or the wife and kids. Gareth's toothless grin was on show as he and Barry ambled out. As I watched, my guts turning over at the prospect of playing for England for the first time, that display of complete and offhand calm I found amazing and disturbing. It was as if those two great men were expecting to win from divine right.

As England trotted down the tunnel, at least five other people were feeling as tense as I. Also winning their first caps were Mike Beese, Alan Old, Jan Webster, Alan Brinn, and a long-haired giant from the Rosslyn Park club called Andy Ripley. For me, my first cap was the culmination of eight years intense effort. Now I had all the satisfaction of being one of the élite: I had become an international footballer. There had been plenty of pitfalls and controversies on the way – even though I was later to discover that my rise from England possible-for-the-future to England prop was a good deal easier than remaining an England prop. But at Twickenham on that day in 1972, as I galloped on to the field, I had cause to thank rugby once again for lifting me from some rather tangled origins and putting me in the spotlight. More of England-Wales 1972 shortly. Now I would like to describe the build-up; what actually happened before I took the field at Twickenham.

As that 1972 season came round, I was steadily establishing myself and had been a Gloucester and Gloucestershire player for a long time. I had a sneaking regard for myself, in that none of those players who were supposedly ahead of me in the props' pecking order had ever given me much bother at club and county matches all over the country. Yet there were many other props who were well established in the eyes of the selectors. Keith Fairbrother, the Coventry man, had won twelve caps to date and proved himself adept with propping technique and vocal chords alike. Stack Stevens, the solid Cornishman, had toured New Zealand in the previous summer with the 1971 British Lions, the party who had the great satisfaction of beating New Zealand in their own backyard. Given what had gone before in international rugby, this miracle was at least the equivalent of feeding five thousand people with a few stale loaves and two particularly rancid kippers. Stack had been part of it and his reputation rose accordingly – and deservedly. Fran Cotton, a Loughborough Colleges prop, was also among those blocking my path to the England side. He had played for England in 1971 against Scotland and against the President's XV which came over to help celebrate the RFU Centenary. I never thought they were any greater than I was, despite all their England caps and Lions jerseys. People did begin to show interest in me, and not just the Gloucester die-hards, some of whom loyally clamour for their players to be chosen for every representative side under the sun. It seemed I was a definite possibility!

The first hurdle to negotiate for England hopefuls *en route* to Twickers was that peculiar system of trials matches which the England selectors used to use to obscure rather tricky selectorial points with an absolute dense fog, thereby making their already difficult job the next best thing to a pin and a blindfold. Or so it often seemed. Sandy Sanders was the new chairman of selectors, and he and his new panel were about to sweep clean with their new broom and put together a successful England side.

Sometimes the system used to pit an England XV against a regional team, or two regional sides together. This was an improvement from earlier days when trials were held in far away places as a sort of missionary gesture to various outposts; prospective England players had to spend three days on a train and then pick up the sherpas to reach the ground. The first regional trial in 1972 was the West against the North. I played on the tight head in the West team, with Robin Cowling at loose head and John Pullin between. Cowling was still a Gloucester player and had not yet begun his second career with Leicester, with whom he completed in 1981 a John Player Cup triumph for the third successive year. Neither had Cowling won any of his eight caps. Pullin was a Lions tests hooker. Enough said. Out we went at

Coventry to try to impress the men with the vote.

Colin White, Gosforth's captain in the 1981 John Player final, was at loose head for the North with F. E. Cotton on the tight head. Yet we still took six strikes against the head – solid facts for the selectors to work on. On that day, I saw a glimmer of light between the backs of the props I was chasing: I was on my way.

The next stage of the trials extravaganza came at Bristol, where the Probables played the Possibles. Over the years, some selections have owed themselves entirely to one trial. A player who has had a good spell, even a single good run in a trial, has come from almost nowhere into the team. One match should not really be able to change orderly selectors' minds, which at the top level should already be aware of all the necessary information about strengths and weaknesses and not really need trials – but many people have been catapulted into international rugby in this way. Even Phil Blakeway was. He came from trial reserves to Possibles prop to Probables prop all in one trial in 1980 because of injury, and he was then chosen for the England team. Mind you, that is not a very good illustration of my point because he thoroughly deserved to be in anyway, but it was a lucky chain of events which gave him the chance.

I raise the point about trials because round the same time as my trial for the West against the North, a London and South East side had been playing a Midlands team. Sure enough, the London trial threw up a combination almost from nowhere – Les Barlow, the Rosslyn Park loose head, Tony Boddy, the Metropolitan Police hooker, and David Trench impressed as a unit. Suddenly, more runners had entered the Grand England Props Stakes. In fact they had jumped over the fence on to the course as the race went into the final furlong. Therefore, into the Probables front row at Bristol went Trench and Barlow with Pullin, while Stack Stevens and I were given Boddy to keep us company. He was a good, workmanlike hooker who toured with England in Australia in 1972. Cotton and Fairbrother were also-rans for the moment.

A 3-1 tight head count for the Possibles against a front row containing John Pullin was not to be sniffed at by the selectors; so, with England playing the Rest at Twickenham, Mike Burton, Stack Stevens and John Pullin were proud wearers of the white jersey – without embroidered rose for the moment. I set off from Gloucester for the last trial match and an accompanying squad weekend as the man in possession. I was in and someone had to turf me out. I found the feeling tremendously to my liking.

If all my progress through that trials system seems terribly civilised and logical, then I should point out the doubts, worries, over-the-shoulder glances and sheer hard work and effort caused by my progress in 1972. But the tight head prop position was mine, given a decent trial.

The trial did not go well. Time ticked away and I was still desperately trying to get into the game as it drew to a close. I trooped off the field thinking that the crown had slipped: that Trench, Cotton, or Fairbrother would come through. In the dressing room, I wanted reassurance from other people. I think I went round the whole of the senior trial side individually saying: 'You had a good game. You'll be in OK', in the desperate hope that each would reciprocate those sentiments. I think I would have told someone he'd had a good game if he'd given four tries away, just as long as assurance would be forthcoming. This wasn't playing for Longlevens I was talking about, or for Gloucester, it was bloody England; the top.

We filed into the tea room to find something as familiar on a squad weekend as tactical talks or training – sandwiches. Wherever you turn, there they are, piled up on their silver platters with bits of lettuce poking out. When you arrive for a talk, relax after training, or prepare for bed at night, there they are, materialising like the Tardis. Had I done enough, I wondered aloud to Alan Brinn, between mouthfuls. Brinn was the second Gloucester forward who had been plodding through the trials along with me. He was in the Rest for the trial but he was a fine forward, a scrummager and an effective short line jumper.

From Twickenham we left for Lensbury, a sports ground in West London owned by Shell, where the facilities for serious coaching, solitude, and accommodation were excellent. This was where the defeat of Wales in a fortnight's time would be masterminded; where the England coach, John Elders, would formulate the dos and don'ts and build the organisation and team spirit; where we would all tune up for a few days. But before that, the big moment: the team was to be announced. Sandy Sanders had arranged a small room at Lensbury in which all the players gathered. There were about forty of us, including six props. Fran Cotton was recovered from injury and, in fact, it seemed to me that all the props had a fixed gloat on their faces, as if they knew they were in. After my mediocre trial, I began to convince myself steadily that I was out.

Sandy, being a typical Harlequin and English gentleman, wasn't going to put me out of my misery without uttering a few choice platitudes, thanking us for all our efforts and begging our indulgence during the new campaign. Everyone listening wanted to be part of it, of course: it could have been the start of something big. Then heads bowed, people started fidgeting, hearts started sinking. He began to read the team. 'Bob Hiller, captain,' he said. 'Janion, Beese, Duckham, Fielding, Old, Webster.' The forwards – would Sandy start with the back row? 'Stevens', he said, 'Pullin.' Everything went blank. The walls closed in on me, the ceiling sank down; I was in the room on my own, or so it seemed. 'Burton' said Sandy.

I heard none of the remainder of the team. Sandy could have announced the selection of Wavell Wakefield or Geoff Boycott and I wouldn't have heard. The thrill was incredible. I was about to nudge the person sitting next to me but suddenly I realised it was Fran Cotton, who was not in the side. 'And there we are', said Sandy when he finished.

As we all rose, Alan Brinn came up and stuck out a great paw. I took it and accepted his congratulations, not really noticing his extra wide beam. In fact it was not until later that I came out of my private world of delight and realised that my club colleague was in too. 'Brinn', Sandy must have said, 'Ralston, Dixon, Neary and Ripley'.

When I settled down for a period of reflection I realised that there were six new caps and that the new chairman had gone to town. As I have said, they included Andrew George Ripley, who was to go on to win more caps than any of us, and to become just a little more popular than me with Mums and Dads round the country. (I have always been at the disadvantage, of course, of not being asked to participate in *Superstars*. Mind you, my canoe would probably have sunk and they could have timed my sprint from the position of the sun.)

As we went to bed in readiness for a hard day's work, I began to compare the teams and a chill began to grip me. All right, we had a fair side. Those players whose game I knew on the England side were brave, workmanlike performers. I rated Alan Old, for example; and I knew that the forwards would not fail for lack of effort. But look at the Welsh side: hells bells! JPR, Barry and Gareth; Delme and Dai Morris. Old was all right but the man was playing against a legend. How were we ever going to beat that lot? The moment of panic passed, but a respect for the Welsh side remained right through the preparations, through the game itself, and, incidentally, persists to this day.

Next morning, Wales were to be regarded as the enemy to be beaten, not the enemy to be feared, and I regained the competitive attitude which had made me an international prop. We were together as a team, with the coach, and we began the tactical and mental build-up, sharpening minds and hearts for the big game.

John Elders was the first real coach I had come across – everyone else at Longlevens or Gloucester had been someone stepping into the breach and making a few observations and comments, perhaps an ex-player who put on a tracksuit to run around with the lads and then discussed rugby over a beer. He made no attempt, generally, to direct overall playing policy. But Elders was different; he was the real thing, expected to weigh up the opposition and develop our strengths. A silver-haired schoolmaster, he was a very sincere man, and was always prepared to listen. I also felt he was a good coach and found some of his views and little coaching points fascinating. Ultimately, he was perhaps too nice to be coach. He would suffix everything he said with 'OK?'. 'Do this, OK? Do that, OK?', as if he was asking our permission or our assurance that everyone agreed. After the sessions he would sometimes fall into step with a certain player on the way to the changing rooms, bringing up some point which he thought might be helpful.

During the breaks from sandwiches at Lensbury that weekend, Elders formulated his strategy. One of the things he had spotted, as had everyone else who had ever watched rugby on television, was that John Williams was dangerous coming into the line. In 1972, the fearless Williams's effectiveness was at its height. Even though he was the last line of defence, he was also in many ways Wales's first line of attack, too. He could open defences like a crafty burglar working on a safe. As the years went by, other teams developed counter tactics and he found things a little harder. As the eighties approached, he merely settled back and continued as the most courageous and best defensive full-back ever. But in 1972 he was a danger in attack and he had to be stopped. We knew he would come charging at us, launched by the Welsh backs, and Elders knew we had to try to stop him.

We worked really hard on our counter, on our net to catch the flying doctor. The England wingers would stay out with their opposite numbers, so that when JPR came charging, they would not be drawn in to tackle him, thus leaving their man free. The man who would take JPR would be our own full-back and captain, Bob Hiller. Wherever Williams entered the line, Hiller would be up to take him. The JPR deputy we fielded for our sessions was Peter Knight, the full-back from Bristol, even though a greater contrast between the ferocious flying doctor from Bridgend and the religious, quiet man from Bristol could not be imagined. Yet Knight played his part well. He came into the line, and the wingers stayed out; up would come Hiller to tackle him. If he came in between his centres, Hiller would tackle him. If he came outside his centres, Hiller would tackle him. This sort of planning gave me a tremendous boost, and I thought Elders was a magician – I had never before seen anything worked out so deeply and in such detail.

Next we switched our attention to what we would do if Wales attacked on other fronts, concentrating especially on preventing Gareth Edwards and Barry John creating trouble. We wanted Peter Dixon, Tony Neary and Ripley to blot them out. Elders laid the traps again. For instance, if Gareth broke, even flat across the field, Neary would go with him and nail him. He would ignore any dummies and put him down. If he ran off the field and through the car park, Neary would still be with him. If he scissored with Barry John, Ripley would be there to take on John and snuff out the move.

I was even more impressed. I couldn't give a damn what the papers were saying or what my heart had been saying earlier. Now I was confident. The adrenalin was running as we finished laying our traps, worked out some more moves of our own, and walked from the training field for a sandwich.

As I munched, I looked around the lads – my lads. I saw all their good points and their qualities and I realised that perhaps there wasn't such a gap after all. Many of that England side were eventually to be firm friends off the field as well as on it, friendships which I still treasure.

I wasn't too sure about Tony Neary at first, because he seemed to be everything I wasn't. He was cool and good-looking, and a solicitor in Manchester. In those early days in the England side I was self-appointed team joker and all the lads would be laughing away at my 'funnies' wherever we were – travelling on coaches or planes, or in the dressing rooms, or on the training fields of the world. Fran Cotton, for example, used to chuckle away at me with his shoulders going up and down like a demented Ted Heath. Neary used to smile but his reserve never allowed him to laugh. In fact, in my less secure days in the early 1970s I often used to gauge what a player thought of me by the amount he laughed at my attempts at humour. Neary smiled, nothing more. But as time went by Tony and I became firm friends; I always used to find his company enjoyable, and now he even laughs at my jokes . . . Nevertheless, you do not become the leading cap winner in the history of English rugby by being solely a jolly nice fellow. Neary has a hard edge and was a fierce competitor. One Northern journalist told me that he was the hardest man he had ever met. Once, in a Calcutta Cup match at Twickenham, Neary went through a Scottish line-out and tackled their flanker, Nairn MacEwan, so hard that the Scotsman's jaw was broken in three places. That flash of steel surfaced on a previous occasion and shook me to my socks.

It was on the 1972 England tour and a test match was imminent. The Lions hotel was crammed with friends and hangers-on and most of the players were urgently searching for tickets for their particular friends who were floating around. Choet Vissar, the Lions liaison officer, managed a small supply for Neary and myself, including some prime seats and some not so good. Now Terry Byrne (the person who, as I reveal later, almost caused me to join the rugby league), was in the hotel and I decided to hand my share of the tickets to him. He came over and I gave him the good seat tickets. Off went Terry like a dog with two tails.

Neary approached for his allocation and I handed over the remaining tickets. He turned away, but stopped as soon as he realised that I hadn't given him any good seats. 'These are no good', he said, with the fair assessment that I should have seen him all right. 'Where are the good seats?

You've given them to that fellow from Gloucester, haven't you?' I could see the flash of anger behind that smooth exterior. I sped off to find Choet Vissar and begged him to find some other tickets. Thankfully, he did so, and I raced after the glowering Neary to heal the temporary breach. We often laugh about the incident nowadays, but he certainly showed me his hard side when I tried to fob him off.

When Tony went on the 1977 Lions tour to New Zealand he realised that I was terribly disappointed not to be selected. I had set my heart on going. As the tour was approaching its end, I received a card from Tony, signed by all the Lions party – he must have gone round the whole team specially to get them to sign. I appreciated that gesture enormously. Five years before, seated in a room at Lensbury, Neary seemed aloof, but he turned into a real friend and was, of course, a truly outstanding rugby player.

The training weekend at Lensbury ended and I went home to Gloucester with plenty to anticipate. There was another fortnight to go before the Welsh match and on the intervening Saturday I was allowed to drop out of a Gloucestershire county match to rest for the international, in the tradition of new caps. I went along to watch the game and surprised myself when some of the lads tried to entice me to a celebration drink afterwards. I replied tersely in the negative and went straight home for a run.

Though I didn't think anything of it at the time, this period was the first time I really realised just how much an international sportsman has to dedicate himself to reach the top and how much work he has to do to stay there. During the next fortnight, if I ran upstairs and found myself slightly out of breath, I'd panic and think: 'Christ. I haven't done enough.' If I stumbled in the garden a vision would swim into my mind of me lying in hospital with a fractured ankle, watching England play Wales. Yet I negotiated the last few days before the team was due to assemble, and I worked hard at my own training. I also read gratefully the many letters and telegrams of congratulations that my selection had brought; there were several from junior clubs in the Gloucester area, and others from old mentors and adversaries all over the country.

Alan Brinn and I travelled back to Lensbury on the Thursday with international fever reaching critical proportions. On the field, we ran through the counters, the moves, the attack, the defence, the signals, the strategy, putting a final polish on things.

The night before the match drew on, with all the side making such a terrific effort to look relaxed that they managed to look very unrelaxed indeed! But I had a recurring image of JPR being cut down by Hiller, and of Gareth and Barry being cut down by a rampant English back row. I had a further, personal cause for confidence, too. Opposite me in the scrums was to be the

Welsh captain and loose head, John Lloyd. The balding Lloyd was a sound prop but wherever I had played against him, for Gloucester against Bridgend, he hadn't really impressed or frightened me as a world-class force. He was steady and a trier, but the prospect of facing Lloyd at Twickenham next day was a relatively comfortable one for me. One – England were ready to win; two – JPR was going to be hammered; three – John Lloyd was not going to prove a problem. Those were my thoughts as I went up to my room with my cocoa and sandwiches. I did not realise it then, of course, but I was to be proved seriously wrong on all three counts!

Any player will testify that sleep on the night before a first international is a problem, even to such great 'kippers' of our time as Fran Cotton. I remember lying awake as the light blue haze of dawn crept through my window and panicking at images of myself falling asleep on the field or being rendered useless by exhaustion. I next opened my eyes at half past nine, feeling rested but anxious. The anxiety continued as I ambled down for breakfast; my mind and my pulse were racing. When a waitress called out something I said 'Yes'. She was asking me if I wanted a full house – eggs, sausages and bacon with toast and the lot. I just managed to pick up the plate and turn away without assistance. In fact I never usually had breakfast, and I had to get through all that with a churning stomach. John Elders came over. 'Do you eat much lunch?' he asked.

The training field at Lensbury that morning was filled with players strolling round; again, their efforts to look casual were transparent failures. I was walking beside Jan Webster and we must have looked drained and worried. Dave Duckham came over. 'Come on, you two, it's not a bloody war you know.' There was just time for one more talk by Elders face-to-face.

As Elders spoke, people were donning red and white bobble caps and leaving hotels; queues were forming at stations all over South London; underground trains were picking up hordes of happy groups en route for Twickenham; vendors were setting up their boards with rosettes pinned to them; ticket touts were fingering the precious commodity in their inside pockets and hoping that demand would be good; coaches were rumbling in through Hounslow from the west; the Welsh side were listening to their coach and mentally playing the game in their minds; the groundsman at Twickenham was taking his final look at his pride and joy, the turf; the television cameras were testing, the interviews were being set up. All over the rest of the rugby world, people were preparing their TV dinners and standing by to share the occasion beamed straight to their firesides from a fashionable suburb of south-west London.

A rugby international is a great event. It was in 1972 when I first played. One of the great plusses of the game, notwithstanding the squabbles, the difficulties with the laws, the occasional violence, is that rugby has its internationals. Now these create even more fanatical interest, attracting big business and serving as the great shop window of the game.

For once, I wanted to be quiet on the bus to the ground – not to make comments that would get the lads laughing. We arrived at Twickenham, and a gloomy place it was on that day. As the coach stopped and I stepped down, I saw a lone Welshman standing across the way from me, a large puddle between us. His bobble hat was soaking. 'Mike. 'Aven't got a spare ticket, 'ave yew?' The England accents reached me too. 'Come on now, Burton, have a good match', and so on. I couldn't help the Welshman with a ticket, but I couldn't help feeling sorry for him, and identifying with him too. He was working-class and his Twickenham trip had probably divested him of his life savings. He was probably a fanatic who supported the game week in, week out. Despite his red woolly hat and his Welsh accent, despite his cheek in asking an England player to help him go in and support Wales, I felt that I had more in common with him than with many of the English people in the crowd.

I walked into the dressing room and grabbed the number three jersey. 'Look at that', I told Alan Brinn, holding up my jersey with its England rose. Then we went out on to the pitch itself for another little ritual, the inspection of the field – as if it might have disappeared, or turned blue, or suddenly developed large hills and valleys since we were last there. We came up the tunnel to the cheers of those early into the ground and stood there looking thoughtful and important. I threw up a few blades of grass to check the wind and struck my heel into the turf and looked sagely downwards. Just what use all this was to a tight head prop, or indeed to anyone else, I never really found out. All the England team gathered on the halfway line, throwing up bits of grass and sticking their heels into the ground and nodding sagely, like a formation dancing team. It did help to calm the nerves to take in some fresh air, I suppose.

Suddenly, David Duckham spotted something. The stands were still almost empty, since stand ticket-holders do not have to jostle for their position like those on the terraces and come in later. Duckham was staring up into the top tier of the East Stand. 'Look at that woman up there', he said. On about the third row, high above the knot of players, was a lone figure, waving frantically at us. Peter Dixon and Duckham and the others looked up disbelievingly. For my part, since a large coat with wide lapels was not available for me in which to slink off, I had to admit that it was my very own mother! 'She's been here all night', I said, bringing smiles to everyone's faces. I walked a few steps towards the stand and waved back. That provoked a double-handed burst of frantic waving akin to a collapsing windmill as my mother's pride came to the surface. I turned away to find that the whole England team had got the idea. They were all waving, interrupting their mental preparation for taking on a brilliant Welsh side, in front of millions of people, to wave to Mike's mum.

That little interlude, and the fact that I was playing at all, may have made up in some ways for the struggles which she had in bringing me up. It was also the last light interlude that afternoon. We went to the dressing room and the door slammed behind us, shutting out the world and shutting in the team. I jumped on the scales several times and checked my boots for the fiftieth time, as a hundred thoughts flickered through my mind. Suddenly the door opened, and a man I knew only as 'Fergie', who used to help run the Barbarians, looked in. 'Half an hour, lads', he called, and was gone. 'What the hell is he doing here?' I remember thinking as I began changing. Then a parade of well-wishers came through the dressing rooms; RFU presidents, people with bristling moustaches. Flesh was duly pressed and then they departed. All part of the scene. 'Twenty minutes', Fergie called. The atmosphere became electric and the room filled with heavy vapour from the rubs as people went about their stretching exercises. 'Ten minutes' called Fergie. Then, after what seemed like half an hour, 'Five minutes'. Christ, this is it, I thought. '. . . to photograph', said Fergie. I had completely forgotten that we had to take the field in full battle dress for the photographers to take their beloved 'team groups'. I found that I had been champing at the bit, punching the toilet door, rolling my shoulders, stretching my hamstrings, and mentally scrummaging John Lloyd into the turf, all in preparation for the team photograph!

We filed back into the dressing room, and then Fergie was shouting for real. Out we went again, and saw those scarlet jerseys in the ante-chamber where the television people do their interviews and where the band keep their reserve drumsticks. That was all the preparations for the international finished. Tactics – nerves – sandwiches – were all behind.

And that is where we came in to this chapter, my eyes watering from liniment, and that show of confidence from Barry and Gareth as they sauntered out. The build-up I have described set the pattern for all my international weekends: the nervousness was always there, and so were the little disagreements and the moments of laughter. Broadly speaking, it was always the same.

Meanwhile, back in 1972 at Twickenham, I suddenly found the ball in my hands, an untenable position for a prop. England had kicked off, Delme Thomas caught the ball, and I came up and took it straight from him and fed Jan Webster. The television replays show the ball emerging from a mêlée of players but unfortunately the man behind this early scrap of English possession is hidden. It *was* me though – honest!

Then came the first scrum; I was anticipating the struggle with relish. Bang. Down we went. During that game, John Lloyd never once hit me, pushed me without the ball, bit me, gouged me or even spoke to me. But he played like a man possessed – he was a completely different proposition from his club form, like Popeye after the spinach. For the first time I realised what international stimulus could do to a man. Lloyd and I had a real battle and he was a fearsome opponent, but that said, we played soundly enough. Alan Old and Jan Webster linked confidently and in the front row we just managed to shade the tight head battle. There was very little in it, though, and as the game wore on into the last quarter, Wales led by just 6-3. Barry John had kicked two penalties to Bob Hiller's one.

With the game thus critically poised, Wales were obviously going to throw their moves at us when they next won a pressure position. Barry John duly kicked them down to near our line and English eyes turned to the Welsh backs, who were signalling and whispering amongst themselves. Wales won a ball and Edwards shot away straight across the field. All that work on our counter tactics was going to be tested. As planned, Tony Neary shot after him and grounded Gareth. As he did so, the great man slipped a pass inside to Barry John. Sure enough, Ripley was there, and he made a smother tackle on John, ending the move. My belief in our chances and in John Elders was reaching a high.

Then the whole thing was blown wide apart. All our efforts went for nothing as a crucial and mortal thrust was delivered – there are no prizes for remembering by whom. The ball was moved to the right and I saw JPR accelerating to make one of those charges into the line outside his centres. I had faith. I believed. Instead of setting off for the corner flag and anticipating a clean Welsh break, I ran towards the spot where I believed Bob Hiller was going to come up and knock Williams down, just as he had taken care of Peter Knight on the open spaces at Lensbury. JPR took the ball and Dave Duckham stayed out with Gerald Davies on Williams's right. Williams pounded on and Hiller closed on him. This time – tragically and inexplicably – Hiller made a feeble, token tackle. A schoolboy could have done better. Far less than halting Williams and snuffing out the move, he hardly slowed Williams's progress. As he picked himself up, Hiller saw the rear end of JPR descending over the English line. Nearby photographers snapped the joyous expressions on Williams's face and a brave, despairing effort by Peter Dixon to stop him. One important link in the chain had failed miserably, and the whole thing collapsed. We knew what was coming when we lined up before the move: we had even known two weeks before that Williams would come charging: Bob Hiller knew he had to take Williams, but when it came to the high noon of the match, he failed us. We were beaten 12-3 with the try being converted.

After that we were mentally gathering ourselves to try to hit back and to stop that sinking feeling hindering the effort, when Hiller came up behind us, making all sorts of encouraging noises, and some hostile ones, which were supposed to lift us for the last few minutes. But as I looked back at him and saw his clenched fist smack into his open palm, I didn't see England's inspiring captain, but the man who had just let in a vital try. Hiller played once more for England and then retired, after a memorable career. For me, his retirement was just as well, because he would never have carried quite the same authority.

As I lifted my glass to John Lloyd after the match, disappointment steadily eased and was replaced by quiet satisfaction that I had held up my end; that I had played for England and would do so again. In fact, despite my regard for John Elders and for others in the team, we had a disastrous season which ended in a crushing humiliation in Paris. But that is another story which appears shortly. I left Twickenham in 1972 a member of a losing side but, more important, at least a member of the side.

4

GOODBYE ENGLAND

IT is thought in rugby circles that I am the only life member of the Rest XV. This team is the one which contests the England trial matches against the England XV. In other words, the Rest side is the Possibles, and they play against the Probables. I gave a lifetime of devoted service to the Rest because I was always chosen in that team. Even when I thought I was England's tight head in possession, when I was racing favourite to make the team, I was still selected to take up my ordained place with the Rest in the England trials.

This was a particularly difficult way to impress the selectors because, although the side was supposed to be composed of 'possibles', it usually consisted of a desperate combination of just-possibles, highly-improbables and never-in-a-million-years. I was usually given a hooker with a wooden leg to pack down with, a young loose head prop a year out of school, and two genuine home counties locks who used to blow away if the wind got up unexpectedly during the match. In fact for several seasons the Rest provided the only opposition which England could beat, and, given the trials selection, no wonder.

It was from the humble origins of the Rest XV that every year I had to launch my bid to climb into the England side – to claim the tight head prop position which I coveted more than anything else on earth. If playing for England wasn't everything to me, then it was certainly the next best thing. In the previous chapter I described the start of my England career in 1972. It spanned the next seven seasons, yet I played in only about half the internationals which England played during that time. For those seven years I rode a switchback, soaring into the side then diving out, courtesy of the selectors, till I felt quite dizzy and devastated. Some seasons, I played in all the games, but in 1973 and 1977, for example, I missed them all. To say my career at international level was up and down is an understatement. Before I trace the highlights and disappointments of Burton and England, I shall recall a typical year in the life of Burton of England, which illustrates better than any other year what I had to contend with. It is also the year when I decided that I had had enough.

As the trials approached for the 1978 international season, I began my mental preparation to continue my loyal service to the Rest. After all, despite my rather mixed opinion of playing for the Rest, at least it was better to be in the trials rather than out of the spotlight altogether. I went through the usual round of Gloucester and county games.

Sandy Sanders was chairman of selectors. He was the man, you will recall, who had announced my first cap in 1972 in that crowded room at Lensbury. He pleased me a lot less with his choice of the teams for the 1978 trials. In the England side was Robin Cowling at loose head and Fran Cotton at tight head. In the Rest, my side, the life member was dropped completely. How could they do that to me after all my years of service? They chose Barry Nelmes at loose head and Bert Greaves, of Moseley, in my position. It seemed that I was completely forgotten and discarded. I had played in none of the England games in 1977 and now perhaps my England career was over.

But worse was to follow. Cotton suffered a leg injury – one of approximately two hundred assorted injuries to all parts of his body which the big man suffered in his career. Bert Greaves was promoted to the England side and one Terry Pryor, of Redruth, was brought in to fill the vacant place in the Rest. 'Terry who?' asked thousands of people all over the country.

I sincerely hope that I never over-rated myself, and I certainly never saw myself as the front row's first superstar and the pack's answer to Barry John and Muhammad Ali. But in 1978 I was an experienced prop, I had taken on all the world's leading meanies, I had played in South Africa for the Lions, I was at the prime age for a leading prop – yet I was dumped. England were facing their first match of the season, against France in Paris, and I seemed to have no part in their plans.

When he saw the trial teams, John Reason, then of *The Daily Telegraph*, fired off in his normal, realistic manner: 'No English prop is nearly so well qualified as Mike Burton to complete the pool of three props needed for England's match against France in Paris. No one else is either technically or physically capable of taking on the French front row, particularly in the event of injury to Cotton.' Sandy Sanders was forced to reply to such criticism and to the threat of armed insurrection against Twickenham by hosts of Gloucester followers – which might have made Toxteth, Moss Side and the other 1981 riots look like an under-21s touch rugby match. *The Citizen,* the Gloucester paper, carried the story of how one of my supporters had rung up Sandy Sanders personally to give him a piece of his Burton-orientated mind. Poor Sandy probably went ex-directory for all future matches.

Sanders declared that the selectors hadn't ruled me out completely or disciplined me. 'We know exactly what he can do', he said. 'We are aware of his strengths and weaknesses.' These noble sentiments do not bear close examination because if they thought I was good enough, why didn't they pick me? Alternatively, if they did not bother to play people in trials about whom they knew everything, why did they pick Peter Squires, Alan Old, Peter Wheeler, Bill Beaumont, Peter Dixon or any of the others that they knew all about? And as for knowing my strengths and weaknesses, I feel strongly, as do all the props of my era, that the England selection committee had very little idea at all what was happening in the front row to measure anybody's strengths and weaknesses. Nevertheless I had been firmly led out to grass, and I was to be found moodily chewing the cud in my Gloucester paddock, attempting to bite anyone who came near me. I was upset and angry.

Messrs Pryor and Greaves took part in the trial and, with respect, as far as their international pretensions were concerned you could have put them both together, and they still couldn't have hit the snow off a clothes-line with a shovel.

The trial took place and it was obvious that Fran Cotton would take up the tight head position. Then ripples suddenly began to appear on the selectors' little pond. Cotton's leg injury was not improving, and the ripples quickly turned to tidal waves as he withdrew. England faced Paris without him and with the two new stars next in line. The selectors scratched their heads. Remember, they were not nominating a side to go down and celebrate the opening of the new showers at some junior club in the wilderness. They were picking people to go out on to the Parc des Princes to take on what was at the time the most fearsome and powerful pack of forwards in French history. They were nominating forwards to stand up to Gerard Cholley, one of the biggest, strongest and hardest props in history; to Robert Paparemborde, who took time off from charging round the field like a threequarter to scrummage all and sundry into the ground; to Imbernon and Palmie, the locks. They couldn't jump, couldn't handle, couldn't run or kick or pass. Their functions lay elsewhere! All those chosen for this singularly unenjoyable afternoon had to take on that lot in front of thousands of bawling, moaning, whistling Frenchmen under the jurisdiction of a referee quite probably as scared as they were; and they had to do it for ninety minutes without escape. They would still expect a decent burial back in Blighty, too.

Bert Greaves and Terry Pryor sank rapidly beneath the waves, just as they seemed to be approaching the beach. Mike Burton received his call-up papers and was wheeled out of his paddock. Armed with passport, boots and a fairly good idea of what was coming to him from Monsieur Cholley, he was pushed into action. Experiments, the new men the selectors wanted to see, were shelved till somewhat friendlier opposition became available. The selectors came running.

For half a second, I contemplated letting them stew. Then I went to Paris and got to grips with Cholley. I anticipated his butts and he anticipated mine. I pushed and shoved him and he pushed and shoved me. We went at each other like fighting cocks and ended almost on our knees as France won 15-6. Robin Cowling, the loose head, played on with a dislocated shoulder. Total courage was the sort needed at Parc des Princes – courage to the point of recklessness and stupidity. Anything less, and England could have been swept away. After the match Cholley came over and tossed me a bottle of wine. He drank his down in one and indicated that I should do the same. In a masochistic, trembling sort of way, I even enjoyed my four visits to France, to take on Jean Iraçabal in 1972 and 1974 and Gerard Cholley in 1976 and 1978. I never played against France at Twickenham.

Two matches in succession for England already represented a sustained run for me, but Cotton was still unfit for the next match of the 1978 season, a home game against Wales. The Welsh were different from the French: they were not quite as ferocious, especially away from home, but all of them suffered a burning desire not to lose to England. They also regarded victory as their divine right. The current Welsh team is not so affected because they have been unsuccessful, but 1978 was still the golden era. Above everything, they had skill as well as muscle: and they had Gareth.

As recognition for my services against France, the selectors kept me in the side to play Wales. Barry Nelmes, then of Cardiff, was brought in to replace Cowling, whose shoulder was still mending. For me, as tight head, a visit from Wales meant an afternoon with Charlie Faulkner, a hard old prop from Pontypool. Hard and old were two very operative words. Charlie even brought along his mates Bobby Windsor and Graham Price to keep him company. Faulkner was less volatile than Cholley, as I explain in a fuller appreciation later, but he was experienced and would be hanging on against all-comers at the final whistle.

It was a gloomy, muddy, slimy day at Twickenham. Gareth was playing his fiftieth game for his country. It was a hard forward battle, and Charlie and I waded round at Twickenham with honours even. I helped shore up the front row along with Peter Wheeler, the hooker, because Barry Nelmes was in trouble against Graham Price on the other side of the scrum. Nelmes's main strengths lay outside the scrummage. I felt it was one of my better games in the England jersey; once again, I gave everything and backed down from nothing.

It was heartbreaking, then, that Gareth Edwards controlled the match like a conjuror, thereby rendering all our muddy efforts in our little twilight world utterly useless and irrelevant. It didn't really matter who was on top, Gareth kicked the ball down behind us and broke our hearts. We could win two or three balls in succession, batter our way up field and be poised for an attack on the Welsh line: then Gareth would send the ball rolling and trickling into our 25 and we had to start again. Phil Bennett kicked a winning penalty when the score had been at 6-6 for a long period. Bob Mordell, the flanker, playing his first match for England, had been penalised for going over the top in a ruck. (Mordell was never chosen again and joined the League.) Bennett buried us, but Edwards had dug the grave.

With the shattering disappointment of defeat came a satisfying realisation that I had done everything possible in my own sphere and that I had won the respect of Charlie and the opposition. Now, it seemed that a dream might come true once again. In all the time that Fran Cotton and I were vying for that tight head place, which took in most of the seventies, there appeared to many people an obvious alternative. There was never really a fully-established loose head prop, so why not switch Cotton to loose head and leave room for me at tight head? Fran Cotton is one of the very few people who could perform at loose head and tight head with equal effect and at international class: he could even do it at world class. He held down the tight head spot throughout the 1974 test series against South Africa while the Mighty Mouse packed down on the other side. But in 1977, a few months before that England-Wales 9-6 match, he had won a place in the test side against New Zealand as loose head and, with Graham Price on the tight head side, had seen off the whole country.

After the 1978 Welsh match, Cotton reported fit. Surely, with Nelmes in trouble against Wales and with Burton having held his end up, it was going to be Cotton, Wheeler and Burton together, with Fran in his Lions 1977 position of loose head? Over the years, many people called for this front row – former internationals, the press, and especially Mike Burton. If Cotton was at loose head, my chances of playing for England were increased, so why shouldn't I call for it . . . but, seriously, I also felt that was the front row which would serve England best. I genuinely rated Cotton as a loose head, having scrummaged against him in trials and training and felt the power coming from him. I also realised that I was rated by international props in other countries and that the Cotton, Wheeler and Burton combination was not the one that they would have chosen for the sake of their own peace of mind.

Even Fran's family would have had it that way; they always treated me like a prodigal son rather than their own son's front row rival. Dave Cotton, Fran's father, used to come up to me and grab my arm: 'You'll have a good do when they put you and our Franny alongside that Wheeler', he would say.

Fran Cotton himself recently set down on paper his chosen England front row from this era. He placed himself at loose head, and M. Burton at tight – so there for all to see is what the protagonist himself felt. However, as I say, the selectors usually ignored the calls and kept Cotton at tight head, while I developed the square backside that comes from too much sitting round on replacements' benches. I don't believe that I was the only one to see the irony when, just after I retired, another Gloucester tight head prop came on to the scene: Phil Blakeway. Cotton was shunted off to the loose head so quickly that he nearly left his feet behind. Blakeway filled the resulting gap with all the large amount of ability which he has. The result – Grand Slam.

Back to 1978. I was waiting to see if that great leap forward would happen – or perhaps I should say the great leap sideways, with Fran being moved to loose head thus allowing me to stay in the team to play Scotland at Murrayfield. The scene was the lavatory of my house in Gloucester, where I was comfortably seated contemplating my wife's exquisite taste in wallpaper and my own limited ability as a wallpaper-hanger. My son arrived outside the door flourishing the local paper. I took it and retreated to my seat.

In the stop press, under the latest racing results and in the normal smudged, misspelt stop press type, was the England team to play Scotland. The wires of the Press Association had beamed the news across the country and it had landed in the offices of my local paper.

There were the usual mistakes. Z. Cotton, it read. P. Wheeler then B. Nelmes. There was no way that B. Nelmes was a misprint for M. Burton. That sinking, bitter, agonising feeling I had experienced many times came shooting back. The pain was so bad it was almost physical. Although you keep telling yourself it doesn't really matter and that not playing for England isn't the end of the world, you suddenly realise that it matters terribly – and that if being dropped isn't the end of the world then you might just rather have the end of the world. I was out, dumped on my ear after answering the selectors' call and playing two good games.

When it came down to it, it obviously didn't matter how many people said I should be in the team: Sandy Sanders and his selectors didn't choose via public opinion. I thought ahead to Murrayfield. There would be a few square inches of the wooden bench reserved especially for me. I would travel up with the team, train, take in the coach's pronouncements. Then, I would put on a tracksuit and sit on the replacements' bench. It was the difference between riding the winner of the Derby and mucking him out.

There and then, in the smallest room, I decided that this was one disappointment too many. I had won seventeen caps and given grateful thanks for every last one. I had had almost as many disappointments as I had caps and I wasn't going to put my name down for any more. I made up my mind to refuse to act as replacement at Murrayfield and, soon after, I retired altogether from rugby.

My reasons for retiring were not solely concerned with England disappointments, as I explain in the next chapter. I did not want to go into decline as a player and also wanted to see my wife and three children a little more often. Similarly, my decision not to go to Murrayfield was not made solely because I was sulking at not being in the team, or because I detested the role of replacement.

At the time, Gloucester were involved in a John Player Cup run; as I was in the international squad, I had missed several important matches as the club prepared for each round. If I went to Scotland, I would miss the last game before the semi-final match against Gosforth. I had been missing from the Gloucester side for too long and also needed match practice.

So with disappointment weighing heavy, I rang Twickenham. I spoke to Colonel Morgan, one of a whole battery of servicemen, it seems, who administer the Union. I explained that I was not going to Murrayfield. This was hardly the done thing as far as the Colonel was concerned, but I didn't want to begin a telephone argument. My England career ended at that point. I had thoroughly enjoyed it all, but I just felt that it could have lasted a little longer and been less fraught. I retired completely a few weeks later.

* * * *

Seventeen caps at a time when a world-class forward like Cotton was around was a good return and, in any case, I was not considered for some of the games because of injury or temporary banishment from internationals. Nevertheless I am still going to be conceited enough to try to explain why I didn't win more caps, fully realising that many players who just missed one cap after years of struggle are going to call me an ungrateful and whingeing old man. Inevitably, the discussion will embrace the whole question of English selection, which, until very recent times, has been lamentable. Even now, flashes of the old bad selection occur.

Lack of knowledge of front row play hampered forward selection in my time. There was nothing like the disgraceful selection for a match against the All Blacks in the 1978-79 season, when Barry Nelmes was chosen out of position and played very much like a roach on the riverbank; while number eight John Scott was thrown into the second row and told to jump against Andy Haden. If that selection was the fruition of a lot of bad basic selections, then I could see where it sprang from: the selectors never seemed fully to realise the qualities needed in the front row, or the skills. They didn't seem to analyse who was mentally tough enough to absorb all the pressure of an international match and still show his true form – in other words they didn't sort out the bluster from true effectiveness.

It is extremely difficult for someone who has never been an international prop to assess those who could become one. There is no yardstick unless you have a thorough and inside knowledge of what is happening. Any fool can make a rough assessment of hooking ability by the number of times the ball comes back on his side; line-out jumpers can be rated by the amount of line-out balls they win; even open-side flankers can sometimes be roughly summed up by the number of times they arrive first at the loose ball. Yet propping and props are extremely difficult to judge; far too difficult for the selection committees of the seventies. Lack of knowledge is forgivable but not on the part of people who choose international sides.

Yet selection of the whole England side has been hit-or-miss for years now – not only in the choice of players for the very next match, but also the 'B' players and replacements, and the players for tours. There seems to be little early appreciation of who is going to make it and who needs to be brought in for certain specific tasks. All these areas have been riddled with mistakes and England's results have suffered badly in consequence. Bad selection was largely responsible for the 2-0 series defeat in Australia in 1975, although the fact that I was sent off in the Second Test did have a bearing too.

The half-back choices have been the most glaring disaster. Of all the half-backs selected for England in the last twelve years, and there have been hundreds of them it seems, very few have been given a chance to settle down; few have been told to play their own game. They told Martin Cooper to kick when he was really a runner, and when he didn't kick well they dropped him; the same happened to Les Cusworth. Bad selection policies have destroyed more good half-backs than they have provided.

Some of the main errors which I remember provide an overall picture of what English rugby had to overcome. Remember Steve Callum, a flanker from Upper Clapton who was selected to go to Australia in 1975? In fact, he had been to the country shortly before with the England Schoolboys and was only really an overgrown schoolboy when he was chosen for the real thing. Australia in 1975 was no place for inexperience. All the old hands were needed and to hell with policy for the future. If you are always selecting for the future then you never choose your best side for the present. Callum came into the England running largely on the recommendation of Dickie Jeeps – but how a player can play for England from Upper Clapton is beyond me now, and it was certainly beyond most of the England party in 1975. The player may have shone for Upper Clapton and for Eastern Counties. But we needed forwards who had been through the mill and were truly experienced, not experienced because they had played one season in junior rugby and perhaps had hit someone back when they were hit. Experience is gained by coming under the hammer as the Pontypool forwards put on the pressure; by taking on the Gloucester side in full cry at Kingsholm; by fighting till the end as Gosforth, or Hawick, or Bridgend, are giving your side a caning; by doing it year after year, not once each. Callum was not a success in Australia and at international level has entered the mysterious list of people lost without trace.

It was another old England player, Ron Jacobs, who first brought to my attention a lock called Bob Wilkinson. Wilkinson was another Eastern Counties man and I remember being in a circle listening to Jacobs's high opinion of him. In fact, Wilkinson gained a high reputation as a line-out forward at Cambridge University and also turned out for the Barbarians' 1973 match against the All Blacks. He won six caps in the mid-seventies, went to Australia, and was generally regarded as the line-out champion of England. He was chosen over the likes of Nigel Horton and Chris Ralston and other more grizzled specimens who, had they been asked, might not have rated the leaping university lad very highly. I certainly didn't rate him much at all. He was too easily psyched out and was not hard enough mentally or physically for international football. An illustration of this came in 1975. We had returned to this country to lick our wounds having been hustled and kicked to defeat by the Wallabies – and when I say kicked to defeat, I don't mean that they *scored* with kicks. Yet the Australians made a quick return visit, a full tour of Britain. I was chosen for their international against England only months after being sent off against Finnane and company in Australia.

The press made an extremely big issue out of this match. They gave the impression that I was locked in a cage at Twickenham being fed raw meat, and that it would take a miracle for Steve Finnane and his colleagues even to be alive when they reached hospital after I had sorted them out in a vengeful attack. But I didn't see it that way at all. I was conscious of the fact that the Australians hadn't respected our rugby in Australia. I wanted to show them legally but forcefully that our rugby was superior. Even better, Fran Cotton was chosen at loose head and I relished the whole thing as the tight head. Wilkinson was brought into the second row for his first England home match. He had played one test in Australia.

I was desperately anxious that the England pack should do well and that we should win well. Nothing was going to stand in our way, friend or enemy. Early in the game, and although he had a quiet tour, Finnane the Phantom Puncher landed one on Wilkinson. It wasn't Finnane's best shot because they tended to put people away completely. But Wilkinson sat down and stayed there. I grabbed him by the arm and literally hauled him up. 'Bloody stand up', I growled. The fact that he rose with something approaching alacrity made me think that he wasn't so badly hurt and that, if he were a true international forward, he would have bounced straight back up, refusing to give any indication that he was hurt, and then picked his moment to belt Finnane back.

After the match I chatted to Finnane. He admitted that when searching for the soft underbelly of the England side he and his colleagues had quickly discarded Cotton and myself and hit upon Wilkinson. However I had my best game for England, and we saw them off with a bit to spare up front. They wanted to throw Wilkinson off his game and they nearly succeeded. The Australians were generous in defeat and good company. I talked away to Garrick Fay and the others and they quickly got over their 23-6 beating. But they were as street-wise as us: they knew their Wilkinson.

Two more selections which caused me astonishment were made after a trial at Leicester. In the early seventies we were all subjected to a grand tour at which an England side would play the regions. One day I had the tremendous honour of being invited to act as replacement for an England XV which was playing the Midlands at Welford Road. It was a wet and cheerless day and I noticed a squat little fellow paddling round behind the England scrum. His name, I gathered, taking a consensus of the dozen different pronunciations and spellings I was given, was Mike Lampkowski, and he came from Headingley. He was a square young man whose nose had been broken so many times he had lost count. There he was, wallowing in the mud; he had all the guts and the courage anyone could wish for. He would come charging off the scrum and take on the opposition loose forwards. Very impressive. There were, however, two rather important drawbacks to his chances of becoming an international scrum-half: it seemed that he couldn't pass and he couldn't kick. Later in life, Lampkowski found his niche as a hard loose forward in rugby league. I would have put him in with Sugar Ray Leonard and had a few bob on. But he couldn't clear the ball to his own fly-half; he couldn't offer relief by kicking the ball out of defence. He was fatally limited.

Apart from Lampkowski, I was also struck by a bearded, bedraggled figure plodding around behind everyone and walking as if he had dislocated both ankles. His name was Alastair Hignell, eventually from Bristol and Cambridge University. His socks fell down around his boots and he looked like an out-of-work third team hooker as he went about his tasks. I felt sorry for him as he fumbled the ball. Imagine my surprise when both Lampkowski and Hignell were chosen for the England side that year – selection masterpieces, I felt, in the English tradition of the time.

I realise that Hignell turned in some good displays for England, notably one in a losing cause at Cardiff. But I must confess I rarely shared other people's huge rating of him. I never felt safe with him as full-back, whether it was for Gloucestershire or England. Don Rutherford, for example, was rock solid and gave me confidence; whenever the ball went over my head to Hignell I was worried.

I remember listening to a team talk given by Peter Colston, when he was coach in 1976. He finished and then asked if there were any questions, any points that the players wanted to bring up. I said yes. The other players were used to me as the team joker and there was a shout of acclamation that Burton was about to lend his vast intellect and rugby brain to the proceedings. But for once I was serious. I said to Hignell: 'Last time we played, you failed to find touch on far too many occasions. When I see you with the ball I want it to go safely into touch, I don't want the ball to be kicked straight to the opposition to do what they like with it.' In the next game, he banged every single kick firmly into touch about two yards upfield from where he was standing!

Admittedly, teams like Wales were lucky. Their selectors in the 1970s met to pick about two players. The other thirteen were permanent fixtures. They were allowed a couple of poor games because the selection process had weeded them out as basically good players who would soon find form again. Things are not so definite down there now, but a few years ago, they just sat back and chose players to complete a fine team while the England selectors were engaged in a determined attempt to find needles in haystacks while afflicted with gross short-sightedness. Even then, they usually found the wrong needles.

Just before the page curls up and self-ignites with the liberal amounts of vitriol I seem to be dispensing, I should perhaps lift the lid on some of the joyous and genuinely memorable experiences of being involved in the England scene. I am certainly not bitter and would always buy any selector a beer if I saw him at Kingsholm – a half, mind you, but still a beer. Here is a whistle-stop tour of events when I wasn't dropped by England!

The thrill of my first cap I have documented in detail elsewhere but I can hardly say that the arrival of M.A. Burton (Gloucester) on the international scene did England much good in that 1971-72 season. In fact, we lost all four championship matches. After losing to Wales, the Mighty Mouse was at his best at Murrayfield and we crashed 23-9. Then we played Ireland at home, with Burton in for his third match in succession, firmly established as the team comedian, and thinking what a fine bunch of men the England selectors were. After the Ireland game I had a slightly lower opinion of Dave Duckham's tackling. We were leading Ireland when they won the ball and, in a perfectly orthodox threequarter movement, an ordinary centre called

Kevin Flynn galloped straight through a Duckham tackle just as in the other home game of the season J.P.R. Williams had galloped through Bob Hiller's tackle.

Panic. We had lost three games and the selectors made changes. They also established once and for all that Paris is not a good place to send a makeshift side – in the last game in the old Colombes Stadium, France crushed us 37-12. End to end play ensued . . . from their end to our end. It was no laughing matter, and don't talk to me about Paris in the springtime.

In fact my first ever win in an England jersey came from an unexpected quarter. We went to South Africa as outsiders ranker than General Custer and we won. The full story of touring in that superb but troubled country, beating off the challenge of Fran Cotton and of the Springboks merits a chapter all to itself, and it gets one later in this book.

I was looking forward with great confidence to the 1973 international season, which included a match against the All Blacks. As I parted with Keith Murdoch, the All Blacks prop, after the match against Western Counties, I called out: 'See you in the test.' Murdoch growled something and disappeared off into the night. He then proceeded to disappear into the outback of Australia, having been expelled from the tour – so if he was going to see me in the test, it had to be on television. As it turned out, I didn't keep the appointment either, although I was chosen to do so.

Fran Cotton had come a close second to me in South Africa during the previous summer in the race for a test place, but when we returned and began to prepare for the All Blacks match, he was approaching his best years and he overtook me. He was chosen to play for the England side, but in training for the match Cotton hurt his back. We walked out into the car park to drive home and he spent ages trying to bend his frame enough to fit the driver's seat. 'I don't know about this one, Michael', he called across to me. 'Bring your boots next week.' Later that week he was in a less jokey mood. His back didn't improve and he was forced to withdraw. By then our friendship had progressed sufficiently for me to feel for him. His international career seemed doomed to some false starting. Ten days before the game it was announced that Cotton was out and that I was chosen to take his place alongside those two West Country pillars of excellence, Stack Stevens and John Pullin.

On the Saturday before the international, the team and reserves assembled at Twickenham for final preparations. The RFU doctor, Dr Leo Walkden, told everyone to go and have a gumshield fitting. Those of us who didn't want to bother or who already had gumshields big enough to fit didn't bother. I didn't want to wear anything which might impair my conversation with my opposite number during the game! Peter Dixon, Andy Ripley,

Chris Ralston and Roger Uttley were among those left behind too, and we went on to the pitch to attempt a few exercises and a few gentle laps. At least, the others thought they were gentle – I was sprinting! And on that immaculate turf, somehow I managed to fall awkwardly. I heard a crack which registered as my studs banging together. Then a pain shot through my leg and I knew that something was wrong somewhere.

Ralston and the others came trotting round and immediately spotted the chance of a lifetime – to pay me back for some of the banter I had directed at them over the years. Clearly they thought I was 'resting' from training, so made some choice and derogatory remarks and went on their way round the pitch. By the time they reached me on the next lap, they decided that my little joke was being a little overplayed. Dr Walkden, and even the RFU president, approached warily, suspecting that I was skiving. By now I felt like the lad who cried wolf, but not even all my never-stay-down philosophy, nor my fanatical desire to play for England against New Zealand, nor all the company of heaven could help me get up and put weight on my damaged leg. I was packed into the RFU minibus and driven off for an X-ray. England had lost another tight head prop. My leg was badly broken, and Frank Anderson of Orrell was called up to play. After all the trouble I had in my career winning selection for England, it was ironic that when I was chosen I had to drop out because I fell over myself while jogging, without any opposition within a hundred yards.

That was a significant point in my England career because I was laid up for almost the rest of the season and my edge of fitness was lost. Road running and continual training was needed to keep a man of my size in trim, and I watched the weighing scales and the television pictures of the rugby with equal frustration. After the plaster had been taken off, I found the leg had wasted badly; it took some genuinely hard effort to build it up and bring my weight down.

By then I had missed the internationals and seemed to be out of mind of the England selectors considering the side to take to Argentina. I did manage a few games for Chosen Hill Former Pupils, a local Gloucester side, who kindly allowed me to work up some sort of match fitness with them. Then I had a call from the Barbarians, one which helped put me back in the spotlight. Geoff Windsor-Lewis, the secretary of that famous club, telephoned to see if there was any chance of my being fit enough to play in the annual Mobbs Memorial match against East Midlands. As it wasn't a death or glory game I knew that I wouldn't be letting anyone down if I was not up with all the Barbarians moves. I played, got back on the road, and was selected to tour Argentina after all. I had clawed my way back.

Eventually, the Rugby Union decided that the political situation in that country was not stable enough to go ahead with the trip, and something altogether different emerged – a tour to New Zealand was arranged at short notice instead. One minute we were going over to investigate an unfamiliar dog in the district with every hope of keeping him under control: the next, we were going straight into the kennel of a huge mutt who would certainly try to bite our heads off.

The New Zealand tour was an amazing one, since we lost all four provincial matches but still beat the All Blacks in the only test. John Pullin had therefore beaten the world's two great rugby nations on their own territory in successive years. Fran Cotton was playing far too well to allow me to take the test tight head spot and I had to be content with two matches – a 3-6 defeat at Taranaki and a 16-25 defeat by Wellington. Just as England were receiving everyone's votes for New Zealand Whipping Boys 1973, the worm turned. England beat New Zealand 16-10 and Jan Webster, Fran Cotton and the back row of Tony Neary, Andy Ripley and John Watkins were unmatchable. We soon found out that whingeing Poms have nothing on whingeing New Zealanders. We left the country delighted and slightly incredulous. It was good to be part of it, if not such a fundamental part as I had been in South Africa in 1972.

The 1974 season was chiefly memorable for me in that I spent the whole time praying I would make the forthcoming Lions tour of South Africa. I have already said how a combination of determination and stupidity helped me to fulfil that ambition – I played second string to Cotton for the first XV games of the season, David Watt broke my jaw, and then I took the injured Cotton's place for two games against France and Wales with my jawbone in bits and my steak-eating career somewhat curtailed. Yet I became a Lion and ended the season an England player. I had already been dropped quite often but the good times made it all seem worthwhile.

Forward a year. I played just one game in the 1975 season, in the 7-6 run over Scotland, bowed to everyone at Bristol on being sent off and was forgiven long enough to be selected for the England tour of Australia – where I again left the field for Eddie Waring's early bath. All this is fully described elsewhere. Amazingly, none of it had any serious long-term effect on my England career.

In 1976 I even won selection for the senior side in the England trial, which immediately put my life membership of the Rest into question. Even better, the front row of my dreams, with Cotton at loose head and myself at tight, took the field for all five matches. We had a win against Australia, but – whisper it quietly – suffered a complete and utter whitewash in the Championship. Yes, after all my demands for that prop combination, when it finally came about we lost every bloody match! However, not even the selectors would have blamed the front row, or even the pack as a whole, for that state of affairs. We weren't brilliant, but the team was dismal. JPR did his normal duty at Twickenham of scoring a vital try, decided he couldn't wait for two years for the next, and so scored another one in the same match; later Ian MacLauchlan and I fought it out in front of the Queen at Murrayfield – result, retention of pride but not of Calcutta Cup. We lost in Ireland at home due to a late penalty, whereupon all the Irish went to London's West End and celebrated for three weeks; then we went to France, I met Cholley and we were blown away.

By that time, even skipper Tony Neary was losing heart. He stood in the dressing rooms at Parc des Princes and addressed us as the worst side in Europe. 'Everyone thinks we're rubbish', he said. 'We have to show them we aren't.' All Neary's points were valid but he chose the wrong approach. We did not need to be reminded how lacking we were. We wanted our confidence to be built up. Neary, for all his qualities, was not a success as captain. By the end of that season, I feel he did not rate the England coach although he never said so directly. The Elders and Burgesses had moved over and Peter Colston was in charge. The Bristol schoolmaster may have read all the right books, but he never exhibited the right personality for the England coaching job and his face grew more worried and despairing throughout the season.

At the end, Neary despaired of Colston. He felt, I am sure, that things were being done the wrong way. Even then, there was no possible justification for the treatment Neary received in the following season. As reigning England captain, he was thrown out and never even chosen for a trial. Like Ian Botham, Neary was better without the captaincy, but to treat him like that was unforgivable. For me, even that full season in the team without even one 'elbow', did not make up for the pain of poor results.

Fran Cotton played all the matches in 1977 when England were slightly more successful and this did not help my chances of being chosen for the Lions of 1977. Neither did my demolition job on a Gosforth prop, Andy Cutter, in front of the Lions manager, George Burrell, in a cup match. To my bitter disappointment I was left out, and took on some friendlier opposition in America on a Gloucester tour. I was a former England player again. And that almost completes the England cycle. I turned out for the Rest as usual in 1978, Cotton was injured, Greaves and Pryor returned to near-obscurity, and I took on Cholley and Charlie, escaping with two split decisions. Then the England selectors took me on again and I lost. I was dropped for the umpteenth and last time.

Right back in 1972, my game improved steadily. I advanced from one trial to the next, I disposed of one contender after another, then I was chosen.

It all seemed so logical. It was hard work, but the rewards were there. Afterwards, there was enjoyment and delight in being an England player; there was the honour and the effort; and the disappointments. After 1972, it was never so straightforward again.

5

WE, THE UNDERSIGNED, THE GLOUCESTER STORY

IT was a sad occasion. I was seated in the dressing room at Kingsholm, home of Gloucester RFC who were my one and only first-class club. It was the end of the 1978 season and Gloucester had just beaten Exeter in the final match of their programme. Also in the dressing room was a large, gleaming, silver trophy – the John Player Cup, the trophy awarded to the winners of the English knock-out cup. A few days before, we had gone to Twickenham and beaten Leicester 6-3 in the final. The margin may not have been very convincing but we were comfortably the better side and thereby proved ourselves the leading club in England. We had brought the cup home to parade at Kingsholm in front of our loyal supporters, which was in one way a futile gesture – they had probably all been at Twickenham and seen the trophy on the day anyway. Our fans were the best in the country, throughout all the less successful years as well as in the glorious seasons.

This was it though. As well as the cheering for the team, there had been a special cheer for me, because it was my last ever match for Gloucester, the last of the hundreds which I had played for the club. I had been involved in some thunderously hard games, and enjoyed some deeply satisfying times both on and off the field. I loved the aura of such a great club, I loved Kingsholm and the crowd, and they loved me. But I had decided to retire. Considering that I was only thirty-two, a word of explanation may be needed before I go on to describe those memorable years. Thirty-two is not even middle-aged in the active life of a prop forward. Most front row players do not mature until their thirties and then some go on, even at international level, till the mid-thirties. Charlie Faulkner, my adversary from Pontypool, was reputedly a lot nearer fifty than twenty when he finally dropped out of the Welsh side.

One of the main reasons for my decision to go out to grass at a relatively early age was the final realisation that I had no real part in the plans of the England selectors. I always dearly wanted to play for England but suffered countless disappointments as I have said. A few weeks earlier, I had played for England against Wales at Twickenham, on a dark, muddy day when

Gareth Edwards broke English hearts and Wales had won 9-6. Yet I was not completely dissatisfied because I personally had played one of my best games in an England jersey. The next match was an away engagement at Murrayfield with the Calcutta Cup at stake. Fran Cotton, my friend and rival all through the years, was fit again after an injury which had made him miss the Welsh match. Surely, that which all the pundits, all my supporters and even Fran himself had been calling for would now happen – they would play Cotton at loose head and retain me at tight head. Well, as is history, the selectors thought otherwise. I was dropped, Nelmes retained and Cotton brought in at tight head. I refused to sit on the bench at Murrayfield and my England career ended. That snub was one too many.

Apart from the England problems, I was influenced by my own standards. A player of my build needed continuous hard training to keep in trim and a good fighting weight. After even a short lay-off from training I would be soaring towards the seventeen stone mark, thereby reducing my overall pace to something less than blistering. I was concerned that, as I got older, I would be unable to find the motivation for all that training, my fitness would slip and then I would be taking the field unprepared. Not only would this be letting Gloucester down, but I would leave myself open to players of lesser ability. I had a horror of taking a hammering in the scrum from an up-and-coming lad whom, at my best, I could have seen off with my arms tied together.

Gloucester were on top, too, and they had plenty of promising forwards coming through. So I announced that the game against Exeter was to be my last. As I sat there, lacing my boots and taking in the atmosphere for the last time, the dressing room door opened and a man came in. He looked around nervously. He saw me in the corner and walked over. 'Mike', he said, 'we would like to give you this and ask you not to retire. Gloucester needs you.' He held out a bound sheaf of papers. I opened it and glanced through rows and rows of names, in all sorts of handwriting: I turned the page and there were more rows. I was speechless. When I had gathered my thoughts I thanked the bearer as warmly as my surprise would permit, and he turned and left. All those people who came down to watch Gloucester week after week in all weathers, and paid their money to stand on the terraces, had put together a petition begging me not to retire. It was a moving gesture and a typical one. Gloucester fans may not strike others as the fairest in the world to opposing teams, but they are loyal and generous.

I led the side out on to Kingsholm, courtesy of captain John Watkins. There were special cheers for me because it was my last game – not even the petition could change my mind – and because the cup winners had come home. I found it a tremendously emotional occasion.

Fourteen years earlier, on 14 November 1964, I had played my first game for Gloucester at Moseley, and become immersed in Gloucester and its traditions and style. Don Rutherford once told me that if he could choose a team to coach it would be Gloucester, because there are no football league clubs in the city and the whole atmosphere is geared to rugby, just as in the South Wales towns. The club is a real focal point for the people in the surrounding areas. Other players fear the name, not only because of the club's outstanding results but also for its characteristic style of play (having more in common with Pontypool than Llanelli is the best way to summarise it) – forward power, domination by force, the effectiveness of a blunt instrument. From the time I joined the club till I finished playing, Gloucester meant forwards and fierce loyalty to the cause. I shall come to the club's recent remarkable efforts to change that style later in the chapter.

One early illustration of the loyalty to anyone included in the Gloucester freemasonry came when I was watching admiringly from the terraces at Kingsholm, with my own rugby career proceeding steadily at Longlevens. Gloucester were playing Birkenhead Park, and at scrum-half for the home side was sixteen-year-old John Spalding, the local slaughterman (off the field!) and a typically tough Gloucester half-back. On the flank was Peter Ford – later to play a prominent part as a selector in the incident when I was withdrawn from an England side. Ford was balding and lean and toothless, with vaseline shining on his head and legs. Early in the game, Spalding took a savaging from one of the Birkenhead Park flankers and went down injured. Soon after he recovered, and right in front of my viewing position, I saw Ford deal with the miscreant. Neither Ford nor any of the experienced old guard could accept a Gloucester player being roughed up. That attitude was mine too when I was the senior player, and I was responsible for looking after the younger players and the key players. Ford landed one fierce punch on the Birkenhead man and he went down. There was not the slightest trouble from him for the rest of the match, and Spalding was able to go about his lawful business in peace. That little scene was to be repeated many times over the years – the protagonists changed but no one in a cherry and white jersey was put upon for long.

Ford's action helped me understand the sort of people I would be playing with when I left Longlevens for Gloucester. I am not suggesting that a whole pack of murderers took the field and dished out punishment in each match, or that the punishment was always physical rather than verbal – or even that Gloucester won all the disputes against all the clubs. But the pride and loyalty which the Gloucester jersey inspired was an insurance policy against too many defeats, or too much thuggery being directed at us.

I was already drawn by the aura of the club after my first few appearances for the United side, and when I was chosen for the first XV I was floating on air. In fact, in the week before my appearance against Mike Coulman and Moseley (described in Chapter One), I was ill with flu. But I went out to train and tried to run off the illness. It nearly killed me but I made it. I had done what hundreds of players from all the dozens of local clubs in the area would have liked to do. After a few more games, I became accepted by the rest of the team and began my club career in earnest. Even now, a few seasons after retirement, I am still excited when Gloucester take the field: I am still inspired by that jersey.

My early years with Gloucester were salutary. I found that matters were taken far more seriously than at Longlevens. The game *had* to be won; each player would run through opposition strengths and weaknesses and pass on little tips about certain players – how they played, how low their boiling point was. In rugby at a lower level, you meet different people all the time. In the Gloucester side, I would prop against the same man year after year whenever our two sides met. The stalwarts of my early period at Gloucester, in the late sixties, were people like Mickey Booth, the scrum-half, Terry Hopson, a brilliant and underrated fly-half, Peter Ford, Don Rutherford, and the two centres, Ron Pitt and John Bayliss. We used to joke that Pitt and Bayliss were brought to away matches in a cage towed behind our team coach. They had little in common with the Jim Renwick, David Richards, or Peter Preece type of centre. They played like a cross between Ray Gravell and a brick wall. They were hard, defensive centres – crunching tacklers and ferocious competitors. Bayliss was probably the hardest back I ever came across. Such was the type of player looking after me as I felt my way around the first-class circuit. No wonder I turned out as I did!

Now, a day in the life of Gloucester rugby club in my early years. I will take an away match at Neath as a typical Saturday afternoon out for Gloucester, to give an insight into the weekly grind. We used to savour that trip every year in a masochistic sort of way, for Neath were a frightening proposition on their own ground. They had Brian Thomas, the Welsh team's hard man, and Morlais Williams, the belligerent hooker; they had Ron Waldron and John Dodds, the props; and they had Randall Davies, the most forbidding man of all, who was eventually suspended for life. The people notorious in rugby, the Ringers, Finnanes, the Burtons – we had absolutely nothing on Randall Davies, still a legend at the Gnoll. And the crowd weren't too welcoming either. Some crowds are regarded as unsporting if they don't clap the visitors on to the ground. At Neath, large sections of the crowd used to boo loudly as we took the field. It used to be forgiven and forgotten in the bar afterwards, but what we didn't forget was that we had just had a hard afternoon. Each year, we would arrive at Neath, and the dressing room would be a tense place; Mickey Booth, who was captain, would pass among us uttering gruff, mumbling noises. When we were ready, Booth would address the assembly. 'Just give me the ball', he would say. 'I want you donkeys to give me the ball and I'll do the rest. Anything to say Peter?' He always called on the experienced Ford. The man himself stood up, glistening and toothless. 'Just good old-fashioned stuff. Get in and 'it 'em hard' – one of the precepts of the Gloucester legend. Ford was ruthless, and under the old rules which allowed flankers to creep round scrums, he made the lives of many scrum-halves a misery. Sometimes we would just about shade the result; other times, Neath would steam-roller round the field and not even we could hold them. 'Percentage rugby' it would be called today. We weren't worried about percentages unless it meant our percentage chances of survival, and we gave Neath plenty of worries on that score too.

The older players would soon drop the protective screen which they erected round the younger players as we came off the field. Then it was every man for himself, and the team spirit which built up with the après-match activities was vitally important to its success. Ron Pitt would be downing his pint in seconds, and all his younger admirers would be trying to emulate him. Eventually they would drop far behind him in the drinking stakes and disappear into the toilets. Pitt would carry on with no visible effect.

One night at Neath, after a good skinful of beer and a riotous time with the opposition boys, a small section of the team decided to risk a genuine Neath curry. The prime mover behind this idea was Rico Bazzi, a lock who had joined from Hereford and was in the squad. Although the set time for the bus departing from Neath to the outside world and Gloucester was approaching, Bazzi was banking on two things. First, he reasoned that no coach ever leaves a rugby clubhouse within three hours of the appointed time. A long time is always allowed for the worried club secretary to do his rounds. 'Come on, lads, the coach driver's going mad. Please boys.' A gradual drift towards the exits may begin, but there will be people deep in conversation or deep into glasses of beer well into the early hours. Brazzi knew this. Secondly, he decided to take with him the two youngsters, Mike Burton and Charlie Hannaford, then a promising number eight. 'They won't go without these two babies', he thought. So we set off for the curry-house.

We wobbled back after consuming the usual glutinous and could-be-anything pile of Indian goodies, and tottered towards the Neath club. We were just in time to see the end of the coach's exhaust pipe disappearing round one of the tight corners of the sleeping town – with someone who had spotted us, but had decided not to reveal it, waving merrily. The size of our predicament hit us squarely between the eyes. With the greatest respect to the good citizens of Neath, I could think of the odd three thousand places I would rather be at one o'clock in the morning with just a few coppers in my pocket. Bazzi tried to puzzle out where his calculations had gone wrong. After a short trek to Neath station, to be told 'Next train to Gloucester? Tomorrow afternoon, butty!' we slept the night in a bus shelter which rapidly became filled with freezing fog. We had to club together the next day to find the train fare home.

Another small disaster in the after-match celebrations of those early years with Gloucester occurred at Kenilworth rugby club. We had played Coventry that afternoon, taking on Phil Judd, Bert Godwin, John Owen and the rest of those fine players. As usual, we were entertained well, with the balding head of Alf Wyman flitting around dispensing good cheer and alcohol. Waving our thanks, we eventually set off for home. Kenilworth was on the route, and we were most interested to see light and hear music blazing from the clubhouse. The coach pulled up and, at the door, the Gloucester committee entered into delicate negotiations with the Kenilworth committee on the subject of all being allowed in to their disco. But Roy Morris and I were impatient. We walked round the club and saw an open window. I pushed Roy through it and waited for him to scout ahead. In fact, he had walked straight through the window on to the stage — he was quickly spotted and marched out. The second attempt at entry was more successful. We found another open window, and I squeezed through inch by inch, with Morris pushing enthusiastically from outside. Unfortunately, I wriggled head first into a urinal, which, unfortunately, wasn't empty. We arrived on the dance floor, dishevelled and dripping, to find all the other players already in and enjoying themselves.

Don Rutherford, of course, was always agog on these occasions. He was a master at Wycliffe College and a fine full-back, but he was a serious man and a serious student of the game. Why trained athletes should abuse their bodies by all this drinking, carousing etc was beyond him. Outside the disco, as we all left, Mike Nicholls, the Gloucester hooker, spotted a horse. The beer he had consumed gave him the distinct impression that he was Willie Carson. He lasted about two seconds on the horse's back, was thrown far up into the Midlands night, and crashed down on the ground in a heap. We all left Kenilworth in stitches.

Returning from another Midlands game at Leicester, I was walking through a small village where we had stopped on the way home. Gloucester's lock, Jim Jarrett, and I were searching for a restaurant. In the middle of a village we came across a small river and a beautiful stone bridge. In the moonlight we could see a figure in his underpants standing on the bridge, shaping up to dive. There seemed to be plenty of water below but, in fact, it was just the moonlight glistening on slimy mud. 'God. I think that's Nicholls', said Jim. As we arrived on the bridge, we found some other Gloucester players encouraging the captain to jump though no one believed he would. I was so confident he wouldn't, I told Jarrett that should Nicholls do so, I would crawl across the road and kiss a certain ample part of his anatomy. Suddenly, to everyone's horror, Nicholls executed a perfect swallow dive, and ended up head first in the mud with his legs kicking. He was pulled out in one piece, extremely lucky not to have broken his neck – and there, across the road, was Jarrett with his trousers round his ankles. I crawled across the road to keep my promise.

Although I played under some brilliant captains during my career, like Pullin, McBride and others, Nicholls was the best. He was a hard man and an inspiring one. He epitomised Gloucester rugby and was a real giant of the club. Quite simply, his captaincy was brilliant.

Those are just a few of my memories of the years when I was establishing myself for club and county, and flexing my muscles as a possible international prop of the future.

* * * *

As the years went by, the Pitts and Fords, the Rutherfords and the Nicholls began to reach retiring age. To replace them came players like John Watkins, Eric Stephens, and John Fidler, then Peter Kingston, Peter Butler, and ultimately, Steve Mills, Richard Mogg and the others. After ten years of campaigning around the country I was made captain – and led Gloucester in the season 1975-76. We won 34 of our 53 games, lost 16 and set up a club record for tries scored. Peter Butler was our leading scorer and his phenomenal goalkicking won several matches on its own, as it still does now. We were the first major club to reach 1000 points and we beat some of the top sides. Yet it was not a vintage season and I did not seek re-election, handing over to John Watkins. I was not completely at ease in the role.

As the seventies ended, and the first few seasons of the 1980s approached, it was still forward power on which the game was largely based. Mills, Steve Boyle, John Fidler and Gordon Sargent were the kingpins, as was Phil Blakeway when his injury problems allowed. Recently, however, the club are trying to change, to break with their traditions; to reply to criticism of the Gloucester approach by expanding the game and putting more emphasis on the back division. The origins of this remarkable turnaround lie in two cup runs – those in 1972 and 1978 when Gloucester won the John Player Cup, which made everyone, inside and outside the club, examine our approach very carefully. We were criticised, and it hurt. These cup successes indicate what the club is all about, and one match in particular does so perfectly.

In the 1972 campaign, we had the most terrible luck with the draw. We played four rounds before the final, all against leading clubs and all away from home. We finally won the cup at Twickenham without having played one cup match on Kingsholm. Yet we were criticised in the press and elsewhere almost throughout for the forward-dominated, over-vigorous game we played, culminating in the final against Moseley, which, for one reason or another, they finished with twelve men. It was an ugly match, and this in the first year of the competition. The knock-out format had many severe critics – there were those just not interested in that sort of competition, and those who thought that it might lead to too much pressure and thuggery. That final seemed to bear out what everyone was saying, and we got the blame. What the competition really needed in its first year was a match between Rosslyn Park and Bedford which one side won 35-28. But that would have been hiding what cup rugby is all about. In fact, after many teething troubles, the cup has attracted the sponsorship of John Player and is showing signs of developing into something really big.

The first round in 1972 brought us a 12-3 win over Bath at the Recreation Ground, and, lo and behold, we were criticised for our approach. The next match for the maligned Gloucester juggernaut to face was Bristol at the Memorial Ground. A Gloucester-Bristol clash didn't need a cup competition match to give it needle, especially one in a brand new competition in which everyone wanted to impress. We went to Bristol and the 'disgraceful Gloucester' critics were given further ammunition.

Gloucester players were used to cup rugby, since the North Gloucestershire combination, from which many of them had come, has its own competitive cup event. Mickey Booth and the rest of us were under no illusions as to how we were going to play the Bristol game. We were going to win the ball, Mickey was going to kick it just short of the moon, and John Bayliss was going to come thundering up from the centre to blast anyone who dared catch the ball; the rest of us were going to be right behind him. The forwards began well, Booth rolled up his sleeves and barked his orders – and sent another ball soaring over the forwards into the Bristol night. Peter Knight was at full-back for Bristol and he never flinched. But, time and again, Bayliss would tackle him in possession or would catch whoever else had put themselves underneath the ball. Bayliss didn't care for his own safety: 'run right over both of us', he said to the forwards. The juggernaut rumbled on according to plan. Booth was our linchpin and we gave him well-protected ball. Once, the Bristol prop Hamish Bryce burst through the line and came within a yard of Booth. I hit him with a right cross and he never came again. We won 15-4, in terms of Gloucester-Bristol margins a crushing score. It wasn't pretty, but it was cup rugby Gloucester style.

Then the draw was made for the quarter-finals. Gloucester were drawn away to a team who were not only the cup favourites but the most brilliant and attractive club side in the world by far – London Welsh. They had seven of the 1971 Lions: JPR, Gerald, John Dawes, Mike Roberts, Geoff Evans, Mervyn Davies and John Taylor. Internationals like Jim Shanklin were mere sideshows. The club had swept all before them during the season, and were hugely successful even when the Lions were resting at the start of the season, such was their reserve strength. Their playing philosophy was the complete opposite of ours. Although they had the forwards they preferred to run and they had the players who could make the policy work. They were messiahs, and everyone who thought that cup and festival rugby were the same thing, plus all those who disliked Gloucester's approach, began to root for them. That game became the one which typified Gloucester more than any of the 360 in which I played. It wasn't particularly dirty but it showed the club in all its effectiveness; it was also Gloucester's greatest day.

As the match approached, the local press carried stories that there were no more coaches available in Gloucester, and that trains to London were booked solid. On the Friday night we stayed at the Richmond Hill Hotel. There, the number eight, Mick Potter (don't get the impression that everyone in the club was bald, but Potter had yet another Kojak cut) observed his traditional ritual of always having two pints on the night before the game.

Our team talks were simple. We had to win the ball, snuff out their attacks, tackle anything that moved, and pressurise. As Peter Ford had said years before in the dressing room at the Gnoll, Neath: 'Just good old-fashioned stuff. Get in and 'it 'em hard.' Mickey Booth prowled the dressing room as kick-off approached; Robin Cowling, the loose head prop, stared straight in front, dour and unshaven; Potter, a home-bred Gloucester lad who only realised other clubs existed when he arrived to play there on the coach, was chewing gum; Eric Stephens, the normally nonchalant place kicker – even he looked tense. On a visit to the toilets, I looked through the open door of the London Welsh changing room, and saw the thoroughbreds warming up, stretching their muscles. But it wasn't in the Gloucester make-up to fear anyone. Big names and hard tasks redoubled our determination.

We trotted out across the wide expanse of the cricket outfield which separates the clubhouse at Old Deer Park from the pitch. Then we burst through a gap in the crowd on to the field. It was just like being in Gloucester – our supporters had come on their trains and coaches and in their cars and they lifted us.

In the first half, we played against a strong wind and kept the Welsh in check by our fingertips. But we never let their confidence develop and we were on top in the forwards. Some of the spectators did not relish our approach but we turned round 0-4 to a Billy Hullin try. I was propping against Freddie Williams, a former Bristol prop. I hit him early and he returned the compliment a split second after I made contact.

The Welsh tried to run at us in the second half, but whenever J.P.R. Williams or Gerald Davies got the ball, there was a whole tenacious flock of Gloucester players ready to jump on them. We kept winning our ball, Mickey Booth kept kicking it; we ploughed on and kept the opposition in a stranglehold. The effort was shattering. Then we scored a vital try, and one in which two reserve players were prominent. We had been shocked before the game when Jim Jarrett and Dick Smith, a magnificent flanker, both withdrew, because they were key men. We were forced to bring Nigel Jackson into the second row to take on the three London Welsh line-out Lions, Davies, Evans and Roberts, while John Haines took Smith's place on the flank.

Jackson won a good line-out ball midway through the second half, with players and crowd anticipating a great climax. Booth duly put the ball into the air, and Haines charged forward to where the ball was falling and caught the defender in possession. Even I arrived quickly – in fact, the whole pack arrived as one. In a kind of anguished daze, I saw Potter, the unsung Potter, wrench the ball away. He had joined Gloucester late in life from Coney Hill, and there he was enjoying the moment of his entire rugby career. He plunged over to score. Eric Stephens converted, added a penalty goal to make it 9-4, and we were sound and abrasive enough to prevent London Welsh coming back. There were tears of joy on many West Country faces as the whistle went, and an expression of sheer disgust on the face of John Dawes. Mickey Booth and John Watkins cried with joy too.

That result probably represented as great a day in the club's history as either of the two cup finals. We marched on, followed by more accusations that we were unattractive and downright dirty players, and that we were killing the cup baby before it had a chance to grow up. It hurt, but we wanted that first cup and we stuck to our formula.

Anything would have been an anti-climax after the London Welsh game, and we struggled in a difficult away tie at Coventry. In fact the match was drawn 6-6, but Gloucester joyfully entered the first final of the RFU knock-out cup as the away team. In the final, we learned as we celebrated in the dressing room, we were to meet Moseley, who had just beaten surprise side Wilmslow in the semi-final and who had also taken care of Northampton, Bedford and Halifax on the way. They had reached the final with some attacking rugby, so once more Gloucester were the villains for the uncommitted.

The final drew fifteen thousand spectators, most of them from Gloucester. There was a strong wind and driving rain, and we took the field with the normal game plan established in our heads. We were going to win the ball, Booth was going to dictate from scrum-half. There could not have been a more sensational start. Moseley scored a converted try within the first minute and, within the next, were a man short: Nigel Horton, their lock, was sent off for hitting Dick Smith. Then gradually we pulled the game round, with tries by Dix and Roy Morris, son of Digger. Threequarters of the way through the game, Moseley was even more depleted, with Smith and Pringle having left the field injured – and this was before the age of replacements. So it was farcical, our fifteen men against their twelve. But they fought on bravely, and we failed to take the obvious step of changing our pattern. We kept winning the ball, Mickey Booth kept kicking. It would have been far too confusing and alien to us if we had suddenly run the ball with the intention of attacking the spaces where Moseley's back row would have been if they had had a back row. In fact, we only really made the game safe against the Moseley dozen with dropped goals by Booth and Tom Palmer in injury-time.

We had won the cup – and the furore that followed showed that most people were indignant and jealous. The critics pointed to the fact that Moseley finished with only twelve men, and to one or two other incidents, and said we had won with strong arm methods, that it was an ugly final. They said we had bored the competition almost to death with our approach – and I do admit it was stereotyped. The criticism hurt, although it could not take away the pleasure of our win completely. As I said, Rosslyn Park-Bedford and a high-scoring match would have done the competition good and established it: but Gloucester's win showed everyone what cup rugby is about and what Gloucester rugby is about.

Unfortunately, I am sure that the cup final lost Mickey Booth a Barbarians jersey. He had played five hundred times for the club, umpteen times for the county and was as effective a scrum-half as anyone of his era. He gave his life to rugby and I believe that the Barbarians would have recognised that fact. But the adverse publicity in 1972 put him out of the running. All he had to show for his efforts over the years was the knock-out cup.

Proceeding with the story of the Gloucester approach, all that had changed by 1978 were the faces – everything else was as normal. The side was slightly more able in all-round play, mainly because we had a talented left-wing in Richard Mogg and, now and again, he was given a pass. He has become a talisman for all those in Gloucester who believe that we should expand our game. Yet still we based our game around the forwards, and hoped that we could get near enough to the opposition posts to let Peter

Butler kick us to victory. We disposed of Lydney, Gosforth and Wasps, then of Harlequins in the semi-final. That left Leicester, the fashionable Midlands club; once again, it was running rugby against forward power.

Gloucester supporters arrived in their thousands for what was now called the John Player Cup Final. We won convincingly, all of 6-3! I had one of my very best games in a Gloucester jersey and we provided a real glut of possession which was mostly frittered away. Mogg did score a try which Butler converted, and we were the better side. However, the referee, Roger Quittenton, who on his day is a fair and good official, gave Leicester so many penalties that I was afraid to cough in case he gave another against me.

It was just as well that Dusty Hare had left his kicking boots in the cupboard at home on his farm: he kicked one goal but missed hundreds of others, and John Watkins lifted the trophy above his head as Gloucester captain. It was a great moment of my rugby life. Once again, though, the voices were raised. Bad thing for rugby, Gloucester's conservative approach. Many people respected the way we did things and realised we were playing effectively and to our strengths, but the Gloucester image was being perpetuated. The fact that we did run the ball just a little more was irrelevant.

Remember that earlier in the chapter, I said that people at Gloucester have eventually decided to try to change the habits of a lifetime, to move the emphasis away from the forwards? I am sure that the origins for this move are to be found in the aftermath of our cup successes, and also in the publicity brought by other games and incidents underlining the Gloucester approach. People are now working to make the great name of Gloucester as great as ever, but a name associated less with forwards and attraction and more with spectacle and running.

When I first joined, with Peter Ford and Mike Nicholls in charge there was no way that our wings were going to see much of the ball. 'Good old-fashioned stuff' was the order of the day for both, and I too believed in good, old-fashioned stuff. When Don Rutherford became captain, as a back and a student of the game, he made an early attempt to turn back history. He said we could change our approach. This would cost us success for two years or so, he said, but then we would bounce back and win playing good rugby. King Canute was an odds-on favourite compared to Rutherford's chances. He tried, but he couldn't do it. There were too many old dogs sniffing around too set in their ways to be taught a whole load of fancy tricks like running and passing. I remember once I peeled off from a maul in a match in the early seventies and charged downfield, in my best enlightened, well-coached manner. Mickey Booth came puffing up behind me. 'Give me the ball. I'll do the running!' he said. I never ran with the ball with Booth around for seasons after that, and neither did most of the Gloucester forwards.

In the mid-seventies, I had my season as captain and it still had not really dawned on me that there was another type of game Gloucester could play. I was as guilty as anyone of keeping Gloucester on the same road. I held to the stereotype as firmly as Booth, Ford and Nicholls, and it often proved successful that way. I told the young lads to play to the pack – 'good old-fashioned stuff', I probably said on several occasions. I had played with Phil Bennett and Gareth Edwards in South Africa and I still thought the pack was the end of the world. To reinforce tradition, Mike Nicholls had a special job as coach in the seventies too, so that was hardly conducive to a breath of fresh air – and why should it be? Nicholls had achieved success within the Gloucester pattern: why change?

Back to all that criticism, and to all the self-examination that it brought. Alan Brinn became chairman of selectors, and is a prime mover in the brave new movement. For the past few seasons, Gloucester have tried to expand. To use their backs. To let Moggy have a run. The new régime is currently led by Brinn, with Dick Smith as coach and Steve Mills as captain. Now a captain and coach and chairman from the forwards doesn't sound promising. But Dick Smith is an enlightened man who probably appreciates the subtleties of back play more than anyone at the club. He was even more unlucky than Mickey Booth not to win a cap, as a superb flanker. If Budge Rogers is worth over thirty caps, then to suggest that Smith is not worth just one is ridiculous. Yet Smith was a footballer too; he could have played first-class rugby in the centre. And now he is coaching Gloucester with emphasis on the backs – the juggernauts are still there, of course. John Fidler and Steve Boyle add their weight to the second row; Mills is a superb hooker and forward; John Gadd, Malcolm Preedy and Mike Teague are proving that the Gloucester forward production line is every bit as efficient and strike-free as the Welsh fly-half factory. But, nowadays, the other seven players behind the scrum are brought in.

Of course, tradition is not turned on its head without a whole host of teething troubles. At the moment, Gloucester are suffering because attention has been taken away from the old power base and the club has by no means the right players behind the scrum to make the new philosophy a great success. It is no good trying to make bricks without straw and, apart from Mogg, class backs are thin on the ground. Reservations are expressed freely and I am not convinced myself that it is necessarily a good thing for the emphasis to change too much, or for too much attention to be paid to those who say that teams who worship forward play are all bad. Gloucester's recent success is still based largely up front. None of this is the point, however. Gloucester are trying. The All Blacks have managed to reverse their history, and bring their backs into the game. British rugby in general has changed in that brilliant backs are now extinct and forward play takes up everyone's time. Time will tell if Gloucester can free themselves from the shackles of their own heritage and reputation, and good luck to them.

The club did anger me in some ways, though, and still does. Its relations with the myriad smaller clubs nearby are sometimes not cordial. Relations between the junior rugby of the area and the major club should be amicable, because if they are, both sides will benefit enormously. Gloucester are not too good at handling local politics. Neither is the club a brilliant example of commercial drive, for despite all the bar takings, the gate receipts and so on, there never seems to be any good news in the annual treasurer's report. Where does all the money go? Certainly not the way of the players. Apart from a small allowance to buy boots, which at current prices will purchase a pair of laces and a tin of dubbin, they are not half as well looked after as they should be. Even strictly amateur clubs like Newport and Cardiff never leave their players wanting for boots, spare boots, or any other items of kit – or for a few glasses of beer. Gloucester should look after their players better in return for the players' loyalty.

Another example of the inward thinking of the club committee lies in the fact that there is never an annual dinner, that traditional end-of-season occasion which almost every other club of any sort in the world stages – to hand out 'player of the season' awards, to offer special thanks to volunteer helpers, to give thanks for another season under the belt. Friends from outside the club, notably from other clubs on the fixture list, can be entertained too.

Lack of attention to social responsibilities has hit the club hard. The great Welsh club, Cardiff, are surely the first name any committee would like to appear on their fixture list. Yet Gloucester and Cardiff no longer meet, which is a disgrace – a disgrace primarily brought about, I believe, by the fact that the Cardiff committee were not accorded the traditional pre-match and post-match hospitality which any enlightened club must provide. No one on the Gloucester committee looked after them. Aberavon, Llanelli and Neath have also disappeared from the Gloucester list. In fact, the Aberavon match was discontinued following some nasty incidents in a recent match at Kingsholm. Yet a little hospitality, a little personal contact and attention on the part of the committee would work wonders and bring some of the opposition back to Kingsholm. Gloucester's image in Wales is tarnished. Entertaining of visitors is now improved, and not before time.

Happily, the club's good points also remain unchanged. What is still the same, despite the new direction playing-wise, is the pride which being a Gloucester player evokes in the team. The current Gloucester side is a good one and it will not be long before the John Player Cup returns to Kingsholm – or before a Gloucester front row player establishes himself in the England side, like Burton or Blakeway did. Steve Mills, England's hooker in Argentina in 1981, is an outstanding player and not only in my opinion. I am convinced that he is the natural successor to Peter Wheeler.

Mills arrived at Gloucester as a prop, but when he realised that his size was against him he began applying himself to the gathering of experience and knowledge for the hooking berth and eventually became one of the cleverest I ever played with. He has a rare ability to strike for the ball and win it against the head after the opposing hooker has struck. He will wait until the enemy front row have made the initial strike and, before they have managed to scrape the ball away down their scrum, he will strike and rake it away on his side. I was surprised that he went to Argentina as second string hooker to Sale's Andy Simpson, but not surprised in the least when he overtook the Northern man and played in both the tests.

I end the Gloucester story with another little illustration of the hold which the club had on us. As if we cannot escape the atmosphere of the ground, a whole battery of Gloucester families, the Brinns, the Nicholls, the Fords, the Jarretts and the Burtons live within a well-struck Peter Butler goalkick of the ground. My children attend school opposite the ground itself and when I am outside the school gates, I can clearly hear the echoes – the terse voices of Ford and Nicholls, the howl of a Gloucester ground in full cry – and even the clatter of a wing's studs as, finally, after a whole history of Gloucester forward power, he is given the ball to run with it.

6

THROW THE BALL ABOUT

THE rain was hammering down on the windows of the Grand Hotel in Bristol, where the Gloucestershire team was assembled in readiness for an important County Championship match against Devon at the Memorial Ground. After a pre-match luncheon during which I absorbed the atmosphere of the occasion and relished the company of the outstanding players in my first county selection, we all sat waiting for our team talk. Newfangled and confusing people like coaches were far too revolutionary to have entered Gloucestershire rugby at that time, so George Wright, a county selector, rose and stood before the players. He stood with his back to the window and we had to crane forward to catch his words, as the drumming from the storm outside all but deafened us. He began what he seemed to consider a close and analytical look at the game. He was nearly shouting against the storm. 'We're going to have a nice game today', he said. 'There'll be a big crowd. And we want you to throw the ball about', as he gesticulated a pass with his hands.

As a less experienced member of the team, I found this line of thought ever so slightly puzzling. Of course, to the rest of the side it was utterly ludicrous and they were openly contemptuous. The experienced men of Gloucestershire had absolutely no intention of giving even the inside centre as much as a scent of ball leather. Furthermore, the Memorial Ground on a dry day was usually a clinging quagmire; on a day like that one, long studs and snorkels were securely packed in kitbags. Finally, the Gloucestershire style of play often mirrored Gloucester's at club level. That is, they wouldn't 'throw the ball about' on a parched, windless day on a beach in the Mediterranean, let alone on a winter's day in Bristol. Yet there was George Wright, county selector, telling us to run the ball. It seems laughable now. At the time, it was annoying. The upshot was that the match was rained off altogether, postponed until a less wild and windswept day.

Why should I relate that little story first in discussing my career with Gloucestershire? After all, the County Championship is an excellent competition taken seriously there, and the side has always been a well-administered, harmonious part of the scene. Wrong on all counts. I did enjoy the successes which the county had, yet I and a majority of those who played for it with me, or since, had so little respect for the way in which rugby was run at county level that it was often a frustrating and angry experience. The fact that we had no coach, even in the 1970s when the Lions proved that no leading team should be without one, is one symptom of the haphazard way in which things are done. To label the Gloucestershire county administrators as Fred Karno's army is a gross insult to Mr Karno's troops.

You can say I am being ungrateful: that I took advantage of the Gloucestershire team as a shop window for myself, and that many amateur people gave a lot of time to allow me to do it, and so they did. But I am also being realistic. Gloucestershire's successes in the County Championship have come about despite the way in which the rugby has been administered, largely due to the efforts of a group of experienced and knowledgeable players from Gloucester and Bristol.

The championship itself is an anachronism. It creates some interest in the north and in the west. In London, it is a tournament for second-class clubs and has-beens. In the Midlands, where the leading clubs loathe the whole event, it is a weekday stroll around for all those able to get the time off work without really trying too hard. The sponsorship of the Thorn company has given new impetus recently, but it is really no more than the blowing up of a burst balloon: there is no way the whole thing is going to soar away to the heights, because there is a dirty great big hole in it. The RFU have even announced that the event is going to be revamped in the 1982-83 season – again, there may be renewed interest, but the integral weakness of the whole idea will bring it crashing down. The major clubs are the backbone of the game in England, and it is time that the powers that be realised this.

The composition of the RFU, of course, is the reason why the championship survives. Most of its members are representatives of the counties. Their new formula will, for instance, give someone like Peter Wheeler a choice. He could either go down and play for Leicestershire against Dorset and Wilts at Dorchester, or play for Leicester against Cardiff or perhaps Gosforth at home. A difficult choice?

When I was immersed in the Gloucestershire effort, perhaps the championship did not look quite so outdated and clapped out. The county had some great battles and some thoroughly satisfying victories. I repeat – these occurred in spite of the outdated format and in spite of the way the competition was run.

One of the memorable coups of the county effort came in the selection when we reached the finals of the championship in 1971, and faced a home tie against Surrey. The London side were strong because interest in the competition was higher there then than it is now. Their line-out capability was awesome. They fielded Mike Roberts and Geoff Evans, the Welsh international locks, while Alistair McHarg was squeezed into the second row with Roberts moving forward to prop. Mervyn Davies was at number eight, who, as well as being a tank in all-round play, was an incomparable line-out player. Even John Taylor behind him was a competitive player in picking up line-out scraps. When Surrey took the field they looked like a herd of grazing giraffes. Gloucestershire's counter to this was obviously going to be Dave Watt, the 6ft 6in giant who reigned supreme in county colours for many years. But, equally obviously, he had to be given backing – both from people who could support him and from people who could jump themselves. When they chose their team, would the county selectors for once be able to see the wood for the trees?

The side was announced and it was ludicrous. They couldn't even see the forest, let alone the trees. Not only did they not pack the team with line-out men and line-out support men to help Watt, they left Watt out too. It was unbelievable. They brought in Nigel Jackson, a sound and honest forward who was normally a reserve at Kingsholm; he had no hope of taking on the giraffes, who duly romped to victory 14-3. That was our second losing final in succession. David Watt wasn't getting round the field too well at that stage of his career but he was sorely needed against Surrey. He was chosen at the end of the season to go to South Africa as an England lock: good enough for England, but not Gloucestershire.

To this day, the county selectors are still falling over themselves to dissipate the strength of the county and make the task of winning the championship as stiff as possible. Earlier in the 1981 season they were toying with Bristol's Phil Cue as full-back. He is a brilliant running player and a skilful one. But to play him, they had to drop Peter Butler.

Poor Butler is looked upon in many quarters as something of an ogre. He happens to be a superb place kicker and has won countless club and county matches on his own. The poor man just comes up and kicks for goal, and his ability ensures that they usually go over. It isn't his fault and he doesn't rush up and take goal-kicks with the rest of the side angry because they were just about to run the ball. Any other team would do the same. Anyway, in that season, even the county selectors grew tired of it. They left Butler out and Cue played. He also played very well, but left the county lacking a goal-kicking match-winner. As the championship wore on, and Gloucestershire reached yet another final, the selectors had second thoughts. The county faced Northumberland at Kingsholm in the final, and they scratched their heads. They knew that the game would be tight, that Cue's skills might be a luxury, and that Butler's kicking would be missed. They also knew that

Cue's selection had been applauded widely by those with a very firm grip on unreality. So they brought Butler back for the final, dreaded right boot and all. To appease Cue, they threw him willy-nilly into the centre in a crude and ridiculous attempt to relieve themselves of their responsibilities.

Having decided to go for the percentages with Butler back as goal-kicker, however, the obvious thing to do was choose a sound pack to pressurise Northumberland and to make progress in the forwards. Again, the selectors played some typical masterstrokes. They dropped Steve Boyle, the England B lock. Boyle is a powerful man and was guaranteed to get us line-out ball from the front. He exhibits occasional visitations of David Watt-like temperament, but he is a good forward. Another good forward was chosen in his place, Bristol's Nigel Pomphrey: but Pomphrey is a different type of player, a powerful runner and by nature a back row player. What was needed was tight forwards in the old Gloucester tradition. Reactionary, Burton, you may say. Yes, and totally realistic for the job in hand.

Another omission in the 1981 team saddened my heart, which I thought was immune to such surprise and disappointment. I went down to Kingsholm for the final and saw a limited Northumberland side not only beat Gloucestershire, but push them around the field in the tight. Old Gloucester forwards were positively revolving in their graves. Yet seated in the front row of the stand, wrapped up in his replacement's tracksuit, was Phil Blakeway. Not long before, he had been the acknowledged cornerstone of the national pack. He had provided the most vital of the extra elements which made a struggling team the European champions in 1980; the players rated him and his contribution without reservation. He was still one of the outstanding scrummaging props in the world – yet there he was in the stand watching Gloucestershire go backwards.

County committee myopia also contributed fully to one of the worst and most shameful days in the history of the county. On a tour to South Africa in 1976, we were beaten 52-19 by Transvaal in Johannesburg – a half-century of points which some reports said could have been more. *Rugby World* magazine headed their report 'The Day of Desolation'. Yet we were reigning county champions as we prepared to go to South Africa and there were plenty of talented players available: Peter Butler, Alan Brinn, John Watkins, Alan Morley, John Bayliss, Richard Harding. You cannot win even the County Championship without fielding a decent side.

The itinerary in South Africa was of Lions standard and it was intense. We had to play Rhodesia, North-Eastern Cape, Eastern Province, South-West Districts, North Transvaal, Transvaal and South-West Africa. It was a real challenge and one which the players were relishing. Then the administration got busy. They had to choose two tour officials to accompany the party and the glaringly obvious thing to do, one would have thought, was appoint a manager and a coach. In fact, the ability of the manager, or even of half the players, is not as vital as that of the coach. He can bind a tour party together, formulate a consistent playing policy, search out opposition strengths and hide his team's weaknesses. He can point out the major and minor faults developing in each individual's game. He is vital. But the county decided to put their own particular aeroplane into orbit without a pilot: they sent us to take on the South Africans without a coach.

With the greatest respect to all the other decisions made by the county during my time as a Gloucestershire player, which were almost uniformly ridiculous, I humbly nominate that one as the worst. Players like John Watkins, John Bayliss and myself had to take on the task of coaching and it was beyond us. We needed a single figure to whom to turn and to listen. It wasn't that we were all tactically naive, but we had our own jobs to do. To return to the aeroplane analogy, even the most beautiful and efficient and fastest plane still comes crashing to earth without a pilot. The coach of Gloucestershire in domestic matches was then Ted Parfitt, although in the true tradition of those uncommitted to coaching, he was generally regarded by most officials as a vaguely unhealthy influence and adviser to the captain. He was liked by the players even though most of his coaching experience had been with schoolboys. He was helped by Dave Protherough, a man for whom I had the highest regard as a hooker during his playing days and as a coach now. Either man could have been appointed coach. If not, there were others with the qualifications.

The backroom jostling for position among the officials went on and, eventually, they came up with two names. What is needed on all tours is a figurehead tour manager who, leaving the coach to coach, can attend to the official functions, make the speeches, keep order with an iron fist in a velvet glove and have a sense of humour. Doug Smith had it all on the 1971 Lions tour – he is the archetypal tour manager and a model for anyone else. Gloucestershire appointed John Marsh, a man who, as far as we knew, had never been on a major tour of any sort and who confirmed this suspicion utterly with his performance.

The assistant manager was hardly a Carwyn James or a Syd Millar either. Dai Walter was elected, a man in his seventies who, with respect, could only duplicate the limited talents the manager had to offer the tour. We needed a coach more than we needed a hotel, or even a pair of boots: it was like sending a team out on to the field without half-backs.

So the day of desolation was perhaps not so surprising. We won three of the first four games and then lost narrowly to Northern Transvaal. But by then, we were losing our way. We had injury problems, there was no one to sit back and tell us where cracks had to be papered over, and we had only a muzzy sort of game plan. We then conceded the half-century to Transvaal in a defeat which was made only marginally less painful for me by the fact that I was injured. 'A good one to miss' is how games of this nature are frequently described. With a final score of 52-19 the whole of South Africa are still wondering what the hell all the fuss about rugby in the west of England is all about: Gloucestershire? That novice rabble? John Mason, now rugby correspondent of *The Daily Telegraph* and a fair man, wrote: 'The team travelled without a coach, and now both team and management realise this to have been a mistake.' Mason must have been cringing along with everyone else who supported English rugby as he wrote this understatement.

The county malaise was not confined to Gloucestershire, because I can also recall a complete shambles of a Western Counties match in which Somerset were involved alongside our officials. The Combined Counties side was due to play Australia, in a match early on their tour in 1975. Since I had been sent off a few months earlier against the Australians, I was very keen that the game should go well. I didn't harbour any resentment, I just wanted to show the Aussies that Englishmen could play.

All that was needed was for the Counties' performance to reflect the strength of rugby in the area, and that would probably have been good enough. We were not yet in the age, however, when touring teams no longer have it easy. Throughout history, ragbag outfits have taken the field in Britain against touring sides representing areas and regions to which neither players nor followers have much allegiance. The teams are thrown together with local politics in mind rather than the realities of what it takes to hold a touring side. Each area or club contributing to the team has to be represented. The jerseys are often a clown's-outfit combination of the colours of each of the contributing teams, and the team itself often plays like a haphazard combination of clowns too. In New Zealand and South Africa, all the opposition is organised, well-prepared, and a regular team that plays as a province every week. Only now is British rugby learning to provide stiff itineraries and prepare individual teams properly. Yet events like the North of England's complete demolition of the All Blacks in 1978 due to planning and common sense, are rare.

Just before the Western Counties match there was a Somerset-Gloucestershire clash at Taunton. After the match, a Counties official, Curly Gunter, was seen distributing cards telling players they had been chosen or were replacements. Fair enough; I was in and looking forward to it. But no team was announced and it turned out that some positions were still open – the selectors were undecided. We actually met for a Sunday morning training session, for a match against a leading touring side, with the full composition of the team still unknown, rendering the whole practice a complete waste of time.

The side was announced later in the week and was full of evidence that backroom bartering of players had taken place in order to appease all areas. The trump card was the selection of three fly-halves: John Horton, the Bath player, was chosen at fly-half; Chris Williams, the Gloucester fly-half, was chosen in the centre; and Robbie Hazzard, Weston's fly-half, was chosen alongside Williams. The midfield therefore consisted of three half-backs, none of whom was noted for his tackling. To me, reared on a diet of Ron Pitt and John Bayliss, it left a naked feel about the whole team. We should have planned for victory using Gloucestershire strengths – a strong pack, a sound defensive midfield, and then kicked for position. Local politics had given us enough fly-halves for ten seasons. As John Pullin and I looked down the teamsheet, we were relieved to find that they hadn't dropped us and brought fly-halves in to hook and prop as well.

Sure enough, we lost 12-6. We gave the Australians a lesson in forward play in the first half and put them under pressure, but our defence behind the scrum was paper-thin. A cavalry charge of Australians came through the centre on many occasions and poor Alan Morley, out on the Counties wing, was often left to contend with about six Australians on his own. There were so many overlaps that the Wallabies themselves became confused. Morley didn't lay a hand on his opposite number, Paddy Batch, all day. Once again, an English composite selection had handed the game to the touring side on a plate – a game that they would never have won if the home side had been planned realistically. Once again, county rugby in my area caused me great frustration – admittedly after giving me the chance of top-class opposition.

I eventually played forty-three times for Gloucestershire and enjoyed some hard and unrelenting battles, mostly against the northern sides who took rugby just as seriously. It was a real pleasure to find some of those outstanding Bristol players on my side, nice to be backing up the likes of Dave Rollitt and Dave Watt, John Pullin and Alan Morley, Nigel Pomphrey and David Sorrell, instead of watching their every move suspiciously. I played in five County Championship finals and enjoyed the feeling of being one of the champions' team on four occasions.

The first win of the four games in 1972 came after two losing finals, the second of those being the day of the Surrey giraffes. We beat Warwickshire in 1972 under David Watt's captaincy and with a rather useful set of forwards. Mike Burton, John Pullin and Robin Cowling made up the front row, David Watt and Alan Brinn were the locks, and Charlie Hannaford, Dick Smith and Dave Rollitt were the back row. We were all international, or became international, except Smith – and he deserved to be capped as much as almost any of the others. It was no coincidence that the final was largely Gloucester/Bristol versus Coventry. Warwickshire fielded only two non-Coventry players. Both teams were able to develop from a strong nucleus, without trying to patch together several disparate elements.

Yet the county really established themselves as the team of the seventies in the Championship, with three successive wins in 1974, 1975 and 1976, the last of these being our eighth successive final. We beat Lancashire, Eastern Counties and Middlesex, again, mainly with forward domination and the big Butler boot. Each of the three wins was convincing and gave the players a real chance to put their skills on show for the national selectors.

We used to go round the country with our herds of supporters and really gave the competition a fillip. If one team establishes itself as outstanding, then its followers will tag along in all weathers and to all parts: while the opposition will be determined to bring down the high-flyers, with their fans flocking in anxious to see them do it. For years in the seventies the County Championship meant Gloucestershire. It isn't quite the same now, since no single team has recaptured that authority.

As I have said before, on days of success it became easy to forget that we were playing in a competition full of weaknesses and anomalies, and which never provided the great middle step between club and country which it was meant to do. It was easy to forget the fact that the team's job was always made harder, sometimes twice as hard, by some of the well-meaning but totally misguided direction which the team received from its administrators. They were true amateurs in the most damaging sense. Gloucestershire county rugby, successful as it has been, is usually waging war against itself. I have some angry and rueful memories of my county career to mingle with the happy ones.

7

OFF, OFF... Part 1

ONE of the best methods of achieving far-reaching fame in rugby is to be sent off the field. Not many sports have the rule that misconduct can be punished by complete dismissal from the game but those which do need the rule as a safety-valve. Trouble can be rooted right out rather than being left to fester. Sendings-off will always, but always, command more column inches in the popular press than the game itself. You often have to wade through paragraph after paragraph describing the scandal and horror of the dismissal before you can find out who actually won the match. Then there will be a quote from the dismissed player's mother saying that he is a lovely lad really and always used to attend Sunday School.

For the player concerned (says Burton speaking from his unrivalled experience) it is very disorientating. One moment you are giving everything, the adrenalin pumping fast, especially if you have become involved in rough play; the next you are listening to some harsh words from the referee and following the direction of his raised index finger. You find it is pointing to the dressing room. The loneliness of the long-distance walker is keenly felt as the crowd hurl insults at you or at the referee depending on how they feel and how they like their rugby. Then you are clattering in to the changing rooms with a thousand thoughts competing in your head – revenge, shame, disgust, fear among them. You have the pick of the beer cans and first use of the showers. Did it look bad? When will I play again? Will I ever play again? Bloody referee!

I was sent off four times in my career and I am sure that many people remember the four sendings-off far, far better than any rugby I may have played over the years. Burton – oh yes, the chap who punched this man, or late-tackled that man. Hardly the best epitaph for seventeen years of honest effort on the field, but that is partly my fault. My playing philosophy was so abrasive that it would have been even more sensational, I suppose, if I had ended my career *without* partaking of the odd early bath. I am not proud of my record.

Looking back on the incidents I am certainly not going to castigate out of hand the four referees who sent me off, and I am certainly not going to celebrate my tag as a dangerous player. But I would like to take a closer look at the events and the referees – ask yourself, would you have acted in the same way? Would you have sent me off had you been the referee? Or maybe conclude that you are not particularly looking forward to running into me in a dark Gloucester alley around midnight.

H.T. Luxon of the Somerset Society of Referees was the first official to send me off. I had never seen him before the match in question and as far as I can remember, I have never seen him since. In many ways, he was the most honest referee of the four; the man who, in my opinion, made the correct decision. He was also the only referee of the four who dismissed me not to referee in international matches.

The scene was Kingsholm, where I loved the supporters and they loved me. I was twenty-one, had been with the club for three years, and had a sneaking regard for myself in the role of self-appointed wild man of the parish. The man on the receiving end was Clive Farr, who had committed a cardinal error. He had left Gloucester and joined another club. Gloucester, to me, was the only club worth bothering with and for someone actually to leave – well, that made him a fairly dubious character. Actually, he had merely found the competition a bit strong and moved on to Cheltenham. Clive was stationed at RAF Innsworth and returned to Kingsholm with the RAF representative team. During the game, I arrived at a ruck and, with that monumental lack of subtlety which was then my trade-mark, I deposited my size elevens in poor Farr's back as he lay on the ground. From the decibel rating of Mr Luxon's blast on the whistle, I gathered he was not blowing for a slight knock forward! He had obviously decided to send me off on the spot, but I jogged back ten yards with the rest of the Gloucester pack, hoping to confuse him or perhaps for a stay of execution. He called up Gary White, the Gloucester captain, who listened gravely to an almost apologetic speech. Then Gary came over to me. 'Mick', he said, 'the referee wants you to leave the field'.

That hurt me bitterly; walking off from the cauldron of an explosive test match in Australia in 1975 hurt me only marginally more. As I said, I loved the Kingsholm crowd and they loved me. As I walked, I looked up and found their reaction was muted, stunned. I went up the steps to the dressing room needing some kind of reassurance that the sky had not fallen on my head. I found the door to the changing rooms was locked and I looked around in desperation for the holder of the key. Up came the squat figure of Brock Lane, whom I knew as a tough little prop from my Longlevens days. He had become the Gloucester baggage man. Brock fumbled with the keys. He had given me a good deal of useful information about the laws for survival in the front row at Longlevens, and not all of it was within the laws. But as I cursed his fumblings, even he turned against me. 'Ah, well', he said, seeing my distress. 'If you gives it out, you have to take the punishment.' That was a bit like Fagin coming over all moral and law-abiding when the Artful Dodger was caught stealing. With Brock turning queen's evidence, I felt friendless.

The first man to follow me into the dressing room was Ken Taylor, a fine hooker and a senior player when I first joined the club. He was a calming influence on me and proved a comfort. He waited with me until after the match and then we walked round to the bar and clubhouse together, with him prepared to ward off anyone hanging round to tell me what an undesirable influence I was. Just as we passed the main gate, we bumped in to Dr Arnold Allcock, the president of the club. He was then in his nineties but still an active and respected man. He was from Guy's Hospital; and whenever Gloucester played Guy's he would provide a bottle of sherry for both sides to celebrate the clash of his two teams. Ken Taylor walked up to him as the old man was leaving the ground. 'This is Mike Burton', said Ken, and I held out my hand, offering myself attractively high odds against him grasping it.

He came over and took my hand. 'Son', he said in a grave voice, 'all the best ones have walked, even me'.

Even apprentice wild man Burton realised that H.T. Luxon was only doing his job when I reflected in the sober light of the next day. 'Many referees would not have sent Burton off' I read next day in a paper. 'But that is not to say that many referees would have been right.' I was a lot less convinced that I should have been sent off at Lydney by Ken Pattinson.

The Lydney incident was the second occasion for my back to be seen disappearing in the direction of the dressing room. I was not quite as wild but had acquired a good deal more knowledge of all the good and evil things which experience means. Lydney are like many Forest of Dean sides – they always field a vigorous pack of forwards. I never once played on a losing side against them, but neither did I ever play against a Lydney pack which didn't refuse to cave in under pressure.

I arrived at Lydney for the game on one of those mild, late season days when cricketers ferret out their flannels and dream of the glories to come. I was with the rest of the Gloucester side poring over the framed photographs in the club house. 'Remember that old bastard.' 'Look at so-and-so when he had some hair.' Ken Pattinson joined us and we exchanged a few comments in amicable and drifting conversation. Out on the field, however, we quickly disagreed when I clashed with David Pitt, a tall Lydney lock who afterwards went on to play for Oxford. I didn't rate Pitt too highly as either a lock or an attempted villain.

Pattinson had already missed one Burton special in the past during a match between Gloucester and Leicester. I had given one of the Leicester players a really bad black eye when Pattinson's back was turned, but he perhaps realised that something had happened by the reaction of the crowd, and from what he was told after the match. He probably made a mental note not to be caught by me again. His chance came when Lydney won a line-out.

Johnny Morris was at scrum-half for them and I respected no one in the club more; he captained Lydney for umpteen seasons and was a clever and competitive player. Just as Johnny dive-passed away from the line-out, I arrived from the general direction of Mars and landed on top of him. The tackle was hard, but I swear it was not late or illegal. It certainly was a heavy tackle, though, because Johnny was winded and he bellowed like a cow at calving. However, he received no attention and finished the game in lively form. Unfortunately I was no longer around to admire his play by the end.

As Johnny lay wounded, Ken Pattinson approached me with a face like thunder and I quickly gathered that I was to have the beer and showers to myself again. 'Come here; get off', he said, probably in so many words. The added drawback of this dismissal was that it didn't take place at Kingsholm in front of friendly admirers of mine. It took place at hostile Lydney, and if there was one person Lydney's fans didn't care for it was an unfriendly Gloucester forward. As I approached the main stand, the players looked after me with that slightly surprised, slightly ashamed, look, then turned away to resume the match. The crowd were baying like a pack of hounds or a committee meeting where the gin has run out. They called my parentage into question, which as you have read they were entitled to do, but they came out with such a string of obscenities that I stopped dead and looked up into the stand, challenging someone to leave the security of the mob and to tell me face-to-face what he thought of me. Thankfully, for the sake of my career and already tottering reputation, no one budged. To take on the crowd would not have done wonders for the image of rugby union.

My case was heard by the Gloucestershire disciplinary committee. In his report, Ken Pattinson stated that I had tackled Morris and, as he fell, that I had kicked and punched him. He described what he could not possibly have seen because it didn't happen. It was perhaps a genuine mistake, but in the context it was a serious one. The little pub in Southgate Street where the disciplinary hearing took place was full of grave men gravely contemplating what Pattinson had said. I had been suspended for two weeks for my first dismissal, on Kingsholm, so I began to prepare myself for a month out of the game this time at the very least.

Johnny Morris came to the rescue. He was of the firm opinion that what had happened was accidental. He could not attend in person to plead my case but he did send a letter in which he pointed out that he received no medical attention and that he believed that the incident did not warrant a sending-off. The committee almost smiled. They banned me for just one week, which was probably as lenient a sentence as they could dole out without completely undermining the authority of the referee – which is something disciplinary committees never do. I'm sure they would always give out some sort of suspension even though the player in question had a cast-iron alibi that he was in the lounge with a lager and lime at the time of the alleged incident.

The Gloucester club stood by me. I was unable to play on their Easter tour of Cornwall, but they took me with them and, as all players know, playing is not the be-all and end-all of happy touring. Easter in Cornwall passed pleasantly enough.

Two sendings-off in a career is at least one too many, of course. It is exceedingly difficult to erase the stigma; once you have taken that lonely walk you are a dirty player even if you then play twenty years of honourable, fair, and clean rugby. Writers from the popular press, when choosing the games to cover every week, will often opt for a match involving a known or suspected villain at the expense of a match potentially better from the rugby point of view. The muck-raking story will be easier to come by should the villain in question oblige by stepping out of line. My personal newsworthiness was destined to increase even further. I repeat, it was my own fault.

County Championship matches are not renowned for producing sensations. In fact, they are not noted for producing much of anything. But the events during and after the 1975 Gloucestershire versus Hertfordshire match were the nearest thing to sensation you could ever get. The popular press had a field day and even the papers with longer words and smaller headlines pitched in too.

The culprit was M.A. Burton (Gloucestershire), the catalyst was Alan Welsby, a north-countryman who has gone on to enjoy a successful career in refereeing at the highest level. To this day he amazes me and others because he always has a very deep tan. Time and again he used to come out on to the field, on foggy and freezing winter days, looking as if he had spent the previous three months basking in the Sahara. In 1975 he was a promising referee and was anxious to make an impression – just as any young player would be. He had charge of the 1975 South and South-West Division play-off. Gloucestershire had won the South-West group and Hertfordshire the South, so there was a semi-final place at stake. Before I proceed, I should point out that I grew to respect Mr Welsby's refereeing as his career advanced. He controlled some potentially explosive games very well, especially the 1978 Wales-France Grand Slam match at Cardiff.

Gloucestershire were racing certainties to win; our power was going to be far too great for a Hertfordshire mixture of second-class players and the odd first-class maverick. However, as with many others in Gloucestershire history, this certainty was rendered a good deal less than racing by the normal selection myopia. The particular gem of the county selectors on this occasion was to choose Alastair Hignell at fly-half right out of the blue. Hignell was a successful schoolboy scrum-half and later that year was to make his international debut at full-back for England. He had an injury-troubled but useful career in the England side. Before that county match I had the feeling that he had never played fly-half before; after the match, I was absolutely certain he hadn't. He floundered in an unfamiliar role and gave none of the direction and purpose which fly-halves are supposed to provide. Accordingly, Gloucestershire struggled and frustration grew as we failed to put Hertfordshire away in the convincing manner we had expected. Hertfordshire clung on, and tension rose among the forwards.

Three incidents combined to contribute to the dusky Mr Welsby sending me off. Firstly, I ran into a ruck in which Hertfordshire forwards were lying on the wrong side. I certainly made contact with at least one because the Hertfordshire trainer came on. The protracted blast on the whistle duly ensued. Mr Welsby mentioned this incident in his report and during the subsequent disciplinary hearing I did my chances of leniency no good at all by berating the committee. 'You will all pay good money when the All Blacks come over next', I said, 'to see their whole eight forwards rucking like that. Then you'll go away and wonder why we don't breed forwards like the All Blacks.' But Mr Welsby clearly saw my rucking as dangerous stamping, and fair enough. The next time I drew his displeasure came when I shoved a Hertfordshire forward at a line-out. I was away and back ten yards so quickly, however, that I am sure he thought twice. 'What me? I'm back here' I said. Mr Welsby made very little of this incident in his report so perhaps I did hoodwink him. Nevertheless, it now needed a pretty small straw to break the back of Mr Welsby's particular camel.

In the second half I was approaching a maul at my top pace, which would hardly have worried Sebastian Coe. I hit the ruck hard and burrowed in looking for the ball. Alan Welsby really burst his lungs: he blew his whistle so loud that I am sure he caused trains to leave their platforms all over the country. He indicated the dressing room and another long walk into notoriety. The press reached for the red telephone too. Mr Welsby raised his knee to indicate that I had lifted my knee dangerously as I entered the maul. I was stunned, because either I did not do so or else managed to erase all memory of the action within ten seconds. If I did raise a knee it was unwittingly done and, by this time, several of the Gloucestershire team felt that I was being victimised. Although the incident took place near the touchline there was little immediate reaction from the crowd, no one professed to have seen the alleged action and no one received attention. Nevertheless, I was off.

This time, there were neither men of Kingsholm nor men of Lydney in the stand. These were the London toffs incorporated, that species of rugby man which stood for everything that I and many of my England colleagues over the years despised. 'Don't look so bloody innocent', rang out some of the fruitiest tones.

I looked up into the stand for a man with a pound of plums in his mouth. The south-eastern accents rose to a crescendo as I approached the touch-line. I was seething, boiling over with anger and frustration. My feelings were conditioned by the previous summer, when I and the rest of the 1974 Lions had given so much to the cause of British rugby – that person's cause. We were trained like fighting cocks, and one of the reasons for our success was our refusal to be pushed around. We developed a harsh edge to our play and were respected by the Springboks because of it. Perhaps it was naive of me to think I could bring that hardness back to the playing fields of England, and I was duly punished by Mr Welsby. But when those people in the stand started their baying, my whole career flashed through my mind. They had never been down at the sharp end; never taken the stick I had taken, when neither referee nor crowd realised what was happening; never played rugby in the Forest of Dean or in Wales, where rugby is as different from that played in the home counties as basketball is from rollerball. I stopped near the touch-line in front of the main stand at Bristol and, with the public and press looking on, I bowed – a graceful movement like a concert pianist acknowledging a particularly rapturous reception. Then I walked off.

That was my single most famous act on the rugby field – when people have forgotten about the tries I scored, the balls I won against the head, even the punches I threw, they will still remember the bow. My obituary in *The Times* will read Michael A. Burton, subheading: Bowed at Bristol.

David Frost, the immensely respected rugby correspondent of *The Guardian*, wrote: 'Burton's actions were those of a bemused man'. Rarely will he write anything so accurate again. People said, of course, that I was thumbing my nose at the committee, being rude to the RFU; making light of and basking in my dirty play; celebrating what a hard man I was. None of these suppositions was true. I had no idea I was facing the committee box, no idea that RFU committeemen were there. I was distressed, confused, disbelieving, and the smokescreen of humour came in handy. In fact, I have spent much of my life hiding behind humour. I often crack a 'funny' when meeting other businessmen for the first time. I could joke my way out of a locked room. That bow was nothing but a confused retreat into humour, ignoring the fact that for the moment I didn't believe I had committed the alleged offence for which I was sent off.

My anguish continued after the game but I had one consolation. I had already been chosen to play for England against Ireland on the Saturday after I was sent off. In Wales, a man sent off is guilty until proved innocent and is suspended straight away, but at that time in England, there was no suspension until the hearing. So I took solace in the fact that there was positively no reason why the sending-off would affect my England match. That, it was proved, was another large mistake. While I was drowning my sorrows, telephone wires were buzzing, and my abrasive playing philosophy was about to intrude in the most stark and direct way on my England career.

8

OFF, OFF... Part 2

THE dinner after the county match was remarkable for a monumentally ridiculous and damaging speech by J.V. Smith, who was chairman of the county disciplinary committee, and would therefore be hearing my case when it came to 'court'. Smith said that he couldn't comment on the affair as it was *sub judice*. Then he went on in the same breath to say that he supported the referee wholeheartedly and commended him. My prospects of having a fair hearing thereby disappeared without trace. My behaviour on the field during the Gloucestershire-Hertfordshire match was abominable in some ways though not, I felt, at the time of the incident for which I was dismissed. But Smith's behaviour was equally disgraceful. (Incidentally, he is he 1982-83 president of the RFU).

The next morning I travelled to Coventry, where England squad training was taking place for the Irish match under John Burgess, the balding and determined Lancastrian who was then England's new coach. As I was changing, Burgess came over to me and beckoned me outside the room. In a deserted dressing room, we sat down. Burgess sought my explanation of what had happened; I told him exactly.

He listened with a grave expression on his face. 'Normally', he said when I had finished, 'your own speak up for you. But no one in Gloucestershire has spoken up for you. The 'phones were bloody hot last night.'

I realised with horror what Burgess was saying – that people high in the RFU had been discussing the sending-off and the bow, and linking it to my selection for England's team to play Ireland. They seemed to be reviewing my position in the side, although there seemed no reason at all why they should link the two games. But Burgess was also merely confirming what I expected: no one on the county committee had supported me in any way, either to say that perhaps the incident seemed not to warrant a sending-off, or that the bow was not supposed to be a slight to anyone, or that no one had received treatment after the incident; or even that no one really seemed clear that I had entered a ruck with my knee high, intent on damaging the opposition. That was just what I had come to expect from some Gloucestershire officials – the incompetence of some of them was only matched by their complete disloyalty.

Again, please do not think that I am proclaiming my complete innocence. I was involved in several dubious incidents in the match. But much of what happened was misinterpreted, by the RFU and the referee downwards. 'Let's see what happens', said Burgess finally. We left the changing room and went out on to the field at Coundon Road, where we went through our preparations for the Irish match. When training ended and the squad broke up, there was still no word from anyone that my England place was to be taken away, so I drove home to Gloucester with pleasurable anticipation of the Irish and and their special brand of forward play.

The afternoon was a significant one for my children, since it was the day of the annual children's party at Kingsholm. My wife and I duly transported our trio to the party, and they were soon enjoying themselves. Peter Ford, an England selector, was at the ground and we spoke of the incident. He confirmed that the telephones had been buzzing. I also heard from a high source in the RFU that one of the telephone calls made to Bristol on the previous evening, calling me a disgrace to the England jersey, had come from an even higher personage who was, to quote my informed source, 'full of gin'. Ford left Kingsholm for home, and I felt that perhaps the incident was blowing over. I eventually joined a group from the Spartans, a local Gloucester club, and we chatted quietly. Then Peter Ford's bald head reappeared in the doorway. Must have forgotten his umbrella, I thought. But Ford kept on coming towards me. He asked me to go outside, and I leaned on the fence overlooking the ground. 'The worst has happened', he said. 'Don't pack your bags for next week. You are withdrawn from the England team.' Alec Lewis, chairman of selectors, had rung him with the Rugby Union's decision.

He knew, although he was a selector, or perhaps especially because he was a selector, the fight I always had to get into the England side. As I said before, I always had to claw myself in via the Possibles team in the trials. Now I had been discarded without even playing. 'You must be sick', said Ford. 'You've done it the hard way.' I nodded, but could not think of one single word to say. I went back into the club in a daze; I collected my children from the middle of the fun, and drove home with Pat. Then the enormity of what had happened hit me and the anguish I suffered made me feel very sorry for myself indeed that night. The press had another field day and large headlines gave me the news that I was the first man to be withdrawn from the national team in this way.

I was absolutely stunned, because there was no rule then that anyone should be withdrawn just because he had been sent off, although a player sent off today would indeed have missed the match. At the time, I repeat, there was no such rule. I got the impression that I was thrown out by one or two people acting together. No meeting of the RFU committee had been held and everything seemed to have been decided over the telephone. No one ever told me whether they ditched me because of the events on the field or the repercussions of the infamous bow or whatever.

However, later in the week I received the following letter on RFU-headed notepaper from Air-Commodore Bob Weighill, Secretary of the RFU:

RUGBY FOOTBALL UNION

PRESIDENT: K. H. CHAPMAN

SECRETARY:
R. H. G. WEIGHILL

TELEGRAMS:
"SCRUMMAGE, 'PHONE, TWICKENHAM"

PLEASE ADDRESS
ALL CORRESPONDENCE TO:
THE SECRETARY,
RUGBY FOOTBALL UNION

TWICKENHAM
TW2 7RQ

TELEPHONE:
01-892 8161

RHGW/PY. 15th January 1975.

Mr. M.A. Burton,
15 Goodmoor Crescent,
Churchdown,
Glos.

Ireland v England - 18th January 1975

Dear Sir,

I am instructed by the Committee of the Rugby Football Union to inform you that as a result of an incident which occurred during a game between Gloucestershire and Hertfordshire last Saturday, which resulted in you being sent off the field of play by the Referee, it has been decided that you should be withdrawn from the England team to play against Ireland on Saturday.

I should add that this action is without prejudice to any disciplinary action which may be taken by the Gloucestershire County Rugby Union Disciplinary Committee, in connection with your sending off.

Yours faithfully,

Bob Weighill

Note that I had been 'withdrawn from the England side after incidents *during* the Gloucestershire match, which resulted in you being sent off the field of play by the referee.' (My italics.) In other words, Weighill was putting down on paper the fact that I was being withdrawn for events which happened *on* the field, and therefore laying bare the fact that there were absolutely no grounds for the withdrawal in the laws and bye-laws of the union constitution. My treatment had nothing to do with the bow and bringing the game into disrepute. I am sure other members of the RFU expressed disquiet about the contents of that letter too – it pulled the rug from underneath the RFU's feet.

With all the commotion raging in the succeeding weeks, I never actually said a word of all this to the press. In fact, I never said a word about the whole affair to anybody. After a time, I found that I had become something of a martyr. Some papers carried stories claiming that I had taken my medicine with a dignity which must have impressed the authorities. The truth was that I was desperate to go to Australia on the England tour at the end of the seaon, and did not want any hasty comments to be held against me as well as the sending-off. But I thought my chance had gone anyway as I simmered at home, serving my suspension, and watching England's season go by. I also turned down several offers from the Rugby League.

The Irish game ended in defeat in Dublin. A muddle at a scrum near the English posts allowed the fly-half, Billy McCombe, over for the winning score. Then in one of the worst English displays for years – and there was plenty of competition for that title – France came to Twickenham and scored four converted tries, eventually winning 27-20. Fran Cotton was England's captain and his misery must have been almost complete when England crashed to a Welsh side at Cardiff which hardly had to raise a sweat. They were 16-4 up at half time and coasted through the second half to win 20-4. The new régime of John Burgess as coach and Cotton as captain had made precious little difference.

Eventually, my own little débâcle was forgiven if not forgotten. Fran was struck by injury and forced to withdraw from the English team for the last match of the season against Scotland at Twickenham. John Burgess told me that I was chosen to take his place at an England session, thereby ending my exile and putting me right in line to go to Australia. I think my sigh of relief almost blew him over, because I never wanted to do anything quite so much as to play for England. Although I have always been bitter about the way I was withdrawn from the England side, I never let it affect my desire to play. 'Does this mean I'm captain as well?' I asked Burgess, since I had taken the skipper's place. The RFU forgiveness didn't extend quite that far.

The match against Scotland was an important one, even more so than the usual hard-fought Calcutta Cup matches. Scotland had beaten Wales and Ireland and were therefore looking for their first Triple Crown since 1938. They were led by their loose head prop, and therefore my immediate opponent, the Mighty Mouse himself – Ian McLauchlan, fresh from his triumphs in South Africa with the 1974 Lions. He had gone through that country's props like a knife through butter and no one had an answer to him. John Reason, then of *The Daily Telegraph,* wrote that he had 'taken on all-comers with a rasping disdain'. Now that disdain was about to be turned on me as I emerged from the international wilderness. Yet the game would also be our chance to avoid a complete whitewash in the Championship (our second in four years); add to that the places at stake for Australia, and you have a needle match.

The match itself was grim and not entertaining, but we did manage to stop the Scots and prevent the whitewash. Alan Morley scored a try and Neil Bennett kicked a penalty. Doug Morgan missed several kicks which would have given the Scots the Crown, succeeding with only two penalties. The match represented not only a confidence booster of sorts to England and their chances in Australia, but also the end of another episode in my sendings-off series. Actually, the next chapter began almost immediately.

* * * *

The upshot of my recall to the England side was that, to my delight, I was chosen to tour Australia with England. That meant I had visited the three leading rugby-playing countries, South Africa, New Zealand and Australia, within three years, and it also meant that the English rugby authorities didn't exactly wrap their team in cotton wool. Three trips like that in successive years represented some hard work; nevertheless, having beaten South Africa and New Zealand, we had the chance of an outstanding treble, and a unique treble at that.

I was not terribly pleased with the rest of the England party because it seemed that far too many experienced players had been discarded and far too many inexperienced players chosen. Building for the future is all very well, but having arranged a job of work, you pick those who can best carry out the job. The competitive atmosphere of Australian rugby – especially the well-prepared and ferocious Australia which we met in 1975 – was no place to take long-shot hopefuls who might, only might, develop into England players of the future. The concentrated eight-match itinerary also gave very little time for players to develop. Almost every match was a pressure occasion.

Looking back on the players originally chosen, there was no Chris Ralston, no Peter Dixon, no Alan Old, no Barry Nelmes, who was then playing superbly for Cardiff; Tony Neary was appointed captain but he and Fran Cotton, who missed both tests, missed vital matches through injury. To fill in these large holes in the team's experience were promising but ultimately inadequate players. No fewer than seven of the team who had arrived in Australia as England's future never played for the country after the tour. Over half the party failed to win more than five caps each on returning home: Brian Ashton, scrum-half, Steve Callum, flanker, Keith Smith, centre, John Raphael, hooker, Neil Mantell, lock, Dave Rollitt, flanker, and Alan Morley, wing, never again wore the England jersey. So as well as a dismal record (five wins from eight matches), there was not even much recompense from the point of view of hope for the future.

Generally speaking, the selection was a disgrace. Alan Old, Peter Dixon, Barry Nelmes and Ian Oram did join the side eventually as a whole string of injuries did nothing whatever to help England's cause. In most cases it was too late: Peter Dixon, that intelligent and experienced flanker, flew right across the world to play in one game, a meaningless match against a Queensland Country XV. We lost both test matches, crashed against Sydney, and were also beaten by a New South Wales Country XV, the sort of result which made Englishmen in Australia at the time practise Australian accents very conscientiously in the hope that no one would realise they were English. I played in seven of the eight games and have the scars to prove it.

However, neither England's defeats and sad failure to develop into a true international class combination, nor the run of injuries, were the true and immediate story of the tour – the newsworthy items contained almost none of these elements. What did hit the headlines was the obvious decision by Australian rugby, and especially its forwards, that they were not going to be pushed around and not going to continue a run of humiliating defeats.

The result was a tense, ugly, and controversial tour. And I became the first Englishman ever to be sent off the field while actually playing in an international – a record I can most assuredly do without and one which has always caused me a great deal of distress. Australian rugby succeeded in its efforts not to be pushed around, but the whole thing over-balanced into thuggery. Who am I to talk about thuggery? Well, I was bad enough, but I was by no means the most villainous or dirty player in Australia in their winter of 1975, not by a long way.

Trouble began in the second match of the tour, after we had put Western Australia away 64-3 in the first match. We moved on to Sydney where the city side put the whole tour in the melting pot by beating us 14-10, and running up a huge lead on points with some top-class punching from a young prop called Steve Finnane. He put Steve Callum and Bill Beaumont off the field and floored me with a punch from behind. I managed to land a few of my own to dissuade him but he made a real impression. I describe the match more fully in my 'appreciation' of the Finnane phenomenon later in the book, but the match against Sydney set the tone for the tour and especially for the tests. With Fran Cotton out of action and with experienced forwards thin on the ground, I became one of the senior players, and I could not accept the opposition handing out punishment on this scale. The Sydney game shook me up to face what the rest of the tour was likely to bring.

The next match was a quieter affair, even though Finnane was playing. We beat him and his New South Wales side 29-24, with a large contribution from Bristol's flanker Dave Rollitt, who supported the attack and scurried round picking up the pieces in defence in his normal, effective, but usually unrecognised manner. Then followed the tragic and dismal defeat by the New South Wales Country side, who had been exciting a lot of interest by their famous up-the-jumper routine. They would turn their backs to the opposition at short penalties, group together, and then burst away in all directions like a starshell with the ball firmly tucked under the jersey of one of them. They tried it against England too. But, in truth, our display was so poor that orthodox rugby would have done the job for them just as well.

So the tests approached. England were hampered by their lack of experience and by the run of injuries. Australia were fanatically determined that the Poms were going to be beaten, and the hysteria of the whole rugby population of the country was duly stirred by a series of Pommy-bashing articles in the Australian press. The stage was set for something explosive. We took the field at the Sydney cricket ground on what was then a great day for Gloucester, since Peter Kingston and Peter Butler were also in the team. It wasn't such a great day for England, though, as the captain, Tony Neary, and the fly-half, Neil Bennett, left the field – and the tour – injured in the first half. Nor was it a great advertisement for rugby, due mainly to the home side's abrasiveness. There was one memorable all-out punch-up, dozens of niggling incidents, plenty of unfriendly discussion between the forwards, and a convincing defeat for England by 16-9 which could have been worse.

Right from the start, the Australians were more confident, cohesive, and determined. The England tour selection and injuries had produced a ragbag outfit far, far away from the sort of side which would have been truly representative of English rugby at the time. At least three English journalists gave some heavy criticism to the test referee, Mr Cooney of Sydney. One report said that the Australian forwards paid no attention at all to the laws and the referee let them get away with it. The whole game was a low point of a tour with several low points.

Things began a slight upturn after that. Barry Nelmes fitted well into the front row alongside John Pullin and myself, and Alastair Hignell played a sound game as England beat Queensland 29-3 in a satisfying day out at Ballymore. However the referee, Bob Burnett, did not impress us at all and John Burgess said so afterwards to the press. But we were in a happier and more settled frame of mind for what just had to be a win in the Second Test in Brisbane. Alan Old, Jeremy Janion and Peter Preece formed a more solid midfield triangle and we faced the Australians with morale rising. Yet again, though, the situation was explosive. I knew that the Australians would come at us with even more fire and brimstone than in the First Test – they had their noses in front but all their efforts would be in vain if we managed to square things off. A draw in a test series for the away side is a narrow moral victory. They knew that we would be better equipped mentally and physically and that we wanted the victory as much as they did.

The events directly after the kick-off in the test have become as infamous as any other incident on any rugby field at any time. The Australians kicked off, a ruck/maul followed, and the whole Australian pack went crazy. To a man they rained blows and boots on to Englishmen either prostrated or on their feet trying to maul the ball away. Ray Price, the Australian flanker, is seen clearly on the television playback raining punches on Bill Beaumont with the speed of machine-gun bullets, as Barry Nelmes is kicked repeatedly. The whole pack came out fighting in a disgraceful and literal way. That playback is always trotted out in any discussion on sporting violence. It was horrible and frightening and Burnett, the fourth referee in my own particular quartet after H.T. Luxon, Ken Pattinson and Alan Welsby, watched it all. Barry Nelmes was kicked yards. One picture of the incident shows Andy Ripley standing, hands on hips, a few yards away; he is taking in the whole scene and the expression on his face betrays his total disbelief – he had been labouring under the naive impression that rugby was a game for fun and not a risk to life itself. Burnett took no action.

The Australian pack that day was MacDougall, Horton, Finnane, Smith, Fay, Price, Loane and Shaw, and there were not very many of that group who did not land a boot or fist on an Englishman. By the time I had arrived at that first fight about six England players were lucky still to be alive.

The Australian sportsman always fancies himself as a hard man, often with justification, and I admire the philosophy which they hold. But on that day, they set out to intimidate us deliberately, they had no respect for us as international players and visitors. They took some of my own philosophies of the game and ran away with them completely.

It needs very little imagination to forecast my own feelings as the fight eventually subsided. I was storming, livid, boiling. I had to take action, to stand up to them. We went to the first line-out and I picked on Stuart MacDougall, the Australian prop. 'I'm going to smack you here. You're going to have it.' If Burnett had not seen anything to send a man off for in the last few minutes, it was fair to assume that he was never going to send anyone off in the whole of the rest of his life. When I threatened MacDougall, I was threatening all of Australia. I was also following a habit of mine – in such circumstances, I was always prepared to take a warning from the referee in order to impose myself, realising that the official probably wouldn't send me off first time. That is the philosophy behind most of the opening exchanges in pressure rugby matches these days.

MacDougall did not feel up to the challenge himself. He called out to his team-mates as the line-out formed, using a typical Australian expression. 'Hey lads. Burton's got the biff on', he shouted. Sure enough, Burnett came round and stood next to us in the line-out. I was still raging. I had to hit MacDougall now or my credibility was gone. I had recurring images of the earlier brutality. The ball came in and I did hit him. Belting a player under the referee's left nostril is not the cleverest thing I ever did on a field, but I still cannot bring myself to regret landing that punch. MacDougall went down, and rose to his feet quickly. Obviously, he had been influenced by his own Digger Morris. I turned away and saw that the whole English pack were receiving another pummelling from the Australians. The 1974 Lions '99' call had nothing on this. As the fight wore on, MacDougall and I became involved in a rather unloving embrace. I actually managed to pull a little trick on him. I wrapped my arms tight around him and nodded over his shoulder. 'He's behind you', I said. As MacDougall relaxed, I butted him. The law of the jungle once again, and a disgraceful thing to do, but I had to make a stand. Officials and non-players will hold up their hands in horror. People who really understand test rugby will understand me.

John Pullin had resumed the captaincy, replacing Tony Neary. The referee called Pullin over. He pointed to me and said that I had started the fight. Of course, I had provided a spark which helped to light the fuse, but the Australians had not only provided great sheets of flame to light the fuse as well, they had been busy laying dynamite and detonators with great forethought and care. Remember, Burnett had completely ignored the first punch-up when England were almost kicked into the stands.

The next item of actual rugby was a drop-out, and while we were preparing to take it I had a conversation with Ray Price, the long-haired Australian flanker. He fancied himself as a hard man, but did not show up quite so much when he came to England the following season and found there were players every bit as hard as he was, who did not make half as much fuss about being hard as he did. His play usually ranged from over-vigorous to hysterical. Our little chat did little to calm me down. The drop-out went way down field into the Australian 25 and I followed up with the adrenalin and anger driving me on at well above my normal shambling pace. I was charging like a wounded elephant. Doug Osborne, the Australian wing, caught the ball and kicked to touch. He was well advanced into a spot of self-congratulation at his sound defensive play when I arrived and knocked him flying with a late tackle. Burnett ran up and stood with his back to the tunnel. He gestured over his shoulder. 'Get off', he said.

Now I had completed a quartet of sendings-off, but the other three, even the county dismissal, had nothing on this. I was disgraced in the England jersey and there was to be no bowing nor other humorous antics on the way off. I was shattered. I went into the England dressing room and sat down shedding tears of shame, anguish and disbelief. My attempt to help England stand up to the Australians had misfired. Not only had I been prevented from playing my part but I had left the team a man short for a crucial international match.

Phil Blakeway and Fran Cotton arrived from their seats in the stands to try to bring some solace. Cotton was terribly missed out on the field. The injury he had suffered in the match against New South Wales had devastated England's chances. With Cotton and I together in the front row, and no disrespect to Barry Nelmes and the other England forwards, the Australians may just have thought twice. But the big man was out. I cleaned the vaseline from my legs and drank a can of beer. Then I broke down completely. Cotton nodded to Phil Blakeway, who understood and left the room. He was a big man in my opinion and he never mentioned the incident again, never embarrassed me. Cotton and I were left together with the misery and frustration of the whole affair. We had another shock when studs came clattering down the corridor and the dressing room door swung open to reveal Bill Beaumont. 'Christ, they haven't sent you off as well', we said. But Bill had come in temporarily for stitches in a head wound caused by one of the Australian attempts at domination by force.

I envisaged a complete ban on me from England rugby and perhaps even from all rugby; I cursed the Australians for taking me to boiling point. Cotton suggested we went up to watch the second half, but there was no way I could bring myself to do so.

The final whistle went on a 30-21 win for Australia and a 2-0 test series victory. In fact, England had fought on bravely in my absence. They led 15-9 at half-time. Uttley and Squires scored tries and Alan Old put over some fine goalkicks. Bill Beaumont coped superbly with life in the front row as my replacement. But the extra man told, especially when John Hipwell began to attack the two-man England back row. We lost, inevitably.

The headlines were predictable and correct. They called the game a disgrace, a brawl, explosive, shameful and sick. They said that my dismissal had rendered the Australian victory a hollow one; some also said that my dismissal must have been embarrassing for the Australians, since they were the instigators of almost all the rough play and I was the one singled out. One report said that Australia had clearly made up their minds to intimidate before the first whistle had blown. Later, Australia's coach, Dave Brockhoff, said that it was not planned for the team to go out and knock us about. He told Fran Cotton that it wasn't premeditated and I am prepared to believe him. But that does not excuse what happened, or my reaction to it. You wouldn't kick a dog the way they kicked England; they thought we were soft, and didn't respect us.

As the players came off I went into the Australian dressing room and shook hands with MacDougall and with the wing I had late tackled, and some soothing noises from each side took away some of the atmosphere, though not my immense sadness. Bob Templeton, the coach of the 1981-82 Wallabies as well as many other Australian sides, came up to me. He took me away from the ground to a small pub where we both sat down. He was trying to remove me mentally as well as physically from the whole situation. In Australia, although they have glasses for the beer, they sell it in large pitchers. Templeton bought two and banged them down on the table. 'Right, we're not moving till we've drunk these', he said. We talked about many things. He described his business in stock dealing and discussed anything except the match itself. I gradually came round – and we finished a third pitcher. He asked if I was ready to go back and face everyone. I said that I was. Templeton is a gentleman and I haven't forgotten his kindness and foresight whenever he has come over to this country. As a coach and a players' man, he knew how I felt and the best way to deal with it: I returned to face the music. I rang my wife. 'You've been in trouble again. Are you all right?' she asked. I wasn't, but it was nice to be asked.

England's manager, Alec Lewis, was a quiet man and incapable of great feats of anger. He took me to his room. 'How could a senior player like you do something like that?' he demanded, having seen his team reduced to fourteen men. That was his way of giving me a severe reprimand. I arrived at the dinner to see the referee in the middle of a group of the Australian side chatting away over a few beers. Alec suggested that we go over and speak to him. He was not suggesting that I go over and grovel at his feet, or apologise and beg forgiveness, neither did we want a forgiving reaction. We just wanted to show that I was big enough to shake hands and that I didn't harbour thoughts of murder. I walked towards him as meek and mild as possible. Yet he came across as a perky, arrogant man; he gave no sign that he appreciated us shaking hands. He finished his drink and said: 'I'm off to the trots', which were Australian trotting races. And off he went.

The England party's opinion of Mr Burnett therefore reached the same extremely low level as our opinion of his refereeing ability. No one gave greater momentum in world rugby to the call for neutral referees than he.

I rated only one other referee on a par with Burnett, and that was Gert Bezuidenhuit, a South African who was the most biased I ever came across. He took charge of the Northern Transvaal-England game in 1972 so I was able to give the 1974 Lions a full briefing on him when he came to take charge of the Orange Free State match in 1974. Every time we got into their half, they had a penalty to clear their lines, or so it seemed. I met Bezuidenhuit again on the 1976 Gloucestershire tour. I spent some time discussing various points with him, and disagreeing with some of the opinions he put forward, just as any two people discussing rugby do. The next day in the papers there was a story about Bezuidenhuit complaining because I had criticised his refereeing. In general the story was a complete fabrication, misconstruing everything I had said. If everyone promptly rushed into print with anything that they were told during a private conversation in a rugby club, there would be a permanent ban on some people, while others would be in Pentonville for gross defamation. Committeemen would all commit suicide because no one loved them, and a high percentage of rugby players would be divorced on the grounds of adultery. No, Bezuidenhuit didn't impress me. He had actually come down to see us in an official capacity, to advise on interpretations and so on, which made the fuss even worse. Neither did he impress others. Edmund van Esbeck, correspondent of the *Irish Times,* said to me after a match in Bloemfontein which Bezuidenhuit had refereed: 'Incompetence I can stand, dishonesty never.'

Continuing for a moment this digression on referees, there were others whom I rated as extremely mediocre. I had particularly angry memories of the refereeing of Peter Hughes, a Manchester dentist. He took charge of an England trial on a Saturday morning at Twickenham between the South-West and London. Hughes was so determined to keep me in order that he forgot about the rest of the game, and seemed to be watching and penalising me throughout. He may as well have put a saddle on me and ridden me around the field. He warned me and then even told the South-West captain, hooker John Lockyer, that he thought I had deliberately put my fingers in Terry Claxton's eyes during a hand-off. I became tired of his incessant attentions. 'You're only refereeing one man', I said to him. He turned away and carried on. Meanwhile the London team were laughing themselves silly because they could see what was happening. Adrian Alexander, their flanker, called out 'mind my eyes Burton' at one ruck when we were yards apart.

Another Hughes classic was a Gloucestershire-Somerset match on

Kingsholm. He decided to penalise collapsed scrums by awarding a kick against the loose heads alternately as the scrum went down. This meant that when it was their turn for a penalty, the tight heads of each side just dropped the scrum and were awarded a kick. Hughes had little idea what was happening. He may be a superb dentist, but how he came to be a leading referee, I cannot fathom.

Max Baise was another controversial referee. He was a South African and took charge of leading games on the 1974 Lions tour. He disallowed what seemed a good try in the Fourth Test, which was therefore left at 13-13, destroying the Lions' one hundred per cent record. Max himself was very upset at the criticism he received. Yet he need not have worried: we found him a referee of flair and distinction, and no one thought he was anything other than a fair man.

In fact, I should say that I have had great respect for most 'puffers'. Just because I often found myself in trouble with authority didn't mean I didn't respect that authority. I grew to admire Alan Welsby, Roger Quittenton and many others. I even admired greatly a bastion of the RFU like Larry Lamb, now the special adviser on the laws but formerly an international referee. He is a high ranking RAF man and I had some fascinating conversations with him on the subject of Britain's defences – and I mean guns and missiles rather than strong tackling centres. 'You see Mike, we must have strong arms as a defensive policy', he said. 'What if the Russians invaded Berlin and said "We are taking over here and here are our tanks". We could then reply "No you are not. Here are our tanks." Our armaments are our insurance policy' he went on. 'And insurance premiums are high.' Larry is a charming and civil man – and a referee!

Back to 1975. The disciplinary committee convened after the test match, being composed of the president and vice-president of the Australian Union plus Alec Lewis. They decided that to be sent off in an international match was sufficient punishment and I did not warrant any further suspension, for which I was relieved and thankful. I even played in the final tour match, a romp against Queensland Country, and scored a try. The tour was over if not the repercussions. Australia had played rough and I had stood up to them. England and I had taken punishment and I had returned it, so Burnett had singled me out. Not many years after, Wales had trouble with both Australia and with Burnett. They found Finnane and his cronies still around. They lost people with serious injuries, including a broken jaw suffered when Finnane punched Graham Price.

The man in perhaps the most difficult position of all as England flew home was John Burgess. He was a hard-working coach, but a poor season in the Championship had been followed by a dismally unsuccessful tour of

Australia. At that stage, with his job very much on the line, I was the one thing he didn't need. I represented controversy and disrepute. Nothing would have been easier for him than courting favour with the Union, the people who appointed him, by dissociating himself completely from me, and in public too. He could have slated me and rightly so. But he didn't, and although I already had a high regard for him, he became an even bigger man in my estimation.

At Heathrow, we waited in the lounge and Bob Weighill and Colonel Morgan approached with smiling faces, to greet the RFU president, Ken Chapman, who had accompanied the team. They walked straight past Burgess and myself towards the president. 'Don't worry son', said Burgess. 'My head's on the block too – but they'll be sitting on the fence till they hear what the president thinks.' Burgess was soon dismissed as England's coach but, thankfully, is chairman of Lancashire for 1981-82, their centenary season, and is a powerful and effective voice within the RFU. He has shaken quite a few people with the good sense of the report which bears his name on the need for restructuring the game in England.

Ken Chapman actually gave me some support in the end, suggesting that I was a little hard done by and condemning publicly the approach of the Australians. He even suggested that they might not be invited to fulfil their proposed tour of the United Kingdom later that year as a protest against their style of play and brutality. That was strong stuff, coming from a man in Ken's position, and although the Australians did come, I am sure they were primed by their own union to take great heed of his words.

So my spluttering England career eventually spluttered on. I had been sent off four times and was well-established as the villain of rugby. It was equally well-established that I was prepared to give everything for the cause and that I was not going to be dictated to on the field. Sadly, if people tried to dictate to my team, I was often tempted to go right overboard to stop them. I was the only Englishman to have been sent off playing for his country, and it didn't feel good. I was an object of distaste to officialdom and many onlookers, and I am not going to try to defend my actions to leave myself blameless. But I carried grudging respect from players from Lydney to Australia: which wasn't a bad end result of some harsh incidents.

9

SOUTH AFRICA - A PROLOGUE

THE system of life in South Africa known as apartheid has been viciously attacked over the years. Internal pressure on the South African government has been increased by the statements of some black community leaders that they have given up hope of finding a non-violent solution; in other words, they are declaring war on the whites if what they see as oppression doesn't stop. External pressure is also growing, as it has been for many years. A variety of people – churchmen, human rights agitators, fair-minded people and people preaching sinister variations of the communist theme – have combined to raise the anti-apartheid cry to a new level of stridency, hoping that the South African government will be deafened. Some of these groups seek merely the end of apartheid; others, probably, seek the complete demolition of the country to prepare the ground for the spread of communism into a place currently a bastion of anti-communism.

All the groups involved in the anti-apartheid movement (including those merely anti-South Africa or anti-sport) have found it easier to go about their demonstrating business outside South Africa rather than under the eyes of the South African police in the country itself, where those disagreeing with the government have a habit of landing up in jail and being asked questions afterwards. So small groups of South Africans outside their own country have become easy meat. Annoy these small groups, create havoc with whatever they plan to do, notwithstanding the fact that they are law-abiding citizens, and the press and television will give the matter acres of coverage, coverage which will filter back to South Africa. Thus sportsmen have come under the hammer, and the intensity of feeling against South African sides leaving the country – even those selected on a truly multi-racial basis, as was the 1981 Springbok team in New Zealand – is enormous. They are harassed and hampered.

When a tour by a South African side is announced to any country and in any sport, but especially in rugby, lobbying from black nations, threats of boycotting of trade and loss of goodwill, blacklisting and violent demonstrations follow. If the tourists eventually decide to go, they may face quite an ordeal when they are supposed to be enjoying themselves following one of their chosen hobbies or professions. As a result, South African national sides in all sports have been ostracised. Their cricket team would have been one of the world's strongest in the 1970s, with Eddie Barlow, Graeme Pollock, Mike Procter and Barry Richards at their best: but they never even took the field. Teams intending to travel to South Africa are bombarded with criticism and accused of supporting a dastardly regime. International contact has all but ended in either direction. Except in rugby. Teams still visit South Africa with the frequency of earlier days. The 1974 and 1980 Lions defied all the shouting from all over the world and completed their tours. After a long gap, a South African Barbarians team ventured to this country in 1979 and the predictions of trouble at every turn went unfulfilled save for the odd carpet tack being scattered on pitches where they were due to play. Then the Springboks went to New Zealand in 1981 to resume the titanic series of matches between the two countries.

Rugby is now in a very important position. It is the spearhead for those who believe that politics has nothing to do with sport, and it is the monster upon which all the many groups who oppose South Africa for any reason can focus their determination, and their indignation that rugby is defying the weight of their opinion.

All this has put a tremendous amount of pressure on the administrators of the sport – people good enough to spend most of their spare time arranging fixtures, attending meetings, choosing sides, balancing a few books, arranging the odd tour, and then sinking a pint before they go home. Suddenly, people who have been serving in this way have found themselves arguing with politicians and others over matters in which they have no experience. The media and assorted nutcases, among others, have forced them to make public pronouncements on matters outside their field. They have to make tremendously difficult decisions on whether to entertain South African teams or perhaps whether to send a team to be entertained in South Africa. If they decide to stop a team playing, they may be letting rugby down; but if they decide to go ahead, the implications are enormous. The acceptance of one invitation can now sever diplomatic relations between your country and another, cause all sorts of other international repercussions and anger, and demolish a host of major events in other sports. The country's sportsmen can, on inviting South Africa or announcing their intent to go there, find themselves every bit as ostracised as those of South Africa itself. Some of the barking of protestors and demonstrators and politicians has been found a far worse experience than their biting, but, I repeat, rugby is in the vanguard.

The hierarchy of the game often appears slow-witted and limited in its response. The uttering of the stock 'we all hate apartheid but we believe in building bridges' phrase is too often trotted out in place of more reasoned, rational and, ultimately, more passionate arguments. The old platitudes suffer when set against the skilful propaganda of the other side. But, as I say, the administrators are being forced to dabble in matters outside their field and, generally, they have done a brave and honest job.

I do not intend a large area of my book to develop into a political tirade and a polarised one at that. But no international sportsman has been unaffected by the South African question and I should like to discuss my career in South Africa and the background to the opinions I have formed about the whole troubled and controversial situation.

I have been to the country four times, each on a major tour and three times as a player. I have taken the time to talk to blacks and whites and see at first hand what people who are creating such a fuss elsewhere have never seen – not because I set out to crusade around the country talking politics, but because people came up to me and discussed their own lives and beliefs. In 1972, the anti-Springboks people were still euphoric after a major victory. The 'stop the 70 tour' campaign had helped to cause the cancellation of the proposed 1970 South African cricket tour to Britain. The campaign's members, it was said, were breeding locusts to let loose on the pitches. An image of a bearded twerp shut away in his college laboratory breeding little insects is laughable and sinister at the same time. Such images kept the Springboks at home.

There was pressure on England not to visit South Africa in 1972 but it was resisted comfortably and off we went after a dismal season in domestic rugby. I had just completed my first season as England's tight head. I must confess that withdrawing from the tour on moral grounds at that time was something which did not occupy my thoughts for a great deal of time! What the hell did Sharpeville have to do with me – or any of those other names which people were quoting at us? I was a newly-arrived international sportsman and I wanted to take on the Springboks. Why should I worry about a few blacks cooped up in small houses? There were plenty of people in Gloucester and the valleys of Wales cooped up in small houses and scratching around the poverty line too. Even if I disagreed totally with something which was happening in the country, why should it stop me playing rugby there? I could have been going to the moon and I still would have looked forward to it if it meant extending my rugby career.

I gained a slightly wider knowledge of the whole question in the days after the party arrived. I saw the petty apartheid system at first hand: the toilets for blacks and toilets for whites; the beaches on which no black feet could be set; the awful sight of thousands of black people crushed into a small area of each rugby arena, while the whites enjoyed the comforts and decent viewing positions. I couldn't believe it or understand it. Yet the Afrikaaner people whom we met were magnificent hosts and during all my tours they proved generous and accommodating. They were continually wanting to explain what was happening in their country, trying to justify in some ways their government's policies. They were anxious to hear what we thought but also wary. In many ways, they were paranoic.

The actual rugby I deal with later in the chapter, but an incident after one of the games is an illustration of the harsh apartheid of the early seventies. We had just played the second of two games against coloured teams. The seven-match itinerary contained historic games against two non-white teams, the South African Federation team in Cape Town and a Bantu XV in Port Elizabeth. After the match in Port Elizabeth, we were taken into the black area for the reception at the Town Hall. The match itself had been memorable for the enthusiasm of the players and crowd and for their absolute delight that we had come, and the reception was an enjoyable affair at which both teams mixed freely. Ties and plaques changed hands and English and Bantu-accented speeches gave thanks for the occasion. The coloured lads were grinning away as the real business of the reception came round. Large tubs, packed with ice and beer cans, were dotted around at strategic points in the hall. One of the Africans went to a tub and came back with about six cans which he distributed around the group as we talked away.

I took great delight on that tour from the company of Tony Richards, the Fylde and Lancashire wing who was later to move to London to captain Wasps. I had already christened him Arthur, which was his second christian name, and wherever I went in South Africa in 1972, my mate Arthur would be with me. Having polished off our cans with alacrity and seeing that the opposition had done the same, we made an expedition to the nearest beer bin and came back armed with replacements, which we handed out. The Africans were thunderstruck. They were astounded that us white people could put ourselves out in this way, even though Arthur and I were merely following the ancient ritual of standing our round, even though no money changed hands. They were conditioned to being the servant rather than the served. Their interest aroused, they began to question us about life in other countries, especially our own. They were not used to being treated as equals, and we had no idea that we were making a special gesture: that was South Africa in 1972. I still didn't believe the fact that I was there was supporting the régime or hampering the lot of the non-whites. But some of the things I saw off the field were not particularly attractive.

However, I have noticed progress in every one of my subsequent visits to the country. The petty apartheid has been steadily lessening and from the rugby point of view, the non-whites have far more opportunity to advance. In 1981, Errol Tobias became the first non-white Springbok and those who said this was a cosmetic exercise were wrong. Tobias can play.

The 1974 tour by the British Lions was notable for the fact that we were almost completely disowned by the British government, who didn't want us to go. They made tremendous attempts behind the scenes to make the Four Home Unions tour committee change their minds and cancel the tour. The demonstrators sounded off and, once again, sometimes through individual letters, they tried to make the selected Lions feel as if they were actually wielding a whip and belabouring the non-white people personally by daring to go to South Africa. Peter Hain, leader of the 'stop the 70 tour' movement, seemed to be the acknowledged leader of the groups attempting to have the 1974 tour called off. He became the man all trendy television producers had to have on their programmes to propound his smug arguments.

Although I had experienced the way of life in South Africa and sympathised with some of the conditions suffered by the non-whites, I still could not see what good our not going would do. The government ban also had the terribly sad effect of our embassy in South Africa being ordered not to have anything to do with us, not to stage any official functions or extend any service to us. This, of course, meant that the team did not have to spend hours decked up in formal gear with small measures of sherry in large fists trying to make polite conversation to the sixty-seven-year-old wives of leading diplomats while holding sausages on sticks delicately between sausage-shaped fingers – which really was a tremendous loss. It has always been a major sadness to all the 1974 team, even though we had some consolation in crushing the Springboks and having a wonderful, memorable time in all other respects!

In 1976, during the Gloucestershire tour, I again saw a relaxation in the lesser aspects of apartheid. Another revealing incident in this context came when we visited an ostrich farm at Oudtshoorn. As the long-legged birds paraded back and forth, Bobby Windsor was making the ritual jokes about certain birds being a lot faster than the Springboks team and that they should be chosen for the next test. Then one of the birds shot past with a small coloured jockey on board. 'Christ', said one of the watching Lions. 'Look at that kaffir go.' The South African journalists were with us and they smiled. Quintus van Rooyen, one of the home-based writers, said: 'We have been trying all the time we've been in your company not to use that sort of language.' The South African whites were wary; they were careful not to give us even the slightest cause to fault them for being disparaging to the non-whites. They cared deeply what we thought.

By 1980, I had retired, but made the Lions tour as leader of a group of supporters from Gullivers Travels, the Tewkesbury-based travel firm which had employed me. My wife Pat came too, with her head full of what she had heard about the vile injustices of life in South Africa. When we arrived, she was amazed. So many of the visible signs of apartheid in the big cities had been removed. Whites served blacks in the hotels and restaurants. 'What's wrong with this place?' she asked in puzzlement. 'What is all the fuss about?'

We arranged a trip to Soweto, that sad and combustible township, so that Pat could see for herself what some of the fuss was about. We duly observed the squalid conditions; yet we also saw, not far from the township, non-whites living in large houses, watching their televisions under huge chandeliers. So what did we conclude, and what sense can I make, after my own experience of rugby touring in the country, of the whole muddled question of sporting links with South Africa?

Firstly, I cannot subscribe to the view that just because a sportsman plays against a South African team he is in any way supporting the South African government. And why does one country take all the stick anyway? If you are going to stop playing against South Africa, then you will also have to stop all further encounters with Russia, Iran, East Germany and several other countries. Those who believe that Britain is occupying Ireland would then presumably refuse to play Britain at anything. Rugby should certainly not blunder around in its contacts with South Africa, taking no account of the protests and the arguments, but neither should it cave in under threats. I would always play sport against anyone in the hope that I was doing some good. I think that external pressure has affected South Africa, in life as well as rugby; but I don't believe for a minute that had I and my colleagues at Gloucestershire, or in the England and Lions teams, not gone there, the lot of those people in Soweto would have improved. I would merely have given satisfaction to those who want to use sport as a scapegoat, and a scapegoat to further their own ends.

* * * *

A deep breath now before I recall some of the events on the field in 1972. For that tour, and a momentous one it was for English and world rugby, was the prologue to the greatest tour of all in my career – the 1974 Lions campaign. The match details of 1972 I do not propose to cover in depth, as a laboured resumé of tries scored, kicks goaled and injuries received has no appeal for those who, by now, know all the details off by heart. Perhaps, though, I can throw a bit of light on some of the more controversial or happier incidents. As that fellow Boyce always says: 'I know, because I was there.'

SOUTH AFRICA – A PROLOGUE

When the preparations for England's tour to South Africa were taking place, the whole thing was termed 'mission impossible', in much the same way that the aforesaid Boyce would view an England visit to Cardiff Arms Park. The Springboks had played little international rugby since they failed to win a test in Britain and Ireland in 1969-70, but that was history in 1972. Now they were on their own ground; they were not the vulnerable, demo-plagued Springboks of 1970. They were, so we thought as we prepared, the men of steel, the unbeatable, immovable Springboks who had beaten all-comers, from Britain or New Zealand, throughout history.

England were also holders of the wooden spoon. We had lost four internationals in the 1972 Championship, and to say we lost to France in the final game of the season is not really to do the occasion justice. We came third, 12-37.

Yet none of this worried me. In fact, the pre-tour predictions of disaster caused me as little pain and anguish as the fulminations of all those who felt that we shouldn't go because of the South African government's policies. A party of twenty-three set out, managed by Alec Lewis and coached by John Elders, the quiet man whom I respected so much, yet he was unsuccessful at the time of the tour. The captain was another quiet man, John Pullin of Bristol, who had succeeded Bob Hiller as England captain. Thankfully for our hopes, the normal, even statutory, deployment by the selectors of a large number of no-hopers and overgrown schoolboys was not too widespread. There was the odd representative of the England selectors' grand benevolent effort, but not half as many as, for instance, made the trip to Australia in 1975. On that tour, anyone over twenty-five with more than three caps was considered a wizened old codger.

The props were Stack Stevens of Harlequins and Penzance and Fran Cotton of Loughborough Colleges – and Mike Burton of Gloucester, making a mental note to impose himself on that bloody college boy Cotton and win a place in the only test of the seven-match programme. Mission impossible, they said. Well, despite my refusal to be pessimistic, we did face four very strong provincial teams and a test, together with those two matches against non-whites, in a concentrated programme. Despite the reassuring presence in the side of people like Pullin and Stevens, Neary and Ripley, I did have some doubts. Jeremy Janion and Chris Ralston, Peter Larter and Jan Webster – did they have what it took to beat the Springboks? With a twenty-three-man squad, it meant that more than two injuries would leave us one replacement short of the six that usually sit on the bench. As I met the other Gloucester players on the tour, fly-half Tom Palmer and flanker John Watkins, to leave for Heathrow, I turned such thoughts aside. I was even beginning to wear a hole in my own determination.

Even allowing for the fact that my rival, Cotton, scored the first try of the tour, we began well with a win over Natal, 19-0. Then came Western Province, whose pack was reputedly large and unfriendly, and who were going, so the locals said, to make us rue the day we took the field at Cape Town. The tour had been going well from the social angle, and obviously the Western Province game was going to indicate whether we had any chance at all of toppling the Springboks in the test. John Pullin said a few words and we went out into the tunnel. The home side ran past and Stack Stevens and I, the props of the day, looked at each other. Morné du Plessis, the giant number eight, went lurching by, followed by Immelman and de Villiers, the huge locks. Stack and I were searching for the numbers one and three on the Western Province backs, so that we could size up our own opposition.

Then the sun set, and darkness fell over the face of the earth – or that is what seemed to happen. Actually, blotting out the daylight were van Jaarsveld and Walter Hugo, the Western Province props who were thirty-seven stone and over four yards between them. They were monstrous. Stack was not big by some standards but compared with those two he reminded me compellingly of a starving maggot with me as his slightly larger, elder, but also starving brother. Cockrell, their hooker, was no midget either. As they lumbered past, Stack's jaw dropped. 'I don't like the look of yours much', he said, revealing his considerable ability to crack jokes in terribly unfunny situations. Nevertheless, they had to be dealt with to put the tour on the road.

For the first three scrums, the giant Hugo bore down on Stack and put so much pressure on him that John Pullin was unable to strike. Yet Stack's experience and determination were equal to it. 'We'll have to go low', he kept muttering during the stoppages, and low we went. We scrummaged with our noses only inches higher than the ground, down where Hugo and van Jaarsveld could not scrummage comfortably or bring all their strength to bear. We lost the tight heads 1-3 but held on – and won the match. The impossible mission was possible after all and we had a wonderful night; Burton, with Arthur in attendance, gave South African lager a thorough examination, not as an irresponsible celebration, but with the realisation that the rugby was going well.

The tour next took in the two matches against the non-white teams, where the infectious enthusiasm of the black crowds and of the home players were not quite matched by the teams' ability, although the games provided a happy experience. The climax was approaching, with Northern Transvaal and South Africa to be met on successive Saturdays and the awareness on my part that Cotton and I were fighting for the test place on the tight head. Stack was surely going to be the loose head. In fact, Cotton seemed to take a slight lead in the prop stakes. He led the England side against the Bantu team and in the Northern Transvaal match formed a front row with Stevens and

All set for my inglorious first appearance on Kingsholm – a 0-40 thrashing in a sevens match. The Longlevens side is (left to right): back row – Warren Fortey, Mike Burton, Roy Morris, Tony Peters; front row – Ken Pugh, Mike Tocknell, Keith Smith.

Above

A gathering before a Gloucester tour to Cornwall in 1967; the assembly includes many of my mentors, and others who played a significant part in my life. Right to left: Don Rutherford, Charlie Lynd, Mike Burton, John Dix, Colin Teague, Mickey Booth, Gary White, Jim Jarrett, Ron Pitt, John Green, Dave Owen, Nick Foice, Derek East, Nigel Jackson, Jack Fowke, Brock Lane, Alan Brinn, John Bayliss, Terry Hopson, Eric Stephens, Dick Smith and the man himself, Digger Morris.

Left

Gloucester's most famous win, bar none. Burton tangles with the incomparable Mervyn Davies during our knock-out Cup win over a brilliant London Welsh side in 1972. Afterwards, Gloucester men cried. *Colorsport*

Above

Who me? Alan Welsby warns me for an offence I am trying to persuade him I didn't commit in the 1975 Gloucestershire-Hertfordshire match at Bristol. *Colorsport*

Left

The bow. I acknowledge the abuse at Bristol. *Colorsport*

Left

A unique picture: Mike Burton within 20 yards of Barry John for the only time in his career. The match was my first for England, at Twickenham in 1972. *Colorsport*

Bottom left

A Lion at last! 1974. *Colorsport*

Right

Willie. Bill McBride inspiring us; despite appearances, I am hanging on his every word. *Colorsport*

Below

Attacking the Quaggas at Ellis Park in 1974.

Bottom right

A bitter match explodes and I am sent off in the second Australia–England test in 1975. *Colorsport*

adidas

Top left

Steve Finnane. He wasn't concerned with swinging warning punches, he really tried to put you away the first time. *Colorsport*

Top right

Keith Murdoch – a formidable, difficult and irascible man and a psychologist's dream. *Colorsport*

Left

Gerard Cholley towers above me, but for the moment only. *Colorsport*

Above

Action from a controversial knock-out Cup final (my first) when Gloucester beat Moseley and rugby lost too. *Colorsport*

Above

Steve Mills hoists the second knock-out Cup of my career – this time, it was called the John Player Cup. Two old stagers, myself and John Watkins (left), savour the feeling of victory. *Colorsport*

Left

Burton, Wheeler and Nelmes against Wales in 1978. Afterwards, Burton was dropped, Nelmes stayed, and that was one rebuff too many. *Colorsport*

Pullin. We could only draw but we came back from 13-3 to 13-all and that against a formidable team, not far short of test strength itself. Cotton was associated with the success.

The test place became a burning issue to us both. Neither of us had a tremendous amount of international experience and neither of us knew then that we were to go on to become gnarled veterans of England and Lions rugby. All that mattered was wearing that number three England jersey against South Africa. Anything else was uncomfortably near the end of the world.

I had one last chance to further my claims. There was one provincial match left after the one against Northern Transvaal – Griqualand West at Kimberley. I set myself to play the match of my life. Despite the superb hospitality of our hosts, the warm friendships which I made within the England team, the respect which I had among the tour party and the selectors, I felt that if I didn't make that test side, I might just as well have stayed at home and trimmed my lawn. As it turned out, I did impress in the Griquas match; I was well on top in the scrums and tore about the field. Mind you, I didn't stand out half as much as Alan Old, who kicked 24 points at fly-half. We won 60-21, and were thus unbeaten in all our provincial matches – which was far better than many people had expected.

So the test approached. Even with those confidence boosting wins, there was still no great optimism for England's chances. It was only one year after the Southern Hemisphere superiority in rugby had been challenged by the outstanding 1971 Lions. British teams defeating South Africa and New Zealand on their own ground had yet to develop into a habit.

We trained hard for the match, and then crowded into one of the dressing rooms at Ellis Park, Johannesburg. The whole party waited expectantly for the team to be announced and I quickly ran through my chances. Cotton and I were both at the top of our form; he had done well against Northern Transvaal, while I had helped take care of Hugo and company for Western Province. John Elders was seated in the corner of the dressing room, talking quietly. I was in the opposite corner as he began to read down the chosen side. In fact, I didn't have to wait for him to reach the front row. Behind Elders, crushed into the corner, was Tony Boddy, the Metropolitan Police hooker and Pullin's second string. He looked over Elders's shoulder at the team list. His eyes met mine as they came up and he gave a slight, almost imperceptible nod. I was in. Round one of the confrontations between Fran Cotton and myself had gone to me – even though Cotton eventually won a good few more rounds than I did as the battle proceeded. Elders finished and looked round; he told us of the importance of the match and of his belief that we could win it. As I have said before, he was almost too polite to be a coach – he was not as forceful as a John Burgess or a Syd Millar, but he was respected by the players even though, despite the 1972 tour, he was ultimately not a successful English coach.

That afternoon we went out on to Ellis Park to train. Fran Cotton formed part of a makeshift pack which had been formed to scrummage against us. He packed down opposite me and immediately the scrum practice started, I could feel the anger and frustration and force coming through him. That may seem the most inauspicious start for a friendship. When a player is competing for the same position as you at international level, you usually hope that, in as painless a way as possible and with no lasting effects, he breaks his bloody leg. Yet as he walked off after the session towards the tunnel, Fran came over to me. 'All the best', he said. 'I hope it goes well for you.' And he meant it. It was then that we cemented a friendship that has lasted throughout the years, and spanned a long period when it was Cotton or Burton for the England side. The boot was literally on the other foot in South Africa in 1974 when Cotton played at tight head in the tests, but we did play together sometimes when he was switched to loose head to make room for me: though not half as often as we should have done, in the eyes of Fran, myself and many other people.

Yet on 3 June 1972, almost ten years ago as I write, I was the man in possession. The lambs to the slaughter became lions: we beat South Africa 18-9. The Springboks, that virility symbol of Afrikaaner manhood, were well behind at the finish and England, European wooden spoon packed in their travelling bags, had astounded the world. A year after British rugby beat New Zealand, it had beaten South Africa too. A period of British supremacy, which included test successes and some superb International Championship matches, was well established. Sam Doble, the Moseley full-back, was at the height of his powers as a goalkicker on the tour and he banged over four penalties and converted a try by Bristol wing Alan Morley. We took on the Springbok pack and sometimes brought them to their knees. Doble, sadly missed after his subsequent death from cancer, swung that immaculate right boot and kicked England into history.

The surprising success of the party depended on several key factors, but rather than analyse matters like balance of power in world rugby and effectiveness of English tactics and so on, I should like to assess the tour through an appreciation of some of the players, both as players and as friends. There were people who contributed every bit as much as Big Sam and his boot.

One of these was John Watkins, a colleague of mine at Gloucester and eventually the winner of seven England caps. He had attended Linden Road school in Gloucester and risen through the ranks. He only toured in South Africa at all because Roger Uttley, the big north-easterner, had withdrawn due to injury; but a list of one person who was outstanding above all others in South Africa would certainly contain J.A. Watkins. At first, he seemed a little overawed as a new boy amongst established England players, but he soon tore into tour training and played every match as if it was a combination of an FA Cup final and his last act on earth. His confidence grew as he mixed with the party off the field and did a fine job on it. He was by no means a big man by the standards of international flankers but he was a genuine player and a dedicated one. I have never come across anyone who played so few bad games.

In the test match, while the large South African forwards were powering about the field, Watkins was grubbing and grafting at the heart of rucks and mauls and was always first to the loose ball. He was up against two of the most famous flankers in rugby history, Jan Ellis and Piet Greyling, who had won well over fifty caps between them, but he matched them in his first international. Greyling never played for the Springboks again.

A good illustration of Watkins's courage came in that test. We were in the lead, narrowly, when Stack Stevens sustained a nasty head wound, and had to leave the field for some fairly prolonged attention. At least to try to protect our own scrummage ball against the Springbok giants, I switched to loose head to take on Stack's man, Theo Sauerman. That left a great hole under Pullin's right arm – the tight head side. But even as Pullin was mentally running through a list of candidates to fill the role, Watkins appeared, draped Pullin's arm around himself, and prepared to pack down in the front row against Nick Bezuidenhuit, who was a large and powerful man. His feet never touched the ground, such was the pressure that the Springbok applied, but such were the lengths to which Watkins would go.

Another test hero was scrum-half Jan Webster, the tough little man from Moseley. He had played twice before for England before the test, and went on to win eleven caps in the kind of chequered career which the England selectors of the time always used to impose on their half-backs. Webster's tenacity typified the effort of the whole side and he was a scrum-half I came to admire greatly. When I was contemplating the team before we left, I had a question mark against that position: it quickly disappeared.

Another key man behind the scrum was Jeremy Paul Aubrey George Janion from Bedford – all those names and a home counties club were hardly likely to give him an immediate place in my affections. South Africa's trump card in the test was their centre, Joggie Jansen, who was a powerful man and who was supposed to run all over our home counties softie and his test partner, Peter Preece. But Janion was like a rock. He kept Jansen out of the game, going straight past him on several occasions. Janion suffered just a little from inconsistency but had a useful England career. He was also, contrary to what I had expected, a very nice man and tremendous company. He was a rational, sensible type with the dry sense of humour typical of the typical Englishman. If he was watching a game and the man in possession was flattened by a double tackle, absolutely crucified and laid out on the floor, Janion would say: 'My word. That was a hard tackle.' I took great delight in his company.

Peter Knight, who had played stand in for J.P.R. Williams earlier in the season when we were developing our counters to the flying doctor at the England squad sessions, was a different type of character again. He was a serious student of life and a religious man who didn't drink or swear, or believe that rugby was everything. The test match saw him on the wing, although he was normally a full-back at club level. The test aftermath saw him almost a non-participant. He couldn't understand, for example, why some people were considerably anxious to take advantage of a friendship with members of the opposite sex in a relationship that lasted just one night.

My question marks over the forwards mainly concerned the locks, who were Peter Larter, of Northampton and the RAF, who already had over twenty caps; Chris Ralston from Richmond, who was finishing his first full season in the side; and David Watt, the giant from Bristol who had won four England caps five years before the tour. We seemed to lack an aggressive front jumper and grafter like Alan Brinn, who had been left at home, and I had serious doubts about all three. Ralston and Larter seemed to lack the 'devil' for test rugby and Watt – well, he had always been a law unto himself. He was a temperamental man, potentially a superb line-out forward but, on bad days, alarmingly inconsistent and easily upset. Once again, as with several other players on the tour, my initial feelings on the trio were proved wrong. Ralston was another dry, and slow-moving man, but again, I grew to rate him as a player and enjoy his company. In fact, in Fran Cotton's autobiography which appeared late in 1981, Cotton selects Ralston in his best England team above such giants as Nigel Horton and Maurice Colclough, which is a great tribute to the man. Ralston was England's line-out champion throughout the first half of the seventies and was to have his reward with a Lions test cap in the final test of 1974. He was outstanding in the 1972 test and secured his immediate international future. He has only recently stepped down from his regular position in the Richmond side.

Larter was a revelation to me. My suspicions that he was a loose player went unfounded on the tour. He had 'bottle' and he proved it; and I told him so. He sealed up the front jumper position in the test and proved a powerful forward. The test itself was probably the height of Peter's career because he gathered himself and decided to prove everyone wrong who said he was too soft. He was also a fine footballer, and a rarity among international forwards, someone who could run and pass the ball.

Dave Watt, as always, was a target for home supporters with his slow-moving, grimacing style. He was overtaken by Ralston in the race for a test place and he was hampered by what was either a back injury or what people in Gloucestershire used to call a 'Wattism'. But he was a great character and made a full contribution to the tour.

That left Pullin on my mental list of heroes. Despite the lack of success he enjoyed at home as captain of England, there are not many captains who can claim to have taken sides to New Zealand and South Africa and come back victors. In fact, there are none except John Pullin. He was an inspiring captain in his quiet way. He was single-minded and determined but he never made a fuss and never involved himself in a fracas on the field. When he spoke to the team, he always looked people in the eye. He would demand attention and respect despite the fact that he was talking quietly. He was a man's man. Not least, he was one of the finest hooking technicians ever. He was one of the last hookers with the inclination and ability to strike for the ball and win it against the head.

Before the 1972 test, he addressed the side. 'If any of you can come off the field thinking that there was something else you could have done which you didn't do; some way in which you could have helped the team, you will know it when you put your head on the pillow tonight.' That sort of talk helped us to a test victory, aided by Doble, Watkins, Webster and the others, and we left South Africa as England's conquering heroes. Yet the tour was a prologue, not only to another successful visit to South Africa but to another period of English decline. We left a great deal of our determination, ability and success behind; one of the great tragedies of recent English rugby history. As I flew home I was satisfied. I had taken on a combination of demonstrators, Fran Cotton and the Springboks, and had beaten all three. At the time, I was a little green and did not perhaps appreciate the extent of the achievement. When it did sink in, it was a good feeling.

10

WILLIE

A Lion was different from other men. If he had travelled abroad to New Zealand or South Africa with the British Isles rugby union team then he assumed a mantle of indestructibility; he seemed to tower above other players even though he might actually be inches shorter. I used to regard a Lion with something approaching awe, even when I had become one and reached the top of the mountain. Technically, anyone in his own country's side has a fifty per cent chance of becoming a Lion. When selection comes round, for example, two tight head props have to be chosen and there are four international tight heads in Britain: so you could get the vote and enter the record books for all time. As the 1974 tour approached it became my burning ambition to become a Lion, to join the superstars in South Africa and, in some small way, become a superstar myself.

The tour was to mark the end of South Africa's sporting isolation and also a major split between the British government and the Four Home Unions tours committee. The government wanted the tour called off, the Unions refused. But I paid very little regard to the raucous voices raised against it – I had seen apartheid in operation in South Africa. What did that have to do with me? I wanted to play rugby in the country, not stand for parliament there.

The vital season in the International Championship before selection was a remarkable one for me, as I have already described. To recap for a moment: in a club match between Gloucester and Bristol, Dave Watt, the giant Bristol lock, had hit me with such an outstanding punch that it broke my jaw. I completed the match with the injury and then sat back with the grinning agony of it to assess the situation. A week later I was due to sit on the replacements bench for the England-Ireland match. I had already been given hints from above that I was under consideration for the Lions side, but as I sat and fingered my numb jawbone I realised that to drop out of the limelight would be fatal. The England squad was my shop window. If I had a long period out of the game I would be out of sight, out of mind, and sink from the list of tour possibles. It always took a tremendous effort on my part to haul myself into the England squad. I couldn't let that place go just because of injury. So I decided to take up residence on the bench against Ireland, and the rest is history: Cotton was injured in the match and, without realising that my jaw was broken, the selectors chose me to play for England in Paris, then at Twickenham against Wales. The gamble paid off. Although my injury was not even approaching the halfway stage of recovery, I got through both games, did well enough and therefore stayed on the list of possibles. That was how much I wanted to become a Lion. I had been associated with a draw in Paris and a win over the Welsh, so my stock rose considerably.

As Lions selection approached, I began to lose heart. After all, Fran Cotton had beaten me to the tight head spot in the England side. I was only second choice for my own country. Yet the press were flying their kites and telling me I was going to make it. Then, on a Monday morning, the telephone rang in my home. On the other end was Chris Lander, my friend and the rugby correspondent from the *Daily Mirror* – a brilliant, untiring and generous tourist. 'You're going', he said. My mind tried in vain to cope with about three thousand different thoughts as Lander continued. He had obviously only just seen the team list himself and was probably looking down a Press Association teleprinter sheet. 'But wait a minute', he said. 'Pullin's not going. The hookers are Windsor and Kennedy.'

I cannot remember having much sympathy at the time with those who were left out. I felt like a boxer who has had his arm hoisted as world champion. If that is not a particularly subtle analogy in the light of prior or subsequent events in my career, then I felt like the man who has climbed Everest and is able to shout down the mountain for everyone to come and see the view from where he is standing. The view was staggering.

On reflection, I should have been sympathetic to John Pullin, still then England's leading hooker. He had been one of the great Lions in 1971 and was someone with whom I always got on well and much admired. In his typically quiet manner, he wished the hookers who had been chosen all the best, and went off to spend the summer on his farm.

The other names were glittering. I was going to play with Gareth and JPR, with Gordon Brown and Ian McLauchlan, and, although I did not know him very well except by his formidable reputation, Willie-John McBride, the tour captain. Neither did I know Alun Thomas, the manager from Wales, nor Syd Millar, the coach from Willie-John's Ballymena. But I was sure of one thing: after a few months of being welded together under pressure in South Africa, I was going to know all about everyone.

My mental preparation to take on the Springboks and stand up to everything, no matter what, commenced in earnest as soon as Chris Lander voiced his final congratulations and put the telephone down. I trained with Gloucester and by myself until I was fitter than I had ever been, or ever would be again. The man who helped me tremendously in this was Ivor Oakes, Gloucester's trainer, who is responsible for the club's fitness even today. He has done a superb job with successive Gloucester teams over the years and the club has reason to be deeply grateful to him. In 1974, however, as I built up for the tour, I used to curse him as he ran me up Robinswood Hill, a stiff climb. We would arrive at the bottom by car and Ivor would tell me to set off. Once, I went sweating and toiling up the hill with images of Springboks floating before my eyes, powered up the summit and then tottered back down to the car where Ivor was sitting, desperate for a shower and a rest. 'Back already?' asked Ivor. 'You may as well do it again.' Eventually I was struggling up that bloody hill three times a night, with Ivor, now well into his forties, not far behind me. I went off to join the Lions at assembly in Richmond, so bursting with pride and eagerness that I almost tore apart my Lions blazer.

It is history now that the tour was brilliantly successful. We played 22 games and won 21, drawing the other. We were invincible; in a country where the home side was traditionally insurmountable, we crushed them into their own turf. We won the tests 12-3, 28-9, 26-9 and drew the last 13-13. That represented the biggest hammering ever given in a series between two major rugby-playing nations. We stormed through the country on the power of our forwards. People said we didn't take advantage of the best pack in British history to expand our game and they could have been right. But Syd Millar concentrated on the forwards, on making no mistakes behind, on allowing the genius of Gareth Edwards to run the show – and he developed all those elements into a match-winning and irresistible combination.

Most of the players were real thoroughbreds. If they had been racehorses when they retired they would all have gone to stud: they would have won the Derby. Many people said that our second string, midweek side would have been far too strong for the Springboks. The heroes of the tour were J.P.R. Williams and Andy Irvine, Fran Cotton and Gordon Brown, Mervyn Davies and Roger Uttley – you could go on to embrace almost the whole party. Quite simply, South Africa had no answer to us and they never looked like developing one in time to avoid humiliation. In addition to our successes, we had a harmonious, memorable tour in other respects. We planted the flag of British rugby on the summit, had a super time doing so, and a great reward for a lot of hard work.

Look at the players who never played in a single test – Tony Neary, Andy Ripley, Mike Gibson, Tom David, Sandy Carmichael, Ken Kennedy, Tom Grace. Class players. Selection of the team was rarely tested because whatever team the selectors put out, it always won. It was a pleasure to be part of it all. Of course, all the details will be familiar. But I should like to take you back to Richmond and the Lions assembly, and recount some of the tour highlights and incidents which are not nearly so well known, and which provide an appreciation of a remarkable, once-in-a-lifetime man called Willie-John McBride.

Our Richmond hotel was surrounded by demonstrators, who were trying to persuade us that we were doing terrible harm to everything from the welfare of the coloured man in Soweto to the future of the whole of the universe by going to South Africa and playing against their rugby teams. The television cameras and non-sporting media were there in force, to portray in loving detail every single expression on the faces of the demonstrators and to catch with their notebooks and sound microphones every last word uttered by them. Peter Hain was the leader of those besieging the hotel and making all the noise.

I then had my first experience of the style of Willie-John. We had all exchanged handshakes, and the team spirit which characterises all the best and most successful tours was just beginning to form. People were being allocated everything from kit and badges to the position of tour joker, or target for tour joker. Hain and a deputation wanted to talk to the Lions' management to put forward their views and they stood expectantly in the foyer. Willie and Syd Millar went down to join them, Willie wearing his Lions blazer and puffing on his pipe. He towered above Hain. He listened to the arguments, with a thoughtful and piercing stare on his face. I could not hear the content of the conversation, but eventually I saw Willie's lips move and then the two parties broke up and went their separate ways. The demonstrators had apparently gained the distinct impression that if they returned with bazookas and machine-guns, plus the odd cruise missile, and aimed them at Willie's head, he was still going to go and play rugby in South Africa. Willie's personality dominated the conversation and showed the demonstrators what they were up against. I swear that from that time the voices outside our hotel grew quieter.

During the flight to South Africa, Willie went among the players, tagging on to the various groups and sharing a drink with everyone in the relaxed atmosphere of the flight. Bobby Windsor was the only one who was not relaxed, since a flight for Pontypool's hero consists of hours of sitting with eyes screwed up, fists clenched till the knuckles drain of blood, demanding of the stewardesses to know if the plane has any chance at all of ever ariving safely back on the ground. He had little in common with Biggles.

Willie eventually reached a group which included myself and Geoff Evans, the clever Coventry centre. He sat down with us and puffed his pipe, then opened a can of beer. 'Y'know. It's going to be hard', he said. And he gave me that look – his head bent slightly forward, so that the whites of his eyes were showing. The way that Willie looked at you always made you take him seriously. He went on puffing, discussing what lay ahead and the fact that he had no intention, if he could help it, of going all that bloody way and not coming home a winner. In the end, he held up two great fists, one in front of the other, Marquis of Queensberry style. 'It may come to a bit of this', he said, looking around us. I nodded once. That was supposed to be one of the most eloquent nods ever, because with that one, short action I was trying to tell Willie that I would follow him through the thick of it and right out the other side if it did come to 'a bit of this'. In the event, Willie's prediction came true.

His character and appeal were already making a deep impression on me and we had barely taken off from Heathrow. As we digested the implications of his words, he came out with his most famous line. 'There will be no escape', he said. There was no easy way – we had to give absolutely everything or else we would win nothing. Willie started that tour by meeting it head on and that was how he approached the whole trip.

Syd Millar and Willie ran the whole show. They planned the tour tactics and the selection and they thought alike on playing matters. They were conservative in their approach to rugby but they still developed a winning side and an invincible machine. They also ran the tour off the field. They had been on umpteen of them, and they knew all the problems and the potential pitfalls: they knew the friction that could be caused in such a close-knit, even claustrophobic community like a tour party: they knew that every person was different. They realised that some people wanted to skip off to night clubs, some wanted a quiet drink and that some just wanted to go to bed – and they wouldn't let any of the people in one of these categories interfere with those in another. They would let people have a little leeway, let off a little steam, and then say: 'Listen, we don't want any more of that.' They were the ideal men. Syd Millar was a successful coach and went on to manage the 1980 Lions, the next party to tour South Africa. He is a strong and wise and sensible man, with little time for fools.

Willie became paternal, an almost priest-like figure in our eyes. He was a man's man and lived up to everything I had ever heard of him – either as a player, where he was courageous and formidable and occasionally ferocious, and off the field, where he was a giant too.

One of the best illustrations of the kind of man management of which Willie was capable came when the tour was a month old, and the initial impression we had made was favourable. He called a team meeting and stood up before the silent company.

'Men', he said. 'We have been away from home for more than a month now. One or two people will start getting on your nerves – it always happens.

This is the time to make a special effort, to look around at that person you might not be getting on with and remember that we are here together to do a job. We can do it easier if we are friends.'

All the players who might have had such nagging disagreements searched their souls. There were no baddies or prima donnas or unpleasant scenes on the tour because we all got on well together, but it is a tribute to Willie that he realised what might happen. The response of the 1974 Lions to a command from Willie to jump out of a fourteenth floor window would have been unanimous and instantaneous, so the reaction to his warning was similarly striking. Someone going up for his cup of tea at breakfast would bring five cups over and distribute them amongst the players before returning for his own. When he got back to his seat he would find five cups of tea and six helpings of cornflakes awaiting him. Everybody was falling over themselves to be friendly and helpful.

As the First Test approached, attitudes hardened to meet the challenge. We had beaten Western Province in the biggest match of the tour so far and approached the test with confidence tempered with the realisation that history was against us. In the event, we beat history and the Springboks, and won 12-3 on a wet day which seemed to have been specially imported from South Wales or Lancashire. The First Test was ours and that is a smashing feeling on a four-test tour. In some ways, winning that first match is way over one quarter of the job done. It is a great blow in the psychological battle and puts the pressure on the opposition. They know that with just one more defeat they can only square the series, and it is a difficult matter to motivate and dominate when the eventual prize is mere parity. In the Arthur's Seat Hotel in Cape Town, we settled down in recognition of all this to celebrate our win and the fact that South Africa had to worry about us for a change, not the other way around.

One by one, we walked into our team room. Willie stood by the door and had a word for everybody, because he wanted to involve everybody. He always insisted that those who didn't play in the tests were still part of the show and that their contribution was vital too – even the players who were understudying the real stars and had no chance of a test place felt that they were important. The whole touring party arrived in the room and sat down. Willie shut the door and looked around his men. Until then, we had been fairly well behaved, and if we had wanted to get drunk and cause a noise, we would do it in the team room and not impose ourselves on other people. Besides, Willie had always said that he didn't want to be 'fooled around by players making a nuisance of themselves in hotels and causing trouble generally'. As Willie faced us he was fighting a losing battle to control his instincts to celebrate fully a great victory. For Willie had a wild side. He had been involved in some legendary 'celebrations' on previous tours, although his outward covering of discipline and authority had never slipped so far on this trip. Suddenly he gave in to his baser instincts. 'Men', he called out. 'I take no responsibility until next Tuesday!' He reached up and grabbed an innocent-looking chandelier. He pulled it right out of the ceiling and it crashed in a heap around him, the bulbs rolling away over the floor. We realised then that we were in for some sort of night, and so it proved. It was a magical way to mark a magical test victory. There is no feeling in rugby quite like it.

As the tour progressed, the main controversy concerned the famous '99' call which we used. If Willie or the day's captain called out 99, it meant that we all went in swinging punches to protect the Lion who had come under attack, to give all South African rugby the conviction that we were not going to be pushed around and that thuggery was not going to put us off our game. The philosophy behind the call of 99 and the effect it had on the tour has been seriously misinterpreted; it was an effective, if not a particularly attractive, method of carrying on.

In the Second Test at Pretoria, we buried the Springboks. The 28-9 margin was the biggest international defeat ever, and South African rugby, which is a part of the fabric of the white South African's whole life, crumbled before Willie and the lads. Phil Bennett sidestepped through the Springbok forwards and Fergus Slattery snuffed out any home attacks even before they sparked into life. It was murder. As I said before of another incident, if Harry Gibbs had been refereeing he would have stopped it.

We gave the odd poor display, of course, and we only just scraped past Orange Free State, Northern Transvaal and the Quaggas to keep our unbeaten record. Then on 13 July 1974, at Port Elizabeth, came the Third Test. If we won, we had won the series, and all the efforts of everyone from Syd and Willie down to the baggage-man would be richly rewarded with a place in history. It was an historic day all round. Although the Springboks came out fighting and put the Lions under some fearful pressure, that magnificent Lions pack held on. The Mighty Mouse and Fran Cotton were propping Bobby Windsor; Willie was at lock with Gordon Brown, who was a giant in every sense; and Roger Uttley was in the back row with Mervyn Davies and Fergus Slattery. They were unbeatable and immovable. They scrummaged South Africa off the field as they did all around the rest of the country. J.J. Williams flashed over for two tries to seal it. So it was 26-9 to the Lions, and 3-0 in the series. Game, set, match and half the world to the Lions. Willie was king.

He came off the field with South Africa at his feet. He was lifted high by the players and sat on their shoulders waving and acknowledging the handshakes of victors and vanquished as his procession approached the tunnel to the dressing rooms. There he asked to be put down. He and the other players lined up at the tunnel entrance and looked up into the stand, to where the replacements and the rest of the party were waving with joy. Willie and the whole side lifted their arms towards us to show that we were not forgotten. We realised what his gesture meant, and there were tears in the eyes of myself and of some of the other hardened forwards. It was the pinnacle of everyone's career. The best of British rugby had beaten the previously unbeatable. And, perhaps best of all, Willie-John McBride, after so many disappointments on his previous tours, had reached the top. He deserved all the accolades.

That night was one of the greatest ever enjoyed by any touring rugby team, and there must be some competition for that title. Willie's wild side surfaced again – and although I have tried to let you into some of the secrets of rugby, I am afraid the events of that night after the Third Test must remain a secret. I simply can't remember a thing about it. There was damage to the hotel, I do know; fire extinguishers were set off, beer was spilt, glasses were broken, doors were knocked off hinges. There was quite a trail of destruction.

Next morning arrived with the whole party in the anguished stages of re-entry, and they savoured a day and a night to remember through a haze of hangovers. Down in the foyer, the manager was fretting. Alun Thomas was studying a list which the irate hotel manager was waving in front of his nose. He was horrified that we should have behaved so badly. His instructions from on high were obviously inclusive of keeping the team out of trouble and, Welsh stickler that he was, he was worried.

I watched, wincing at the bright lights and the clanking of the cutlery in the breakfast room, as Willie was summoned to join the discussions between the Lions manager and the hotel manager. 'Look Willie, what the boys have done.' And he went down the list: three hundred rand for this; five hundred rand for that; two hundred rand for something else. It had been quite a night, and it was quite a list. Willie took it and looked down it, with the inevitable pipe puffing away. He looked up at the two managers. 'Are there any dead?' he asked, and walked away towards the revolving doors for some fresh air.

Alun Thomas shuffled his papers and walked away in the opposite direction. As Willie passed me he stopped. 'Sure', he said. 'Last night was priceless. They'll never be able to buy that again with a million rand, let alone the sum they're talking about back there.' Off he went to savour the deserved feeling of being on top of the world. That was Willie-John McBride, the greatest man of rugby.

There were three people on that tour who deserve a mention in addition to Syd, Willie and the players. Alun Thomas is one, and he was a rather solitary figure by the end of the tour. There was no great rift between Syd and Willie and Alun, they just grew apart. They managed the party as far as the rugby went and imposed their own brand of discipline on the tour. That left Thomas to do all the official things, to take care of the administration and the speeches, which he did satisfactorily. He busied himself with tasks peripheral to the main one of beating the Springboks. There were never any harsh words in front of the players, but everyone sensed that the management had grown apart. In my opinion Alun Thomas was often over-officious and too concerned with observing the letter of the instructions he had been given by the Four Home Unions tours committee, rather than observing the spirit of them as Doug Smith had done with the 1971 Lions party.

After one of our games in Port Elizabeth, John Tallent from the tours committee arrived and joined us. We didn't actually rush up and cry 'Welcome John', but he was a good sort of man. One day during training immediately after Tallent arrived, Thomas appeared on the field. He had carried out his managerial duties quite efficiently until then, as far as we knew, but never before had he come on to the field: never had he intruded into Syd Millar's domain. Millar was putting us through some exercises and the whole session was warming up when Thomas stalked out to the middle of the field waving a piece of paper. It was pretty obvious to us all that he was trying to impress the newly-arrived Tallent, because there was surely no item of Lions business that could not wait for a few minutes till the end of the session. Syd Millar sensed that too, and began calling for exercises in different parts of the field. As the players sweated and grunted their way upfield, Millar followed them and walked away from the approaching Thomas, leaving him trailing and switching direction like Phil Bennett at his best. When the manager eventually caught up there was a very brief conversation indeed. Thomas departed and was never seen on the training paddock again.

Another man integral to the party was the liaison officer provided by the South African rugby union. This is a key job on all major tours, because he is the only link between the tourists and the country. He arranges and advises, taking care of the social and official programme for the team. Our liaison officer in 1974 was the most charming, helpful South African gentleman you could ever hope to meet. His name was Choet Visser. When I first met him in 1972 with England I wondered why I should trust him; he had a different, alien accent and, after all, he was one of them. I could not have been more wrong. As long as the team was happy, Choet was happy. If there were problems, and the lads were irritable, Choet's brow would furrow and he would beaver around putting things right.

Another man whose name cropped up often on the tour and afterwards was John Reason, who was one of the press covering the tour. He was then the rugby correspondent of *The Daily Telegraph* and is currently the correspondent of the *Sunday Telegraph*. He is an outspoken man and tends to rush in where others fear to tread. This has often made his opinions disliked, but disliked usually by those who are afraid to admit that what he is writing is the truth. Amidst all the joy and happiness and sense of achievement which we had, his was the one dissenting voice. John Reason seemed to think that the Springboks were so weak that our test victory was devalued, and he never even believed that Willie should have been given the captaincy. His book of the tour is the usual admirable and often amusing record which he produces, and I have always enjoyed his writing and my conversations with him because he is a challenging man. But the book's conclusions were the complete opposite of what everyone else was saying in print at the time.

Basically, he said that there was no point in going overboard because we had beaten the Springboks, as their rugby had sunk to a pitifully low level and that they were the blind school. He said that British rugby would have been good enough to choose a completely different side and still thrash the Springboks. He said that England had put South Africa away after arriving in the country in disarray after a dismal season. He compared the 1974 side with the one which had gone to New Zealand and won in 1971, and while paying credit to the dominant 1974 pack he said that the team was inferior, especially in the backs. He compared the task which the two sides faced and concluded that the 1971 task was in a different league. Finally, Reason castigated the conservative approach of Syd Millar as coach. He said that the Irish approach, a refined version of kick and rush based on strong scrummaging, came to be forced upon the Lions because Millar and McBride were the major influences. When the approach wore down everyone, including the Springboks, Reason argued, why on earth did the side not remain true to the past traditions of British rugby and play a more expansive game? After all, after years of trying to run bad balls, now the good ball was around it was being kicked. Reason's words were strong, challenging stuff – and were very unpopular with both the Lions management and the rank and file.

The barbs hurt members of the side, and there was a rumbling sort of resentment against Reason, which culminated in a direct reference to him and his views on the tour in a speech which Willie gave after the Third Test. This was all a great shame, because Reason, as well as Millar and McBride, had and still has a great deal to offer rugby with his analytical approach and absolute refusal to get carried away by taking things at face value. He did seem to go overboard on this occasion and not recognise what genuine achievements there were on the tour. The very fact that we had reversed a trend and won so easily was praiseworthy in itself, and I still maintain that there is no such thing as a terrible Springbok side. Even if the players lack ability they will fight to the death for the cause – the cause of the Afrikaaner people and the country itself. The truth of the whole matter lay somewhere in between the gushing torrents of praise heaped upon the Lions and John Reason's hosepipe fixed firmly to the cold water tap. There is still great respect for the man and his writing, and journalists have told me that from the technical point of view, he has few equals. I would like to think that I can count some of the others members of the British press who criticised and praised me over the years as my friends too.

While Willie was working his magic and the Lions were sweeping through South Africa, and Alun Thomas and Choet Visser were going about their business, what on earth was Mike Burton doing? As I say, I never made the test side. I remember what Jeff Young had said to me in the weeks prior to the tour. I met him after a London Welsh-Gloucester game at Kingsholm. Young had been a Lions hooker in 1968 and a powerful Welsh forward. We were discussing the forthcoming tour, and I told him that I didn't care about the test side, I was just delighted to be going at all. He knew better. That's what you might think now, was the gist of his words. But when you get out there, you and everyone else will be living and dying on the test selection.

So although I did rate the tour as the pinnacle of my career, and knew that my contribution as a player and diversionary humorist was valued by the management, I did have the frustration of not playing as large a part in the rugby as I could have done. There were many reasons, the first and most obvious being that Fran Cotton was in the test side playing at the towering height of his abilities. He was chosen as tight head in the test side although he had been brought on tour as a loose head. With Fran in for the big games, it meant that the two players selected as tight heads had to jockey for position in the Wednesday games.

But there were other reasons why I became confined to the dirt-trackers, the side which used to play in the midweek games and not in the more pressurised and usually more difficult games on Saturdays. Early in the tour I took a heavy fall and injured a leg, which was described in press reports as a training injury. In fact I had hurt my left knee during off the field horse-play with Tom David, which made it all the more annoying – in Stilfontein during the very first week of the tour. It took a long time to get better, and I missed the first three games and did not play till the win over Eastern Province. All players are desparate to be first off the blocks, first to impress on tour and by the time I was off and running, the others were a long way down the track and they took some catching.

Then I was troubled with a scratch on my cornea. I had originally received it during the previous domestic season in a club match against Newport. It was completely accidental but painful. During the tour, some lime from touchline markings reached the scratch and aggravated the injury substantially. I was in tremendous pain and for a few days had to parade around swathed in bandages. Really I needed a parrot for the full effect. The first injury at the tour's outset had already prevented me gaining any momentum and I never made a serious bid for the Saturday place. The eye injury hampered me still further, and I played in just three of the first fourteen games of the tour. That was sheer frustration and my depression sometimes threatened to overtake my delight at being a Lion at all. I also thought of the people at home. I could hear the Gloucester lads saying 'Good old Burton. He's not playing much rugby so he must be on the beer in a big way.'

A match against Rhodesia in Salisbury just before the Second Test became a goal for me. I just had to take part in it – to get my personal tour on the road and put myself back in the minds of the selectors for the future. The title 'forgotten man of the tour' is not a coveted one among Lions.

My eye injury was at its worst in the days before the game, but I was told that if I left the bandage on till the actual day, it might heal enough to enable me to play. The selectors, too, sensed my frustration and disappointment and they chose me for the team. Some drops seemed to improve the eye, and I made as many soothing noises as possible whenever members of the selection committee were around.

On the morning of the match, I was lying in my room contemplating removing the bandages to check on any improvement. There was a knock and Willie entered. 'I want you to come to my room', he said, and turned away. I jumped up and caught him at his door. As we entered I perceived quite a gathering through my one good eye. I found Syd Millar, Dr Ken Kennedy, and Gareth Edwards, who was captain for the Rhodesia match. They were all hopping from one leg to another and looking embarrassed. They said they were worried about my eye. They had sensed my desperation and they didn't want a half-fit player doing harm to himself or the team. I said there was absolutely nothing to worry about, which was not altogether true. I had the full use of my hands, and I wanted to get to grips with some Rhodesians. There was a silence and everyone stared at the ground as if watching a heat of the ant olympics with particular interest.

Willie spoke up. 'We don't think you should play with that eye.'

'Look, I'm all right', I said. 'What's the matter with you all?'

Dr Kennedy decided on a test. He unravelled the bandages and, as they came off, my eye was obviously blinking, trying to adjust to the light. It was a gorgeous, clear day and the sun streamed in as Kennedy opened the curtains. He told me to look up near the sun. By this time, both eyes were weeping, but especially the bad one. 'No wonder', I protested. 'Your eyes would do the same if you looked straight up at the bloody sun.'

Gareth took the bit between his teeth. 'We know how keen you are to play and it's great to see', he said. 'But yew're not playing an' that's it.'

I was shattered and upset as Kennedy wound the bandages back on. As I walked towards the door, Willie stopped me. 'Micky. I have been on tours when I have seen men do their damnedest to get out of playing a match; men who have no backbone. I want you to know that your attitude has registered with us.'

I can't say Willie's words made it any better. I was really dejected. People who have never made a Lions tour might not understand, but ninety-five per cent of the players who have would rather be at home than taken round the tour as a passenger. It always crosses your mind that you would be best going home. The worst part was that I had absolute confidence that I could take on the Springboks and be too good for them. I had done it in 1972 with England and was never in any trouble in the games I did play in 1974. One of my last chances really to make an impact on the tour was gone with that Rhodesia game and the sun streaming in through Willie's bedroom window.

However, from that point on I did play every week – in five of the ten remaining matches, including the big match against the powerful Quaggas and the fixtures against the South African Leopards and Border. My zest for the tour returned, and when I reached home I was hailed with the other players for the job we had done. It was unforgettable. The worry of the preceding months brought on by broken jaws, broken legs and broken eyes was made worthwhile. I was one of Willie's conquering heroes, and had joined the ranks of the indestructibles.

11
AFTERMATH

IAN Botham, one of the most famous current cricketers, has spent a great deal of his life away from home since he arrived in the England side in 1977. One day, when he was battling away against Australia as another English winter took a grip, his son Liam went missing. Mrs Kathryn Botham eventually came across him in his bedroom, curled up on his bed and in great distress. In his hand, he clutched a colour photograph of his father, who was thousands of miles away: Ian's absence was obviously a disturbing and disorientating experience for his young son. No blame, of course, to Ian, for taking on the Australians, the West Indians or the Indians, because cricket is his profession – he is well paid for it and no doubt enjoys it.

Nicholas, Andrew and Claire Burton definitely didn't enjoy it when I was away, which was for long and frequent periods. I spent six consecutive summers away from home and family. I went to South Africa (1972) and New Zealand (1973) with England, to South Africa (1974) with the Lions, to Australia (1975) with England, to South Africa (1976) with Gloucestershire, and America (1977) with Gloucester. Those seven years were an important time in the lives of my young family, and, in fact, I missed a good deal of their younger days.

All those readers in fits of jealousy that a player can tour the world for free, should rest assured that I am not going to launch into a lengthy description of the pain of being abroad. I am not going to bemoan the fact that the nasty old rugby unions dragged me away from my poor, neglected family to further their own ends. I enjoyed touring, and found it a memorable experience. I made friends, saw the world, downed beer and accepted challenges thrown down in many countries. As a failed apprentice panel beater, and an unsuccessful bread delivery man, I am rather grateful for rugby's contribution to my life. Besides, I can hear voices being raised that if I didn't want to tour, why didn't I say so earlier so that someone else could have jumped into my seat on the plane!

At the same time as I accept all the good-natured descriptions of me as a permanent tourist, however, I would like to dispel just a few of the notions that the aftermath of a major rugby tour is all wine and roses, congratulations and champagne, and trans-village drives in open motor cars. Up to a point, it is all these things, but it is also a potential domestic minefield. Ask any of the Burton brood.

In 1974, for example, my daughter, Claire, had an experience as upsetting as that of Liam Botham. She was gurgling away happily in the kitchen of our home in Gloucester when a strange, large, and forbidding figure came towards her, waving its arms and, as it must have sounded to her, growling ferociously. Claire's screams probably disturbed half the county. She was not to know that the ghastly apparition was her father returning from afar. I had just arrived back from South Africa, as one of Willie-John McBride's conquering heroes. We had left in May and returned in late July – an absence that was too long to be spanned by the memory of little Claire, barely one year old. While I was away, her life was full of women – her mother and grandmothers – and she had grown used to the lack of any male presence. My wife, Pat, had brought Andrew and Nicholas to Heathrow to meet me, and after the helloes and goodbyes and the ceremonial unveiling of presents, we had driven home to Gloucester. They were older, and able to understand. But with Claire it took many weeks of holding her on my knee and making an assortment of soothing noises before she took me back into her confidence – before I was accepted again as her father.

In fact, I missed Claire's birth and early life altogether. In the summer of 1973, England had toured New Zealand and Fiji – a pleasant outing thoughtfully arranged by the RFU after a projected tour of Argentina had been called off due to the political situation in that country. (It was to be another eight years before an England team finally went to Argentina, under Bill Beaumont.) There was a vital decision to be made in the Burton household: should I tour or not? For Pat was pregnant with our third child, who turned out to be Claire. Frantic calculations seemed to indicate that Number Three would arrive before I had to leave for New Zealand, and furthermore, we decided that I might never have another chance of a trip to that country. So with typical selflessness, Pat encouraged me to accept the invitation, and then tried to make me feel less guilty about doing so.

My conscience was further helped by Dr Mick Molloy. Not only was Dr Mick a powerful Irish lock between 1966-1973, he was also one of the nicest men in rugby. We met on the traditional Barbarians' Easter tour of Wales in 1973, and I consulted him about my dilemma. Would everything be all right? Would my absence cause problems? 'It should be OK', came the reply, buried somewhere under that lovely Irish accent. 'As it's the third child, everything should be fine.' Needless to say, everyone in the predicting line was well out with their calculations; the day arrived for my departure to the other side of the world, and Pat had still not produced. It was in Fiji that I learned, via the impersonal, staccato style of a telegram sent by my mother, that my first daughter had been born and that all was well. So I had to raise a glass of champagne in Fiji in celebration of an event which had happened thousands of miles away, and which I had missed completely. For me it was a sad by-product of the joy of touring that I missed the first few days on earth of our daughter, all the fascinating and gratifying experiences provided by a new arrival.

The preparations for the 1974 tour affected another of my children in a more direct way. The trip gave rise to all sorts of pre-tour fuss. Everyone in my family and circle of friends had spoken of nothing else for weeks as the assembly date for the party drew near. Almost everything else was pushed into the background. Even though my reputation as an international prop was commanding enough, I still felt somehow that you had to be some sort of superman to be a Lion. Now I had been selected to join them and I couldn't wait – after all, you are not a Lion until you pull on the jersey. All I wanted to do was to get on that plane wearing my Lions blazer; to set foot in South Africa; to find out if those Springboks were as hard as they were supposed to be.

Andrew was then five, and had just begun school at Brockworth Primary in Gloucester. He seemed unaffected by the bustle of tour preparations and by the obvious fact that something big was happening. He wasn't off his food, was making no trouble at school. All that changed very quickly. Suddenly, almost overnight, he began to cling to his mother and became insecure and frightened. Every morning he would become dreadfully upset when Pat left him at school. He knew I was about to disappear, and that something big was happening which did not involve him. Three months is three years in the mind of a five-year-old. He fired away with all sorts of questions. 'Will you be coming back, Daddy? Will the plane be all right, Daddy? Will I be able to come and see you? Will you write to me?' He sensed my own excitement and, although I never neglected him, he was becoming ever more anxious.

The pride of 1974 was to assemble one May morning in a London hotel, where the final little details were to be settled. As a salve to Andrew's growing bewilderment, I took him to school myself that day – and quickly realised the problems which Pat had been experiencing. When I took a step towards the door, having made my farewells, he became terribly upset and made a tremendous commotion: so much so that, momentarily, I wondered if I should forget the whole thing, and go home and unpack those carefully packed cases. The only thing which made an appreciable difference to Andrew's distress was when I solemnly promised to return later in the morning, actually en route for London, next stop South Africa. This was not merely a ploy. Even the school staff thought I should keep my promise. The whole cycle therefore began again later. As I approached the classroom, Andrew saw me through the window. One tearful, shattering goodbye and I was away, with my mind on the immediate past as well as the exciting immediate future.

Andrew was rather slow to get started in school, and it was some time before he caught up with the others. The anguish of those early events no doubt played a part. Now, apart from his bravely-borne habit of breaking bones while engaged in various activities, he has come through to be a well-balanced and intelligent boy – rather highly-rated by his parents! Again, no thanks to my touring, and it could have been worse. The fact that Andrew shows even some of his father's aggression on the rugby field may be thought bad enough by some people!

Ian Botham and I are far from being the only ones whose family life has been disrupted by our decisions to further ourselves in our chosen sports. I shared a room in 1974 with the Mighty Mouse, Ian McLauchlan, when the news from home came that his son had taken to wandering off and that Mrs McLauchlan was quite concerned that he was becoming unsettled. In 1977, the first Andy Irvine saw of his son was a photograph sent from Scotland: he was taking on the All Blacks in a foul Southern Hemisphere winter when his wife gave birth.

Ian McGeechan, another fine player and character in 1974, had enough trouble with the tour's effect on himself. His wife once told me that on returning from South Africa, he had become so accustomed to the daily round of socialising and activity which a tour brings, that he felt the urgent need to continue the social whirl and go out every night! He carried on till that hyperactive edge which the tour induced had eased.

By now, it will have become dazzlingly obvious to anyone that I have my wife to thank for the fact that my family life returned to normal. You can depict a rugby player as a finely-tuned athlete and a single-minded sort, but in many ways he also has to be selfish. In my own case, after all those summers away from home, I didn't even retire because I wanted to spend more time with my family. I retired because England didn't want me to spend more time with them, and also because I wanted to leave the game at the top. I had no wish to be pushed around by up-and-coming hard men whom I could have taken care of blindfold at my best. I can safely say, therefore, that among the considerable number of mistakes made by Mr M. Burton during his life, marrying Mrs P. Burton was not one of them. She coped superbly well. She detached herself enough to realise that I would settle down eventually and she had the ability, bordering on the magical, to give me a free rein while keeping the rest of the family together. I now realise what a contribution she made.

Another great misconception about people who have been away on a major rugby tour with their country or the Lions is that, somehow, they have suddenly become very rich indeed. People expect to see Maurice Colclough moving into a nineteen-bedroom mansion, or Gareth Davies driving round in his Rolls Royce. Very often, as I was walking round Gloucester, someone would stop me and discuss a recent tour. Invariably, the conversation would end: 'Well, you're OK now Mike, got a few bob in the bank!' Cricketers and footballers may well bring home the bacon from their tours, but rugby tourists are extremely lucky to break even. The pittance which goes under the heading 'tour allowance' is generally adequate to cover a half of beer per day plus a hamburger (onions extra), and many tourists pay a high price for the honour. Self-employed people, like Swansea's Clive Williams in 1977 or Bridgend's Ian Stephens in 1980, lose out completely. A one-man business can hardly thrive if the one man is away. Other players lose their jobs to make a tour: their employers cannot afford their absence, or perhaps don't want their employees frolicking around a nasty country full of baddies like South Africa, or have no particular need for a famous name in their business. 'A few bob in the bank' is the metaphorical way for the legions of amateur tour analysts to suggest that returning players are rolling in it. In my experience, the few bob in the bank can be taken literally.

Since I retired from playing and moved into the commercial world, working for a travel firm and representing sporting people, I have become, if not the West Country branch of Rothschilds, comparatively affluent. (I also have two big dogs, for the benefit of those who might care to remove some of the trappings of affluence.) I am able to take my family abroad on holiday, whereas for several years, the furthest we ever managed was Cornwall, which is not so different from Gloucestershire anyway.

Furthermore, since Pat and I have not yet entered the divorce courts on the grounds of unreasonable touring, and since she still often speaks to me, and since Nicholas, Andrew and Claire Burton are a delightful trio (not solely on the testimony of their parents), I should conclude that all is well in the Burton household that ends well. I should also remind everyone that touring is an experience to treasure. But there are drawbacks, quite apart from the reckoning on whether the tour itself was a personal success. There are moments of agonising and distress, times when the tourist has to bear selfish neglect on his conscience. My family could have paid the price, were it not for good luck and, above all, my wife.

12

BLACK AND WHITE

ONE of the wonders of the rugby world is the hostility, suspicion and jealousy which exists between the two codes of the game. You would hardly think that rugby union and rugby league are in the same family, if only related as half brothers. Until recently, leprosy or typhoid fever had nothing on joining rugby league, as a means of becoming estranged from old friends in the union game. Many people still have an image of a furtive old man in a flat cap prowling union clubhouses and engaging a likely player in whispered conversation in the lavatory. This is the rugby league scout, pantomime villain for committees, unions and governing bodies all over Britain.

The laws of rugby union go to extreme lengths to ensure that, should anyone catch the incurable league disease and go north, then he will have to live with his mistake for ever. If a player signs as a professional, he can never play rugby union again. Never darken these portals again. Until recently, he was also banned from many clubhouses. He may have been a dedicated servant of his club, and given so much to the cause that his job or marriage suffered; or he may have been so badly off that he just could not resist the wads of tenners which rugby league scouts traditionally wave in the aspiring player's face. Yet when he signs, he becomes a non-person. His mates look up and down the street before they talk to him. The club for which he gave so much disowns him, sometimes with an official and high-handed letter. An extreme example, you might say: not in my experience.

Until very recently, if a player took part in amateur rugby league he was tarred with the same professional brush; but not even the frightened men who run rugby union could make that bye-law hold water. Now, amateurs can switch sports, even though they can still not be members of clubs of both codes at the same time. You can play union and join a golf club, or a squash club; you can play union and join a cricket club; you can play union if you have just left Pentonville Prison, where you spent the last twenty years for murdering six people, but you can't play union after joining a rugby league club and being paid to play.

One of the pities is that union has very little to fear from league, save perhaps where top clubs in each code exist in the same town – commercial considerations will then obviously apply because they will be competing for fans. Otherwise, union is a blossoming and worldwide sport which is booming despite teething problems. League is rooted firmly in the north of England, though there are odd outposts – Fulham, Cardiff, Australia, New Zealand, France and Papua New Guinea are some of the outer reaches of the league empire and only in one of these locations, Australia, is league a bigger sport than union. The league game has nothing to compare with the International Championship or the gladiatorial major tours of the Lions. Yet still the jealousy of league exists.

As I have said, some of the barriers are breaking down. But take the example of David Watkins, hero for a million Welshmen in the 1960s and one of the nicest men in rugby. He received a letter from the Welsh Rugby Union thanking him for his services when he left Newport and Wales for Salford and the north. He has become such a respected figure in the union world and the league world (as well as in business) that he seemed to cross the great divide and move easily in both. Reality did eventually dawn, though. He is now involved with the Blue Dragons, the rugby league offshoot of Cardiff City's struggling football club. Cardiff's union club quickly withdrew an invitation to him and his wife for a club dinner – proving that prejudices don't die, they only fade away. 'And my wife never even played rugby league', reflected Watkins at the time.

It may come as a surprise to some people, but I risked the ferocity of the powers that be and had a league career of my very own. Mine was not quite as illustrious as that of David Watkins – in fact, it lasted only eighty minutes plus the odd training session. I only hope that the Barbarians don't pay too much attention to this revelation either: they have a habit of drumming league players out of the exclusive club of members, and I do treasure my Barbarians tie and fought loyally for their cause.

But seriously, there was a time when I thought long and hard and agonisingly, before I turned away the considerable interest which several clubs took in me. There was even a furtive bloke in a flat cap flourishing his tenners on behalf of St Helens.

The first time I was approached by a league club came when I was living in Gloucester, and didn't actually have my walls papered with pound notes. Early in 1965, when my Gloucester career was taking shape, I had read in the local press that I was going to become some sort of player. Then a pal of mine picked up a chance remark which almost changed my life. Terry Byrne was a northern lad himself, and often used to discuss the league game with me. 'I wouldn't mind having a go', I told him once, more or less as a throwaway line.

Tug Wilson, a Gloucester forward, had just lifted his bank balance by the odd £5000 when he signed for Oldham, and the prospect of such a clean and easy way out of financial embarrassment did have a certain appeal. But I didn't actually sit round thinking about it, weighing up the advantages and possible pitfalls. 'I wouldn't mind having a go', was meant to be non-committal. But Terry Byrne set things moving. It wasn't long before a Mr Worthington was on the telephone, wanting to know if I would like a trial with his club, Warrington, with a view to uprooting some well-established roots and taking the dread step northwards.

This is when all the suspicion of the league game which is inbred in young union players comes to the surface. I had heard stories that league clubs arranged secret trials, and then if you didn't want to sign for them afterwards they tipped off the Rugby Union. Even a trial makes you a professional in the eyes of the people who uphold union bye-laws, so with the revelation that you have done the dastardly deed ending your union career, you may as well take up the offer of the people who have ratted on you.

The thought of the money remained attractive though, and I decided to travel to Warrington. People going about their honest business at Cheltenham coach station in early 1965 would have come across a burly figure with his collar turned up waiting for the Liverpool coach. Off I went to make my fortune, hunched in the back of a vehicle of the Black and White bus company, with a pair of boots and armfuls of foreboding. The Mike Burton of that era regarded the trip to Warrington in much the same light as Burton 1982 would regard an overland safari to Outer Mongolia. It came as something of a surprise to find that the people in the north looked the same, used, broadly speaking, the same language, and that they had a Woolworth's and a Marks and Spencer's too!

I was uncomfortably settled in a hotel just outside Warrington and, again, comparisons with the 1982 Burton are instructive. I have now been involved in the travel business for some years and have stayed in hundreds of hotels. That hotel on the outskirts of Warrington was the first I had ever stayed in. Nowadays I progress through them like a forest fire, waving my American Express card. Then, I signed the name of Mr Ashcroft, the Warrington manager, at the bottom of what seemed astronomically huge bills, and hoped for the best. Mr Ashcroft told me that I was to play for Warrington the following day in a match against Swinton.

My inbred suspicion of rugby league and the people in the game was steadily dispelled from that point. They were fair and respectable people – and were keenly interested in me. A group of men in large Russian hats and large overcoats gathered round as I arrived at Warrington's ground. 'Can you play in any other positions, lad?' they asked. 'What weight are you now lad?' and so on. They were obviously having to back the judgement of the coach with the necessary money, and they fired away with their questions.

The coach had to provide me with a lifetime of knowledge of the league game in about three minutes as we sat down together before it started. 'Stand back ten yards', he said. 'Then come up and take your man. The others'll come in wi' dooble tackle.' The unfamiliar faces of the Warrington side did not hide much in the way of love and affection as they filed into the dressing room, taking note of the awkward stranger on trial. After all, one good game from me could take away the livelihood of one of the forwards.

As kick-off time approached, I was given a pair of shoulder pads, and one or two desultory handshakes; then I rubbed my hands in some resin which was broken up on the table. I went out to play an alien game, where front row players had to play almost like union centres. They had to run and handle, and tackle, tackle, tackle.

Even in the scrums, where I should have felt more at home, it was different. There was a blind side and an open side prop; one pushed and the other pulled, and instead of the well-knit driving of the union scrum, there was this crabbing mass of flying boots and heaving shoulders. The rain and the heavy pitch combined with the unfamiliarity of it all, and I hardly expected the officials of Warrington to come rushing into the dressing room with suitcases full of money for me, flourishing their new Parker ballpoints.

However, perhaps I had shown enough ability to convince them that I would be an asset once I had learned the basics of the new game. In fact, I was not the only A.N. Other to appear in the programme for that Warrington-Swinton match. John Isaacs, the Swansea hooker, played against me and his prop from Swansea, Warren Jenkins, was also in their side. There were several other mystery men on the field, too. But they have stayed in the union, and I should not like to curtail their successful careers by naming them here. Warrington won the match and kindly handed me my win money of £50.

I must have impressed someone in the stands with my bewildered display. After the match, Warrington offered me £2500 to join them, and that wasn't far away from being a lot of money. 'Three thousand', I said. I was on firm ground because I was by no means set on signing and I eventually fancied £5000, the sum which induced Tug Wilson to leave Gloucester.

The Warrington officials conferred and eventually increased their offer to £3000, which was quite flattering. Looking back, and taking into account my situation at the time, I find it a little hard to work out why I didn't accept. I was not to know at the time, after all, that I would make an international player and a British Lion. Yet, I turned the offer down; Warrington sensed that a capture was not imminent, that I was window shopping rather than about to commit myself. Black and White Limited duly took me back to the land where there were lines-out and proper scrums.

The experience gave me a respect for the league game and for the forthright honesty of many of the people; and the skills of even the biggest forwards. Later, in the seventies, when my friendship with Fran Cotton blossomed, I became even more fascinated by the game, for Cotton comes from a rugby league family. Mr Cotton senior can still recall his time as a league hooker and tell in the smallest detail his favourite stories. The whole Cotton family are warm, north country people and, on several occasions, I walked off down to Wigan to watch the league with the Cottons *en masse.* Such visits gave me more respect for the players. A loose forward could sometimes become so talented that he could slot into the centre or even full-back. I must confess I never thought of leaving my post in the front row of the scrum to play fly-half.

League people in general became extremely frustrated by the way their game was being portrayed on television. Up to now there has been little analysis, and the victim of a crunching double tackle was usually given only the comfort of Eddie Waring declaring 'He's moved an eyebrow, he'll be all right', as the poor chap was stretched out on the turf. No one stood back from Eddie's little asides to explain things to anyone other than those who were housewives watching just because the film was on afterwards. Perhaps all this will change with the advent of Ray French: let's hope so!

My next approach from the league came in 1972, when I was already an England player. I was a bigger name, and therefore a more costly but more attractive commodity. In the classic tradition, the man to approach me sidled up at a clubhouse. Even better, although he was smartly dressed, he wore a flat cap perched on his head. I had just played for Gloucester in a club match at Counden Road, home of Coventry. 'How about joining rugby league, lad' was his subtle opening gambit. He went on to explain that he represented St Helens, who had just lost their powerful forward, Cliff Watson, to Australia. Fran Cotton later confirmed to me that Watson was a fearsome and effective player, so it was a tremendous compliment to me if they thought that I could fill the vacancy.

At that stage I was already tasting the benefits which a career near the top of rugby union could bring, and was in no mood to put further patronage the way of our friends Black and White. I had a wife and family who were settled in Gloucester and Pat would certainly not have relished uprooting herself to move northwards. I told old flat cap that if he wanted to watch me in a union match he was welcome, but that the cloak-and-dagger stuff as experienced at Warrington was not on. He left Coventry promising to come to Gloucester.

St Helens's answer to James Bond therefore took his seat in the stand at Kingsholm for our next home match; he couldn't have picked a better one, and liked what he saw. We were playing Bedford and they were badly weakened – Billy Steele, the Scottish wing, and Jeremy Janion, the English centre, were unavailable to name but two, and Gloucester won by 47 points. I was cavorting about in the loose and scored two tries, which was about double my normal average for a whole season. It was a loose game.

Yet the talents which most impressed the watching member for St Helens were displayed at a line-out. Bedford won a terrible ball which was falling slowly into the arms of Vic Lewis, their scrum-half. I burst through the line-out and gave him a really heavy tackle as the ball arrived. Lewis stayed down for quite a time. It wasn't an early tackle, but it was delivered with a straight arm, I suppose. In the car park afterwards, my man invited me into the vast interior of his car, which seemed approximately the size of the Longlevens clubhouse.

'I like the way you 'it dummy 'alf', he said. 'You certainly knocked him aboot!' I felt that that remark was indicative of the player they were looking for, and of the type of player Cliff Watson might have been. It was a cheap tackle in my book.

In the resulting negotiations in the car park, I had absolutely nothing to lose. I had no real wish to go north.

'Actually, I want £10,000', I said, half expecting him to faint or fall about laughing.

'You have to be some sort of forward for that kind of money', he said.

The conversation and the interview petered out at that point, but St Helens didn't give up. They rang me a week later and offered something very close to my asking price – but the lure of league was still not strong enough, even for a comparative fortune. The sequel to this story came later, in the signing by St Helens of Mel James, the burly Swansea forward, for £8000. Poor Mel played only a few games before a broken leg hindered his progress, though he did go on to a fine career in league on his recovery.

After the St Helens man purred out of Kingsholm's car park, I often tried to visualise myself as a leading league player. I could easily have succumbed, especially to the earlier Warrington approach when I was short of experience and money. After the sensational incident, described fully elsewhere in the book, during which I was withdrawn from an England team after selection, I was overwhelmed by further offers – but, in the end, that great divide between the two codes, guarded by gun emplacements and barbed wire, was too great for someone half-committed to cross.

Thankfully, my union career flourished instead.

13
WALES, OK?

A Welshman is one of those people you wonder at every two years at the England-Wales match at Twickenham. You look around the ground, take in the sea of red, and then you ask: 'How the hell did they all get hold of tickets?' A Welshman is someone who gives the impression that Wales are playing at home when they are playing away. Welshmen are the people who would come up to me during my rugby career, when they used to beat us every year with a good bit to spare, and say: 'Why don't you combine with Scotland, Mike? You might have a chance then.'

Living so near their country, and crossing its borders so frequently to play against a formidable array of leading clubs, I have discovered a lot about Welshmen and to this day I get on well with them. I have already described how I sympathised with the bedraggled little fellow draped in a red scarf who accosted me when I arrived at Twickenham for my first international, to ask me if I had a ticket.

Not everyone loves Welshmen, and I exclude those who do not purely because they are jealous of them. In victory, some Welshmen are overbearing and unbearable, often arrogant. During the golden era of Welsh rugby in the 1970s – which seemed then to have started before time began, and to be heading into infinity, and which has only just ended – the Welsh team carried their supporters into paroxysms of rapture, and fair enough. The team had no peer anywhere in the world. But wherever they were, Welshmen would try to ram their victories down people's throats. This was usually done in a good-natured fashion, but traces of arrogance crept in. Even the Welsh team itself tired of such adulation; tired of the Welsh fans' collective disappointment if the team won by only ten points, or scored only two marvellous tries. Thousands of people therefore waited patiently for the day when the boot was on the other foot, when Wales would be struggling.

When this did happen, the Welsh attitude caused further anger. In defeat, the team was not always gracious. For example, Wales has grown to resent thoroughly the fact that it cannot defeat New Zealand on the rugby field. The two countries are very alike in approach and history, and have become bitter rivals: but Wales cannot win. It didn't even win when the team murdered the New Zealanders in 1978 and won everything except the match. 'New Zealand cheats' they said in 1978, when Oliver dived from a line-out, and 'blind Irish referee' they said in 1974, when England beat them and the whole of Wales said that Wales should have won. The supporters said that J. J. Williams had scored but John West, the referee, ruled that David Duckham had touched the ball first and therefore minored it.

Some Welsh people find a compelling excuse for every defeat, but they have to accept that sometimes they *are* going to lose. They don't make things easy for themselves – they don't allow themselves to be liked, which is a tragedy because there are few races who, deep down, are so likeable. Yet when they win, the phrase 'you can tell a Welshman but you can't tell him much' is often used. When they lose, and gripe, people say that you never beat Wales, you merely score more points. Wales has become a highly controversial rugby nation, maligned often but sometimes with justification.

I should perhaps emphasise again at this stage that I get on well with Welshmen. I travel around the world with them on business for my firm, and I am often in Wales for midweek games. I have spoken at many dinners there, too. I am considerably more at home with Welsh people than with high-ranking Englishmen who believe that rugby is still based in the nineteenth century and that players should be seen and not heard. I still enjoy the jokes at my expense. They tell me that when I was playing for England, a chap they knew played for Wales against us and came home to be awarded the OBE. 'What was that for?', asks Burton the innocent. 'On Beating England', they reply. The next time their man came over and won at Twickenham, they awarded him the CBE. 'What was that for?' I ask. 'For Consistently Beating England', they reply, with great beams of satisfaction.

Even the most sophisticated Welsh people lapse into general hysteria on occasions. A knowledgeable man like Bleddyn Williams wrote that our win in an unforgettable game in 1980 – unforgettable for its violence – was disgraceful because Wales had scored two tries and were singled out by the referee, and so on. You had to delve deep to find the final score in his report. Welshmen are a complex, sometimes cautious and defensive race. But there any criticism ends, because in rugby they can also be generous, superb company and, more important, leaders in most aspects of the game. They pioneered squad training and were the first country to appoint a national team coach and a coaching organiser; at last, playing strengths could be harnessed and the team performance would finally be equal to the sum of the abilities of all the players. It took the other countries a long time to catch up.

Not only are the Welsh pioneers, but at their best are probably the most attractive side playing-wise. Lately, the authority and confidence has gone but, for a long time during my playing career, Wales was the only team providing any spectacle or open rugby in the International Championship – and even in the whole rugby world. They are innovators and achievers, and nothing is more certain than that the present somewhat limited Welsh side will soon develop, find plugs for the holes, and go on to rule Europe again. Through the efforts of their first coaching organiser, Ray Williams, the game of mini-rugby evolved. Thousands of excited children have taken up the game, and thousands of excited parents have shouted them on.

Rugby is an expression of the whole Welsh way of life. An excellent illustration of the typical Welshman, even though he probably has a few pounds more in his bank balance than his average compatriot, is Max Boyce, a former club folk singer in Wales who now fills huge concert halls all over the world with audiences of all nationalities. I once spent the weekend of an international in his company. Max was cracking all the usual funnies about rugby and the England-Wales rivalry. From his act he told us of the occasion when the Pope, Billy Beaumont and Gareth Edwards were needing to cross a lake without a bridge. The Pope dashed across the water and plunged straight down to the bottom. Billy and Gareth, meanwhile, powered across the lake and arrived safely on the other side. Max says that Billy turned to Gareth. 'Pity the Pope didn't know about those stepping stones, Gareth.' The great man turns to Billy. 'What stepping stones?' he asks.

Sure enough, Max had us all chuckling away, and we realised that when he was taking the mickey, there was really nothing nasty or personal about it. But when he had run through some of his repertoire, he settled into his seat and came over as a very warm and sincere person, and one with a deep knowledge of rugby. He really is a typical Welsh fan, who enjoys the jokes and his pint, but who is able to laugh at himself and thus be likeable as well.

Another typical Welshman, and a man quite unlike the arrogant image which some Welsh people have brought on themselves, is Dai Morris, the Shadow himself. Dai is, quite simply, the nicest bloke I ever met in the game. He won 34 caps between 1967 and 1973, and was one of those players whom the spectators and press thought was a very good player but whom the players thought was bloody brilliant. He was an unobtrusive flanker, was always in the right place, was brave and determined and one of the most self-deprecating and selfless human beings ever. He never toured with the British Lions, which was unforgivable, and one of the great injustices of the 1970s. When he eventually finished playing for Neath, his club, he went to Rhigos and continued on active service, passing on the benefits of his wide experience to the junior club and turning out weekly.

I once played with Dai at Llanelli, where the Barbarians were to help celebrate the club's centenary season in a special match at Stradey Park. The team were inspecting the pitch and, with the time moving on towards kick-off, Dai had not appeared. The Barbarians' committee glanced anxiously at their watches. Eventually, Dai came striding over the field towards us, dressed in his overalls, a bit of a contrast with our blazers and Barbarians ties. 'Sorry I'm a bit late', he said to the officials. 'But I had to work late, you see.' The Barbarians nodded their understanding and Dai went off to change with that quiet, reserved, almost resigned attitude of his. I often had just a short, sharp conversation with him – because Dai wasn't the sort to carry on through the night discussing anything and everything. I have yet to meet anyone in rugby who does not believe that Dai Morris is a good bloke and a loyal Welshman.

I have also found that there is no better company on a rugby weekend than a group of Welshmen. When I lead their trips to Murrayfield, Lansdowne Road, or Parc des Princes, the occasion is always memorable. The Welsh away matches are pilgrimages – thousands of people attend the shrines and then save up all their spare money in preparation for the next big match. And they go whether Wales are brilliant or desperate. Sometimes they go and stay with Scots friends they have made: the Scots provide the tickets and the hospitality, and then in the return fixture the Scotsmen will go and stay in the little houses of the Rhondda and the other valleys and are entertained royally. Friction, even if Wales lose, will be minimal. No other sport has an occasion like the International Championship, no other country has fans like the Welsh.

On the bus to the matches, the laughter is endless. There is always one joker, a complete extrovert, and the others spend the whole time laughing at him. There is also a statutory team dummy, off whom the joker bounces all his jokes – and who always catches a bus to Lyons rather than Parc des Princes, misses the match completely together with the flight home, and arrives on the following Thursday in his local. 'Duw, caught the wrong bloody bus, didn't I', he says. Such events and such trips become legends: many Welsh supporters have figured in more legends than King Arthur.

In my time I have consoled Welshmen in tears because they have no ticket, I have dealt with hundreds hot foot from their hotel where they have just been thrown out, demanding to know what I, as their travel manager, am going to do about it. And in the end, as they board their trains at Paddington or climb into their cars at Heathrow, they always hold out their hands and thank me for a memorable time. They might not have slept in a bed, they may be penniless, they may feel terrible, they may be going back to a dragon instead of a wife, Wales may even have been thumped: but they still had a good time. In many ways you could even say the Welsh are puritanical. Let slip a swear word in a working mens' club and there will be a tap on your shoulder. ''Scuse me, Butty. There's ladies present yer.'

When they are entertaining, the Welsh can be excellent company. I have been to speak at dinners or play charity matches all over South Wales, at places like Tonyrefail and Garndiffaith. You just can never drink enough beer, hardly putting your empty glass down before another has been pressed into your hand. The ladies' committee – Welsh rugby clubs have almost as many committees as players – have provided delicious food, and it is difficult to drag yourself away from the warmth of the clubhouse.

I once arranged a match between a 'golden oldies' team from New Zealand and a club called Hollybush, who had a small ground near Tredegar. I desperately wanted the New Zealanders to have a good stay since my travel firm had arranged the whole trip, and I was uneasily aware that relations between New Zealand and Wales in rugby circles are not quite as cordial as they could be. Hollybush were unbelievable. They mobilised all their infinite resources, laid on a full four-course meal, dispensed club plaques and ties, and in a torrent of words expressed their delight that the visitors had come. About thirty New Zealanders almost settled in the town for good. It was a lovely occasion.

Those are my considered views of Welshmen. In my days as a player, of course, I had very little time to contemplate such matters as the make-up of the average Welshman, to analyse the contrast between the hospitality he offered and the arrogance which he could show. My time was fully used watching them like a hawk on the field. Nowhere is there such a concentration of large, successful and competitive clubs as in South Wales, and Gloucester used to play them all – at least, it seemed that way at the end of the season. The approach of Gloucester and the Cardiffs, Neaths, Newports and Aberavons of this world is remarkably similar. Genuine respect reached across the River Severn, but that didn't mean that we turned our backs on each other for a moment or that we wouldn't try every move within the laws, and a good few without, to win our games. They made it memorably difficult for us down in Wales, and we returned the compliment when they came to Kingsholm. A famous definition of a good player is one who is still piling in in the last few minutes of a wet Wednesday night match at Aberavon. I am proud to say that I never dropped out of such a clash with a feigned injury as some have done, and I was always piling in well into the final seconds. And that goes for Neath, Ebbw Vale, Newport and the others as well.

Early in my career with Gloucester we came up against Cardiff, with their formidable array of hard men. Their props were John O'Shea and Howard Norris, while they had Lyn Baxter and John Hickey and the others to back them up, too. Norris was a giant with great craggy features and a typically grating Cardiff accent. He was the kiddie at the time having come back from the 1966 Lions tour. I remember delving around in a ruck when I felt someone's fingers in my eyes. Cardiff or no Cardiff, I had to be true to the man I thought I was or, against Cardiff, the man I thought I needed to be. I stood up and smashed Norris across the face, not knowing whether he was the guilty party or not. 'Any more of that...' I warned him. Norris nearly collapsed in astonishment that a young Gloucester lad had landed one on him. We formed up for the next scrummage and, as there had been no retaliation, I quickly decided that Norris was very frightened and would be like a man walking on eggs for the rest of match. I didn't notice him slip his right arm off his hooker, Billy Thomas, as we went down – and neither did the referee. As I bent my head to enter the scrum, I ran into a clenched fist travelling speedily in the opposite direction. I went down on one knee and, as usual, jumped straight back up according to my first rugby commandment. I jumped up like a boxer who doesn't want the referee and judges to realise that he has been hurt, so intent on showing everyone how well he is that he manages to forget that he isn't quite sure which month it is. Everyone in the whole ground had seen the incident with the significant exception of the referee. As I bent my head into the scrum again, blood began to run out of my nose, and as my head was nearly upside down, to gush into my eyes over my forehead and into my hair.

'Or'right son', said Norris. 'Yew've 'it me an' I've 'it yew.' (Wyatt Earp used to say that if he got a gunman to talk in a tense situation, he knew he had the upper hand, and I summed up Norris's accurate assessment of the situation as fear on his part.)

'Whassamarrer then, scared are you?' I asked. The whole Cardiff pack shook with laughter, and I gathered that I had slightly misread the situation. But I suppose it ended all-square on points, and I had provided the information that, for future reference, I did not intend to be pushed around even if I did lose the odd clash on the way up.

Another incident which I will never forget came at Aberavon, where the local side used to take the field in their red and black jerseys at the Talbot Athletic Ground and tear into us, and where the mother of Billy Mainwaring, one of the locks, used to tear into us too – and the referee – with some barbed remarks which carried clearly to the players above the din of the crowd. Mrs Mainwaring was eventually given an award for services to rugby by the Welsh rugby writers' society. Only the Welsh could have done that – and I mean no disrespect to the likes of Bryn Thomas, the amazing, generous and prolific writer from the *Western Mail*. He has taken some criticism for some of his views over the years, but would anyone like to take over his job? Welshmen are so argumentative on rugby that whatever he writes, half the population vigorously applaud him and the other half demand that he be certified insane. Yet he seems to come up smiling with the game itself close to his heart.

Back to Aberavon. I know many clubs who, when faced with a day out down there, have found several of their players discovering urgent business appointments, muscle twinges and dead grandmothers needing burial. 'Damn. And I was really looking forward to playing down at Aberavon.' Gloucester players, on the other hand, tended to take what was coming and try to hand out something in return. One day, we were travelling by coach into the town and we passed a policeman, who looked very familiar, on point duty. It turned out to be Omri Jones, a legendary Aberavon flanker. Sure enough, Omri jumped on to the bus and took us to the ground for the match. His most arresting feature was a savage crewcut. Today, he would be called a skinhead – preferably by someone of Olympic class as a sprinter. He was neither born nor made, I often felt, but drawn by a cartoonist searching for the archetypal hard man. He stood with his socks rolled down at the end of the line-out, perusing a menu of scrum-halves for starters and anything else available as other courses. Phil Morgan and Dai Whitlock were the props, with Billy Mainwaring and Max Wiltshire the locks in the game in question.

During play, I broke through a line-out and pole-axed the Aberavon scrum-half – giving him a really heavy tackle. He was taking a bad ball for the pack and I hit him as he took it. As the scrum-half recovered his breath, Omri stood quietly by, gathering his thoughts. 'I'll see you about that, butty', he said, and walked off. I countered in the verbal battle with the promise that what the scrum-half had received was available for Omri too, and at no extra charge.

As we formed up for the next line-out, Billy Mainwaring looked across. 'Nice set of teeth you got there, butt', implying that some haphazard dental work was soon going to follow. The ball was thrown long, over the back of the line-out, and I followed it at my top speed. The momentum given by my weight helped the whole effect. The ball bounced high and I stretched up for it. As I did so, Omri hit me in the midriff with his shoulder in a ferocious and perfectly fair tackle. It felt like the tackle of all time, and I went down in a heap. As I slithered around on the floor, Omri trod on my hands with his studs before passing on his way. 'Or'right now, butty', he said. I always knew I'd had an afternoon out with Omri and his friends.

I certainly do not want to leave the wrong impression, though. I had the greatest respect for the likes of Omri, and I am not suggesting for a moment that Welshmen always started it, or that Welsh players are necessarily any dirtier than any other players. But my experiences in Wales were eye-opening. The tit-for-tat philosophy may seem dangerous or childish, but it is practised by many of the leading forwards all over the world. If not, they may not be leading forwards.

Any book on 'your hundred best hard men', would undoubtedly include Brian Thomas, the Neath lock who played for Wales over twenty times as I was beginning and developing my Gloucester career. In fact, the book would carry Thomas on the front cover and probably contain a foreword written by him: it might even be called 'Brian Thomas and 99 others of your best hard men'. Since Brian Thomas also attended Cambridge University he was that most dangerous species, an *intelligent* hard man. One day at the Gnoll, after Neath had taken the field, in their jerseys which were supposed to be black but which always seemed a washed-out grey, Thomas started dispensing a little bad cheer. Those were the days of double banking and Thomas was knocking us around in the line-out, taking liberties with the Gloucester players. He even hurt Peter Ford, the hard Gloucester flanker. 'You wait till you go down', said Ford, as he pointed his finger over the scrum.

Several Gloucester players were waiting their opportunity to dissuade Thomas, and mine came at a line-out. I popped my head through a gap in the Neath wall as Thomas caught the ball and was preparing to feed. I hit him straight on the side of the face, and felt it was a worthy effort. Thomas then did a very surprising thing – absolutely nothing. He never looked sideways, tottered, or gave any indication at all that he had felt a thing. He fed the ball to his scrum-half and got on with the game. He didn't even look sideways to see who had done it. He so upset some of the Gloucester players during the game that many of them refused to drink with him or converse with him in any way in the clubhouse afterwards. But as he brought round the jug of beer and approached me, I stuck out my pint pot, pleased to join him. I understood him and respected him, too. Perhaps I understood Welshmen better than the others.

I look back fondly, if ruefully, on my experiences in the company of Welshmen, both on the field and off it. Yet in many ways, the generation of superstars fielded by Wales thoughout the seventies made an even bigger impression on me. Never have so many world-class players existed at the same time in the whole world, let alone in one country. Barry John and Gareth Edwards, J.P.R. Williams and Mervyn Davies may well be the best players of all time in their positions. To back them up, they had a whole host of players who were merely excellent. That quartet probably managed two bad games at international level between them; when they were at their peak, you could have filled the rest of the team with schoolgirls and they still would have won their matches. I had some strong views on Edwards and Williams especially.

For example, one of the reasons I rated Gareth Edwards so highly was not for his great tries, or kicking ability, or even for his dominant personality. I respected him for his dogged approach when the chips were down. He was a match-winner, and a real artist when things were going well. He was virtually unstoppable, playing havoc with any side which showed the slightest weakness in trying to keep him quiet. Yet he was also brilliant when Wales were struggling for rhythm, or when the Lions were under pressure. In other words, his performances were superb on the days when it was hard to be good. Edwards would be cornered, but would come out breathing fire like a wounded dragon. When he was knee-deep in mud and his pack were winning bad ball; or when the Irish pack were storming all over the field in Dublin and knocking him about; or when New Zealanders or South Africans were pincering in on him because they knew he was a danger and a springboard for the team, he would still be effective. He could stand on one leg and still get his kick away safely to touch. He would scramble away his long pass to Barry John or Phil Bennett, tackle as well as take what was coming to him, then spring back up with a combination of his ability as a gymnast and sheer guts. He always fought to keep his team's head above water and, so many times, would be there when the pressure was eventually turned off to deliver the mortal thrust.

In South Africa in 1974, he fitted in superbly with the tight sort of game which Syd Millar wanted the Lions to play. His kicking destroyed many of the home packs, even in the tests. His strength held the opposition at bay and he took all the heat away from his partner, Phil Bennett, who was a skilful but slight man who could have his effectiveness diminished by too much pressure being exerted on him. Gareth rarely allowed anyone to lay a hand on Phil Bennett. At that time, Gareth was so far ahead of any other player currently in action anywhere in the world that it was laughable.

As I have mentioned before, it was Gareth alone who beat England in my last international. His brilliance under pressure broke English hearts. When I looked at him, with the mud plastering his jersey and with the glint of battle in his eyes, I saw, not the brilliant player and my hero, but one bloody nuisance. He would send the ball soaring behind me, and I would have to turn and trundle back again. He was a unique player. That was his fiftieth cap and one of his last; he succeeded in almost everything he did in rugby, and it is hardly a surprise to me to see him prospering in the business world now.

JPR somehow had the more glamorous role. He would come steaming up into play, either bursting into the line or taking the high ball, his long hair flying around to add to the dashing and stirring sight. He dominates my memories of England-Wales matches more than anyone else. He always did well against England – always scored the vital try, always had his picture in the paper diving over the line with an expression of double delight on his face as he bit the dust to make a clinching score. Sometimes, he decided to repeat the dose in the same game.

England played to JPR far too much over the years, putting up those hopeful high balls which it was ordained, as if in the Bible, that he would not drop. When he caught them, he would come running back upfield, too – kicking to touch or marking the ball was mundane, unheroic, inglorious. I did think that things ran his way in the England matches which he played, but there is something significant in the fact that, when he missed the England match in 1974, England won. It was not that his replacement, Roger Blyth, threw the game away, because I rated Blyth a very good player: it was just that the scourge of England wasn't around. As did Gareth, Williams took what was coming to him. He caught the ball, was submerged under wave upon wave of All Blacks, Springboks, Scots, Irish, French, English – and he came up immediately.

The controversies which followed the publication of his life story, and the decline which his play suffered in the later stages of his career until he was merely an excellent full-back, should not dim the memory of the most remarkable full-back ever. My own memories of that annual dive across the line at Twickenham and Cardiff, and the accompanying smile of delight, I shall take with me to that great and well-filled stadium in the sky where no one ever loses.

Just before I get carried away and become accused of favouring the dreaded Welsh too much, I should say that on the field I disliked them as much as I disliked any opposition. But I am very glad that I saw beyond the rivalry and the bluster, and met their supporters and their superstars off the field. Their contribution to all aspects of rugby is indispensable and may even be unequalled. They are undoubtedly a complex race, but I am grateful that I managed, through years of contact, to reach past the veneer of arrogance and aggression to have the ultimately rewarding experience of finding the true Welshman.

14

PROPS AND PUNCHERS Part 1

FRONT row play is in a world of its own; a place for experience and sheer, iron strength; at the top level, it is vitally important. In many ways, propping can only be learned in the heat of the scrum: there are so many little tricks of binding, foot placement and sheer villainy. Like coal mining, it is so hard it gives rise to a certain wry humour, largely because there is so little to laugh about. A side on top in the scrummage through the superiority of its props gains a tremendous psychological boost as well as a practical one. It is satisfying to see the opposition struggling from the scrum where all the action starts, and, also, the side going forward finds it easier to keep up the momentum in the resulting play. The side being put under pressure in the scrum are back on their heels – the forwards have to run backwards to rejoin the game when they get up.

Quite naturally, international prop forwards are a different breed; they are even supposed to have their own trade union. Over the years I set myself on some collision courses, because while I was considered an aggressive prop there were plenty of others who fancied they were every bit as effective. This made for some bone-crunching confrontations, some nasty moments, and some genuinely funny situations. I also came to grips, literally, with some of the biggest, hardest and most single-minded men in any sport. Props are often the characters most loved by the supporters, and the most disliked by opposing supporters. I should like to tell some stories now of my experiences in that dark world. I won't pick my world props, or put them all in order, but every one I met made a strong impression on me in some way or another. Those impressions were sometimes lasting – and often required stitches! I needed all my 'never stay down' philosophy to keep heading in the teeth of some particular gales.

I would need to be one of the world's leading psychoanalysts to do full justice to Keith Murdoch, a forbidding giant who was on New Zealand's international scene in the early seventies. Almost everyone in rugby has his own favourite Murdoch story – always told when the man himself was at least twelve miles out of earshot, a distance just about safe. In bare statistics, he played three tests for New Zealand and toured South Africa in 1970 and Britain in 1972-73. He was a strong scrummager and a lively man in the loose, a six-footer who hammered the scales at seventeen stone. He hated the press, even to the extent of manhandling some of those who begged to intrude on his private world; he was a rather unstable performer once a few drinks had passed his lips. On the field, he was a villain, and a villain's villain, rather like me. When you went out and did an eighty-minute stint against Keith Murdoch in the scrums you were always left with the fairly strong impression that you had been in a match.

Murdoch didn't even have to leave his house to cause a fuss. Early in his international career, he divided New Zealand by dropping out of three confrontations with the 1971 Lions with various injuries; he never faced the Lions in the end and they doubted he even existed. Not even I could rival the controversy, argument and conflict of Keith Murdoch's career. When he was sent home from the seventh All Blacks tour, he disappeared in Australia, never to be seen again in rugby. He left behind a compendium of myths and legends rivalled only by Robin Hood.

On the 1972-73 tour, the All Blacks' first outing was at Kingsholm against Western Counties – one of those mishmash selections which have been fielded over the years against touring sides and which usually bear no relation to the strength of rugby in the area. The visitors were obviously out for an impressive early showing, and they achieved it against a side that did have John Pullin, John Watkins, Dave Watt, Peter Butler and some other sound players. It also contained John Gabitass at fly-half, a Bristol player who was talented but whose talents lay elsewhere than in tackling. The All Black back row came charging off lines-out and round the back of the scrums; they brushed Gabitass aside, committed a good deal of the remaining defence, and then spread the ball wide for two superb wings, Grant Batty and Bryan Williams. Their technique was effective, and showed some of what the side could achieve at its best. They won 39-12 despite that rare occurrence, a Burton try.

Robin Cowling packed down against Keith Murdoch that day, with Jeff Matheson, a quieter man from Otago, against me. John Pullin and All Black hooker Ron Urlich kept the various warring factions apart. Given the similar approach of Murdoch and of Burton, it was inevitable, I suppose, that we should clash.

The first outbreak of trouble centred round John Bayliss. He was a centre who, although he never played for England or ever looked likely to, was respected all around thc rugby circuit. He was a hard man and a tremendous tackler. To cover for the frailty of Gabitass at fly-half, Bayliss stepped inside time and again to tackle the All Blacks' big men. Hamish MacDonald, the lock, was driving upfield when he ran into a Bayliss special – a hard and fair tackle which left both men on the floor. The ball went loose and, in fact, stopped inches from Bayliss's head. Murdoch arrived on the scene and, instead of driving over the ball in the classic tradition of All Black rucking, he took a wild fly-hack at it. He booted the ball forward, and therefore straight into Bayliss's head. The crowd hooted and bayed. Murdoch could have claimed that he was going for the ball, but it was a reckless and dangerous act – and there was absolutely no way that my playing philosophy would allow it to go unpunished. I let a few choice rights and lefts go. Murdoch immediately retaliated. Eventually, Ian Kirkpatrick came over to break up the protagonists and a crowd of other active participants.

From the next line-out on, Murdoch seemed even more determined to live up to his reputation. We were taking a beating as far as the scoreboard was concerned, but there was no way I was going to accept Murdoch's efforts so I threw another unsubtle punch at him at the beginning of a movement which swept away downfield. The All Blacks attacked down the left, and I thundered across to cover at my fairly limited top pace. In fact, Bryan Williams scored, and I slowed down to walk behind the posts for the conversion. 'Hey, matey', growled an antipodean accent behind me. I turned, straight into another Murdoch punch, delivered way after the try had been scored. I didn't think that was particularly disgusting since it was the law of the jungle – frowned upon in public, but somehow condoned by those fully conversant with the jungle statute book. The loony in both of us was coming to the surface in a desperate battle not to lose face. It was as if the whole match was irrelevant. As I formed up for the kick-off after the conversion, Murdoch pointed to me and then to himself, suggesting that we should resume our dispute. There was no way on earth, particularly at Kingsholm, that I was going to disappoint him. The ball was caught by Hamish MacDonald, who was quickly surrounded by those players with their minds on peripheral matters like getting on with the game. We made a concession to sanity of some sort by moving nearer the resulting maul, but then we swapped punches again. It seemed the right thing to do at the time, although looking back our behaviour was on the ludicrous side of amusing and certainly no example to the watching youngsters.

Paddy D'Arcy, the referee, came over to restore order and thereafter Murdoch never came within range. The All Blacks cruised to victory. They were hard players, like all New Zealand sides, but they were generally honourable and dedicated too. We were thrashed, and it was a shame that the side rarely reached such heights again on the tour. The party became sidetracked, unsuccessful and, largely, unpopular.

My friend Keith Murdoch ambled off to have his shower and prepare for something which, I was to find, he detested even more than props landing their clenched fists about his person. He hated any and all of the social events of a tour – the dinners, the cocktail parties, the small talk, the receptions. The composer of the table plan for the dinner which followed the Western Counties match no doubt felt that after a jolly hard game of rugger, everyone would be the best of pals and would like to socialise with their opposite number. It was with some foreboding that I arrived at the New County hotel to find Murdoch already seated, and an unattended place beside him: sure enough, the little card on the vacant place said M. A. Burton. I walked up and held my hand out towards Murdoch. Two elbows stayed firmly resting on the table. 'How're you going', he said.

On that day in October 1972 my touring career had not really started but I knew that, as hosts, it was our duty to look after the visitors as visitors are looked after all over the rugby world. I was anxious to see the All Blacks have a good time and leave with happy memories of Gloucester, so I pressed on with my attempts to communicate. I understood from some short, sharp and recurring words that Keith wasn't too taken with the round of formal occasions and their roast beef and two veg – nor was he a fan of wearing uniform, nor of a whole host of other things. Then Terry Evans appeared.

Terry Evans? Well, all the good people of Newbridge and a good few others round Wales know Terry Evans. He was Newbridge's scrum-half for many years, a lively, talkative, ginger-haired chap who infuriated the opposition by a mixture of aggression and incessant chatter. He is a character. He appeared at the hotel, and stuck his head through a serving hatch. 'Mike', he shouted above the din of the arguments and general chatter, the clinking of glasses and cutlery. 'Gerrus one of them silver fern badges, will yew?' Murdoch reached into his pocket and pulled out a bagful of the distinctive All Black badges. There must have been at least a hundred. 'Here', he said. 'Save me giving them around all . . . day,' Terry Evans clutched his trophies in his sweaty palm and his head disappeared through the secret trapdoor from which it had sprung. Murdoch had discharged all his obligations in one fell swoop.

The dinner wore on, with speeches on the match, obviously written three weeks before, and a few social niceties from the visitors. As Sid Going was receiving a presentation, Murdoch emptied his wine glass. 'Any more of this piss?' he boomed. Floor speakers have made an entertaining contribution to rugby dinners over the years, but 'any more of this piss' has never been handed down as one of the more memorable lines of witty repartee. But, again, I was anxious to please, and I consulted Ken Cottle, a local bank manager who was county treasurer. I explained that the New Zealanders wanted some more wine. Ken hummed and hawed, and did his sums to the nearest farthing as any rugby committee man worth his salt would do. He may even have completed a quiet mental recall of the laws relating to amateurism before he graciously gave dispensation for a largish bottle of red wine to be made available. Murdoch picked it up, drank almost half the bottle straight down, and then handed it back to me. 'Get the piss down you', he said. I took a swig, Murdoch finished it, and I suddenly realised that this was the nearest I or anyone would get to having a vaguely amicable drink with the man. He said thanks and went.

That was Keith Murdoch in my experience. In fact, many people tell me that their relationships with the big man from Otago were somewhat shorter. John Reason of the *Sunday Telegraph* once wrote that the first two words Murdoch addressed to him on being introduced as a pressman were to the point, and left him in no doubt that he was to go.

I should emphasise that I didn't object in any way to Murdoch's behaviour on the field or off it – even though he was rather extreme. I respected him as a player, though I was unwilling for him to dominate either my team or me. I understood the high rating which his team-mates put on him. It came as no surprise, then, when I heard that Murdoch had played a valuable part in the All Blacks' test win over Wales in 1972, or that he had played an outstanding part in a brawling affair at the after-match dinner at Cardiff's Angel Hotel. This effort led to injury to a very large security man and the banishment of Murdoch from the tour. His blazer was stripped of its New Zealand badge, in the same way that people disgraced in the services have their stripes torn off with a flourish. The Angel Hotel incident, some informed sources tell me, was one of those rare tales which was actually more lurid than the legend. Murdoch really ran wild.

The New Zealander's reaction on being 'deported' was to leave the aeroplane on a refuelling stop in Australia on his way home, and to disappear there for several years. Rugby's hard man became its Lord Lucan. Just before we parted at Kingsholm, after a match which seemed to portend so well for the Seventh All Blacks, I said to Murdoch: 'See you in the test.' I was throwing down the gauntlet for the England-All Blacks game later in the tour. Neither of us kept the appointment: I was on my back with a broken leg, but Murdoch just disappeared. The tour management must have realised that they were taking rather a risk bringing him in the first place, and notwithstanding his class as a prop they paid for it with one of the gloomiest chapters in All Black history.

* * * *

French forwards are every bit as hard as New Zealanders, and not even Keith Murdoch could put some of the French forwards I faced in my time in the shade – men like Alain Estève, Michel Palmié, Alain Paco, even Jean-Claude Skréla and Jean-Pierre Rives were hard men. I speak with authority because I played four times against France for England and every time it was in Paris. As I have explained, good old Burton was often dusted off and given a run out against the French, but always in Paris. Sometimes, it was like the Christians being thrown to the Lions in front of a merciless and bloodthirsty crowd: four times I went there and England never won. I sometimes felt I was going to die!

Jean Iraçabal was the first loose head I encountered. He won twenty-eight caps between 1968-74. Most props have terrific strength, but Iraçabal was one of those who had absolute, consuming, iron strength. We met in Paris in 1972 and 1974. In the scrums, I had to hang on like grim death itself to hold the Frenchman, both to stop his technique and strength disrupting our own scrummage and to put any pressure I could muster on theirs.

Iraçabal's successor was Gerard Cholley. Cholley was discovered in 1975 when France made an unsuccessful tour to South Africa, and played twenty-three times up till 1979. In fact, although the French lost the test series, within a year they were hailing the tour as a triumph – because it helped to develop the greatest pack in French history. That pack won France a Grand Slam in 1977 and they came close to two others. Rives, Skréla and Bastiat were in the back row, Imbernon and Palmié at lock, Paparemborde at tight-head, Paco hooking – and then there was Cholley. He was a former heavyweight boxer and, like Iraçabal, was a strong man's strong man. Quite simply, he was the strongest player I ever played against. We met in Paris in 1976 and 1978 and also in a special match between France and a World XV in 1978.

Cholley was a giant of a man. In fact it was his size which eventually provided a chink in his armour for me. He was just too tall for a loose head prop, which made it difficult for all his strength to be applied if he could be forced to scrummage low. I would always try to take him down when I played against him, hoping to make things difficult for his hooker, and sometimes I succeeded. But Cholley would come storming back at me – he would keep on fighting and hanging on, he would dish it out and take it. He would still be dishing it out as the final whistle went.

The first time I met Iraçabal in Paris, France beat England 37-12 and they were brilliant. The first time I met Cholley, France beat England 30-9. Even in the France v World XV match in 1978, Cholley was up to his tricks. It was meant to be a friendly celebration match, and in the days before the game the two sides got to know each other well. Andy Ripley and I were the two

English representatives, and we were determined to show England rugby in a good light both on and off the field. We met the French players at the Folies Bergères and the Lido and even Cholley was smiling away, doing his bit for the *entente cordiale*. When we formed up for the first scrum, I decided that it was no time to get into an argument. Presidents from all the unions, plus the eyes of the world, were looking on, expecting an amiable and enjoyable match.

Cholley hit me hard in that first scrum, and as my senses were returning I remember trying desperately to find reasons why I bothered to play rugby anyway. Battle had commenced!

Like Murdoch and Iraçabal, and like Burton, Cholley's fuse was dangerously short. In fact, the French forwards of the late 1970s were a fairly hard lot altogether. Alain Estève, the giant Béziers lock, had a career of trouble on the field; Michel Palmié was banned from international rugby; Jean-François Imbernon, a member of France's Grand Slam pack of 1981, was nicknamed 'the Godfather' by a British journalist, and it wasn't because he turned up at somebody's christening either. Cholley's *tour de force* came when he laid out several Scottish forwards in a match at the Parc des Princes in 1977: how he remained on the field till the end of the match will remain one of the great mysteries of twentieth century refereeing. Meirion Joseph failed to take action as Cholley went through the Scottish pack like a bus conductor proceeding up the aisle taking fares. The whole approach of the French forwards of the time and the success they enjoyed says something about the qualities that national teams need in the jungle of modern rugby.

Back to Monsieur Cholley. On one of my outings in France I was propping John Pullin and we had had just about enough of his antics. He was knocking people about, and during a break in play, John and I had a discussion which did not include either the state of the French franc or the Common Market. As we formed up for the next scrum, I bent my head with every intention of dissuading Cholley with a butt. He had the same idea, and our heads cracked together at speed. Carwyn James had referred in New Zealand in 1971 to the motto 'Get your retaliation in first'. Cholley and I were getting our retaliation in at the same time. I felt dizzy for hours. Yet, as with Murdoch, I respected Cholley, both his strength and his attitude. He wasn't technically brilliant, nor was he capable of anything stunning in the loose – but I wouldn't have taken him to tea with my grandma. He was utterly formidable.

After the game, Cholley would appear at the dinner with a Gallic grin. He'd throw you a bottle of wine and expect you to drink it straight down like he did. If two people who battled through heaven and hell as we had done could do that after a match, then the rest of rugby may not have too much to worry about.

When Cholley left the scene France were left with not so much a hole as an enormous pit, into which they threw an assortment of inadequate, lumbering giants as the 1980s began. Eventually they found Pierre Dospital to fill the loose head spot in their 1981 Grand Slam team. Dospital is one of those magnificently aptly-named people, only a letter away from hospital. He reminded me that Argentina once had a lively soccer full-back who chopped everything down above roots level – his name was Killer!

During and after the reign of Cholley, and away on the tight head side of the French scrum, was the third prop I would like to discuss. Since we were both tight heads, Robert Paparemborde and I never met in the scrum: so I base my comments on the opinions of others, and on what I saw with my own practised eyes after I retired. He was discovered around the same time as Cholley and is now probably rated the best French prop ever – and that takes in some players. He is a world-class tight head and a forbidding scrummager, yet he is also a footballer. He has scored tries all over the world, and set up numerous others with his charges in the loose. Despite this grievous transgression of all the front row union stands for, I still think Robert Paparemborde is something of a phenomenon. As I write, he is still a pillar of French rugby and a player-selector as well.

In the sense that I played four times in Paris and lived to tell the tale, I am a phenomenon too! When leaving the country after a typical and thunderously hard weekend of rugby, I used to feel that a small boat from Dunkirk would be the most apt way to travel home.

The chapter title is an appropriate one for my next guest. Steve Finnane, the Australian prop whom British players came up against several times, did a good deal of propping but a hell of a lot of punching too. The quality of his propping was low for an international player, for he rarely caused any of his opponents much bother in the scrum. The quality and quantity of his punching, however, has rarely been equalled: when Steve Finnane hit you, you stayed hit. He was a phantom puncher, in that he would hit people from behind and then blend in with the scenery when the concussed victim staggered to his feet, trying to find out who had delivered the blow. I had very little respect for much of Steve Finnane's efforts on the field on either side of the laws. My critics can say that those who live by the sword can expect the old Wilkinson straight through the heart themselves; but even in the jungle there are laws.

Returning to Finnane's technical skills, he was usually struggling. Tight heads like Ray McLoughlin, Robert Paparemborde, or Fran Cotton would have had him for breakfast and still had room for their kippers. It was probably the ascendancy which Graham Price had over him in the infamous tests against Wales in 1978 which caused the Australian to boil over and break Price's jaw with a blow from behind; the rugby equivalent of shooting the sheriff in the back as he walks away into the sunset. Finnane was workmanlike, but not formidable, and the smokescreen thrown up by his misdeeds obscured his lack of class.

English rugby's first experience of him was in 1975, when a ragbag of hopefuls and beyond-recalls set out for Australia for a short tour, which included two tests. The tour was disastrous for England because we lost both tests and because precious few players came through as likely internationals of the future: I have discussed the wider implications elsewhere. Too many players who were internationals of the present had been left at home. It was also disastrous for me personally, because I became the first Englishman in the history of thuggery to be sent off playing for England. Steve Finnane had a field day.

He first announced himself in the second match of the tour, which was against Sydney. We had already beaten Western Australia 64-3 but in the next match we came diving down to earth by losing 14-10 in a match that showed many of the follies of bringing boys to do the job of men. Finnane made his mark, and his version, as later stated in a book which he produced, was that he had sorted out three Englishmen. Well, in fact he did put three of us down. They were Steve Callum, a flanker almost as unknown after the tour as he was before it and he was not yet twenty. Then there was Bill Beaumont, though not the Battling Bill of 1981, the respected and feared captain of England – the 1975 version was relatively mild, feeling his way in international rugby. And there was me. Callum stopped one in the eye and off he went, but instead of wearing his shiner like a badge of pride he spent all night moping. Beaumont also left the field and neither played in the next tour match.

A couple of minutes after Finnane had attacked Beaumont I suddenly found myself on the ground. The Australian didn't use the 'normal' method, where the first punch was a warning and an attempt to win psychological advantage for the rest of the match; he really tried to put you away the first time. Digger's voice came wafting back along with the remainder of my senses. I sprang up and glared round the field, almost grabbing hold of Peter Kingston, the Gloucester and England scrum-half, to demand who had hit me. I was way over boiling-point and I wanted to sort matters out with this youngster who took it upon himself to put English players off the field. To my disappointment I never caught up with him during the match. Sydney won, because England's tactics were poor and also because Ken Wright, their young fly-half, cut through brilliantly for the winning score. Yet that match set the tone for the rest of the tour in that it was a rough battle, not because it contained some gems of rugby brilliance.

John Reason, for example, wrote in *The Daily Telegraph*: 'It was a distinctly physical game. The referee lost control. One of the Sydney props threw so much boot and knuckle that Bill Beaumont had to go off with concussion and Steve Callum also had an eye closed with a punch. Even Mike Burton was floored.' I think that last remark is a compliment! David Frost wrote: 'The spirit in the game was poor . . . and both Beaumont and Callum were injured by punches from Finnane.' Sydney's prop may have been a phantom puncher for those on the field, but he was easily spotted by those watching from the safety of the stands.

I was pleased to see that Finnane was actually to play against us in the next match – for the full New South Wales side, which contained the nucleus of the side which had just beaten us. It was obviously a big game in terms of the whole tour; it was also to be instructive to Finnane on his chances of making more impressions on various eyes and noses. People in the crowd were waiting for him to make his move but he kept himself in check. I shall content myself by explaining that I and one or two of the other England forwards who knew what had happened in the Sydney game managed to dissuade him.

The tour continued with an embarrassing defeat by a New South Wales Country XV. Steve Finnane's bristling moustache and flourishing fists were then in evidence in the first test, which I describe elsewhere. Suffice it to say here that, although he did not stand out as much as an individual assassin as he had done in the Sydney game, it was not for want of trying. It was just that almost everyone else in the Australian pack wanted to emulate him. It is difficult for a giraffe to stand out if he is in a herd of giraffes.

The amazing thing about the man was that he was educated and intelligent. He was a barrister of all things, and I often used to contemplate whether the Australian legal system allows a lawyer to defend himself in their higher courts. Despite the fact that he wasn't in the highest class as a prop, he won more column inches than all the McLauchlans, Cottons, Carmichaels and Prices put together, and rarely seemed to show much in the way of public remorse for his actions. At least I can see *some* of the errors of my ways, looking back!

Among several nasty incidents in which Finnane was involved as his career developed was the one which deprived Wales of their corner-stone, Graham Price, in their tour of 1978. One minute Price was dominating Australia in the scrum, the next he was being led from the field, with blood pouring from his mouth. Gerry Lewis, the Welsh trainer, led him off and one graphic picture of them shows Price holding his jaw, head bowed, and Lewis looking up at the stands bewildered, as if to say: 'What in hell has all this got to do with playing an amateur sport for fun?'

Of course, rugby people tend to forgive and forget. Less than a year after Steve Finnane won several technical knock-outs on the Australian fields, he was in England with the 1975-76 Wallabies. He was still basically the same man, though he kept out of the spotlight and out of too many dubious incidents. He did punch England lock Bob Wilkinson early in the test against England, confiding afterwards that he had reasoned that Wilkinson was a weak area of the England team to attack while Burton, Cotton and others were not to be trifled with. I respected most Australian sportsmen. They were aggressive but, like even Gerard Cholley, were likeable after the event. It was rather difficult, though, to understand or to like Steve Finnane, the phantom puncher of Sydney.

15

PROPS AND PUNCHERS Part 2

MY first chapter on the famous names of the front row began with what is my attempt to discuss the whole philosophy of propping and the fact that people in their right minds need not apply. Just before I move on to examine some of the other exponents of the tight head and right hook whom I met, I would like to discuss propping in more practical terms and reveal just what was happening in those thousands of scrums in which I took part. Very few people have any inkling of what is really happening after the two front rows have come thumping together, with the resulting swaying and bucking. In fact, the only people who can speak with real authority are the players involved. On countless occasions I have heard or read explanations of what has happened in the scrums in a particular match, what I was supposed to have done to their prop and what he was supposed to have done to me, and it seems as if a completely different match has been watched.

I was mainly noted as a scrummager, and I revelled in the battles both physical and psychological. What follows describes the realities of the scrums when our heads locked and the scrum-halves prepared to feed in the ball. It is also, I hope, an insight into front row play as a whole. If you didn't once see me in open play in any match, at least I may be able to convince you that I was up to something in my own little world.

The first of my tenets of front row play was always to keep the other front row guessing, which required a full repertoire of moves and tricks, some of which were allowed and some which were not. I always had to keep one step ahead of the other prop and switch the point of attack if he had developed counters to my last move. As tight head, I was packed down against the opposite loose head on the right of my hooker. On our own put-in, I had to stand as comfortably as possible and take the scrum to a good height so that my hooker would be comfortable too. That was basically defensive, because each team expects to win the ball on its own put-in and had to withstand the pressure from the opposition. I came into my own when it was the opposition's put-in, and we wanted to attack it.

For a couple of scrums, often I would attempt nothing at all. I would pack down with a straight back, standing still and square to my hooker. I would attempt none of my ploys. I might just exert a little pressure on the neck of the loose head, but that was all. He might be packing fairly high and be comfortable, but I would allow that. Then, after a few scrums of inactivity, I would throw out my foot and strike for the ball myself as it came in, just when the opposition were becoming confident and making a mental note that Burton wasn't too much of a handful after all. Of course, on the right of the scrum and nearer the opposition put-in, I was far nearer the ball than the opposition hooker. Often, I was able to hook the ball back through my own scrummage before the ball had got anywhere near their hooker. I'd be striking the instant it left the hands of their scrum-half.

The advantages of winning the ball against the head are numerous. Firstly, it is a blow to the pride of the opposition front row. (After all, there are numerous funny stories told about front rows coming off the field proclaiming victory by 2-0 or 3-1 or whatever; they mean that they won the scrums and omit to mention that their side actually lost the match 66-3!) There is also the obvious advantage that you have provided possession for your side, and your backs may even be given a yard start on the opposing back row, who are perhaps still searching in vain for the ball coming out on their own side as expected. Perhaps most important, it may unsettle the hooker and his props. They don't want to lose any more and may be tempted to press too hard, to infringe.

For example, if I had some success with my strike for the ball, the opposition hooker would often start flapping away with his leg like a Bluebell girl. He would be determined to get his strike in first, and be all too aware that I was having first bite of the cherry – and probably giving him some verbal opinions on how slow he had become. He would strike faster and faster and often be penalised for foot-up. All he had to do to counter me, in fact, was to get his loose head to take the scrum low. If the tight head is forced to scrummage low then his feet have to be placed further back out of the way of the ball as it comes down the tunnel. Once the scrum was low and the tight head's flailing feet were safely back down the scrum, a nice, slow put-in by the scrum-half would enable the hooker to make a clean strike. Yet my snap hooking was often fruitful; teams panicked, failed to use the counter, or were just not good enough to take the scrum down to a level at which I and my foot could not operate.

Mind you, if they did counter me, I had a counter-counter. With my feet right back, I was able to take the loose head even lower, just below a comfortable height for him. He should have been standing firm, steady and comfortable to set up his hooker, but by taking the scrum that little bit lower he would be under pressure and his hooker would be in a worse position as a consequence. As with all my moves in the scrum, I made them in the last few split-seconds before the ball came in. After all, there is no point in charging into the opposition, bucking and fighting like a sumo wrestler when the ball is still in the back row of the stand.

With my man a little uncomfortable, my next move would come when the scrum-half's feet appeared by the tunnel and he prepared to put the ball in. I would then increase the pressure on the loose head to take him down even lower so that he would then be in a very poor position – ideally with a bent back. The hooker would be calling desperately for him to take the scrum back up, and trying to see underneath for the put-in. Then, I would wait for the put-in itself. It is very easy to tell when the ball is coming even if you are low: you can see the scrum-half's knees bend, and you know he is making that final little stoop before he flicks the ball in.

As the ball was coming in I would then increase the pressure to the absolute maximum. The hooker would find his position worsening by the millisecond, and be forced to scrabble blindly for the ball, or be unable to strike for it at all, or kick it straight through our scrum. Most hookers use the 'tap' to indicate to the scrum-half when the ball should be put in. They tap their left hand on the loose head prop and that is the signal for the scrum-half to feed. The hooker does not tap unless he is in a good position: so either my late move would come after he had tapped and it was too late, the damage to his position already done; or he would feel the increased pressure and delay his tap so long that the scrum-half was penalised. If the opposition decided to feed as soon as the scrums came together so that I didn't have time to put on the pressure, I would be ready for that too.

If a front row can continually cause such disruption, the implications are numerous. I have already spoken of the effect on morale and the practical drawbacks of being under pressure in the scrum. But there are other effects too. The scrum-half could quite easily become engrossed in the scrum battle, trying desperately to follow the progress of his hooker's attempts to counter, waiting for the 'tap' and taking in the front row's instructions for a quick ball, a slow ball, anything to put them one jump ahead again. The scrum-half's mind is taken off his own game, and, vitally, off his service to and understanding with his fly-half.

Naturally, not all these moves worked for me all the time. There were front rows around who knew the tricks, and the counters, and had a few ideas of their own. Sometimes, the disruption my front row and I caused was minor. But often we managed to agitate, to irritate, to pressurise and to win the ball. I found that the Springboks in 1972 were susceptible, so it was not only at club level that things came off. I would come out with part of my repertoire and gain great satisfaction if the opposition were fooled. There was always the last variation, too – the eight-man shove. Everyone, the front row and even the hooker, would pack down in a powerful shoving position. We would concede the strike but, as it was made, unleash such a combined drive that we would either cause slow and erratic ball for the other side or even push them right off it and win it ourselves.

Some props, the best and strongest, would attack the opposition scrum by going low with a straight back: Ray McLoughlin, Fran Cotton and Phil Blakeway used that method. All the opposition prop could do was attempt to twist them, and then they would play their ace. When the ball came in, and with the pressure coming on from the colleagues behind, they would raise the scrum six inches. That was the opposite of my move, of trying to disrupt by lowering – but lifting could be equally effective. The opposition would find their position changing at the vital moment. Very, very few props were good enough to do that, though.

Yet things are changing. Until now, a top tight head has needed to have a full range of abilities. He has had to be tremendously strong and experienced, good with his feet, and a poacher of the ball. Ability with a bunch of fives has been useful though not essential. But now the skills of front row play are waning, mainly because they are no longer needed. The eight-man shove is no longer the last resort, nor even a cunning variation nor a frequent ploy: it is the standard operation on the opposition put-in. The tight head is rarely called upon to strike, or take his man up, down or anywhere. He merely has to take his feet back and push like the devil. The day of the skilful small hooker is also over. Today's hookers are big men and wide men – scrummagers first and hooking technicians second. In many ways, an ideal international pack for the modern scrum would consist of eight well-trained gorillas, who all bound tight and pushed as a unit. It may be effective but the skills needed are almost nil.

The recent new laws are a further blow for the tight head. He has to bind on the back of the loose head and is unable to make those small adjustments to the height of the scrummage which cause dismay and disruption. On the other hand, the loose head can bind wherever he wishes, and can even rest his hand on his outside knee if he feels tired. With the hooker allowed to use that 'tap' signal, things are stacked against the attacking tight head even more.

All this is good news, of course, for those who dismiss props and hookers as lunatics who prevent the game flowing freely by their insistence on having their own little game within a game. People bemoan the fact that the skills of thatchers, blacksmiths, master carpenters and the like are no longer needed – so why not tight head props too?

The other great factor in the decline of front row skills (and I am talking about front row *skills* rather than front row *effectiveness*: I'm not saying some of the modern ploys are not effective) is rank bad refereeing. Like those people I spoke of earlier who pontificate on front row play from the tenth row of the stand, referees often haven't a clue what is going on in the front row. Some of them can just about work out when a hooker has struck for the ball too early or when the scrum-half has rolled the ball in crooked, but when it comes to the other laws affecting the scrum – binding, angle of packing, and so on – they are guessing. In one of the scrums at the start of every match, most referees will gravely tap hookers on the back and mumble something about binding. Then they will go away and everyone will go back to infringing their chosen law.

In my playing days, I would stand up and look at the referee with a serious expression, nodding and agreeing enthusiastically as he spoke. Then I would go down and make my move. John Pullin, far from binding over his loose head, had his hand in his loose head's shorts pockets for four seasons, which allowed him to creep to his right a lot nearer the tunnel entrance when going for a ball against the head. And to think I am castigating referees for not applying the laws properly! I must sound like a criminal dashing into a police station and complaining about the lawless state of the country.

Sadly, the rugby world is no longer full of clever tight heads. There are a few in Britain and France, but in New Zealand, Australia and South Africa combined, only Gary Knight, the All Black, has struck me as a player approaching world-class. Ah well. I'll sit by my fireside and remember how front row play used to be.

Having tried to explain what we are all up to in the scrum, I shall now return to some of the people who joined me in the depths of the front row. In the last chapter, I disposed of the likes of Murdoch, Finnane and Cholley and described how they tried to dispose of me. But they were not the only ones. The most famous unit in amateur sports is the Pontypool front row, who commanded the greatest respect from anyone who played against them – and they met some quality opposition in their time. They were superb, and they really worked as a unit. In attack or in defence, in trying to disrupt the opposition or merely to protect their own ball, they acted as one.

When Bobby Windsor wanted to strike, the tactic was that Graham Price, on his tight head, right side, would take the scrum low – lower than Windsor or Charlie Faulkner on the loose head. This meant that Windsor's right arm would be lower than his left, which had the effect of throwing his body and hooking foot nearer the mouth of the tunnel where the ball would be put in. He was then able to strike comfortably and easily with his right foot. Given that Pontypool, or Wales, were going to hook the ball with the technique and ability of Price and his cronies, the alternative which then presented itself to the opposition forwards was to try to drive the front row and their forward pack with an eight-man shove. Windsor was striking, which would leave seven pushing against the opposition's eight. Then Price would use his next counter. If his scrum was under pressure and giving ground, he would wrap the opposition loose head underneath him and skilfully, not dangerously, take the whole scrum to the floor. There has been a great hue and cry about this method of Price's, and it is not a technique which inexperienced schoolboys should emulate. But much of the fuss has arisen because a disintegrating scrum looks a lot worse than it is. Price was (and still is) merely confirming his superiority and referees their ignorance.

The trio were vastly popular with their own fans and vastly unpopular with everyone else's – and there is no better sign that you are doing well than if the other team's fans start barracking you. The Pontypool front row have become part of Welsh folklore, a legend in their own lifetime. Before that legend and the numerous stories combine to dull people's memories, let no one tell you that they were in the slightest over-rated: they were formidable.

Individually, they were quite different. Bobby Windsor was their spokesman and he fulfilled the duty in a rasping, grating East Walian accent. He is a great humorist, and frequently brought the 1974 Lions tour to a standstill with his escapades. Also on that tour, he reached his peak as a sound hooker, a hard scrummager and a fierce competitor in the loose. In many ways, his rise to the Lions test spot reflected what was happening to hookers throughout the world. The 1971 Lions test hooker was John Pullin, the technician, the honest toiler but the expert hooker. He had all the skills and knew all the tricks. Windsor was nowhere near as complete a technician but he got by comfortably enough; he was bigger than Pullin and harder, representing that new breed of international hooker of which I spoke earlier in the chapter.

Price is a quieter man, who goes about his business ruthlessly but with fewer people knowing about it. He is a master of propping and, in propping terms, unbeatable. Anyone who can come into the cauldron of international rugby in his early twenties, take on the whole fraternity of international hard men and put paid to them, is remarkable. Price did all that and ran eighty yards at the end of a game to score a try against France. If he was a fly-half, Price would be bigger than Barry John. As I write, he is still turning in his quiet and devastating displays. There are rumours that back trouble is finally overhauling him and, with the doubts being raised about the rest of the Welsh team at the moment, idiots are including Price on their list of the people who should go: which is hysteria.

Charlie Faulkner is even quieter and perhaps even more remarkable. He was still playing rugby when, in rugby terms, he was an old man. Not even Charlie seems to realise how old he is but by his standards I was barely out of my romper suit when I retired from rugby at thirty-two. I always found Charlie more interesting because he was my man – he was the loose head and the one I always grappled with when Gloucester had their pleasant day out at Pontypool or when England played Wales.

There were stories that Charlie and his mate Bobby would earn some extra money as part-time bouncers at the Stowaway club in Newport in their days with the Newport Saracens. Trouble at the club no doubt showed a sharp drop. Charlie was unique as a prop because he never tried to push me back. He would get into his position, the one which suited Windsor, and with his technique he could hold it against all comers. When the ball was coming in on our put-in, we would sometimes find our loose head held in check by Price while Charlie had walked round me at tight head. This would cause the scrum to slew and disintegrate, which it needed great concentration and strength to prevent. Charlie was vastly under-rated. He became a rather comic character, what with his age and the complete dismay if anyone gave him the ball to run with. He became 'good old Charlie', and even Pontypool fans began to forget that he was a Welsh prop. But I had the greatest respect for him. Sometimes, I had him nearly on the floor as I tried to disrupt the Pontypool unit's methods. I could even take him down in the next scrum too, but he would hold on and come back, and still be holding on and coming back at the end of the match.

One more Charlie story before I move on, otherwise I shall be accused of joining the Pontypool fan club. On the field, I disliked their front row as much as I disliked any of the players I met. I have mentioned before the last match I played in for England, when we lost 9-6 to Wales at Twickenham. Charlie and I had been having a real go all afternoon in the mud of Twickenham and honours were fairly even – though on the other side, Price was putting Barry Nelmes, the England loose head, under pressure. This was expected because Price had had a few victories in the past over Nelmes when Pontypool had played Nelmes' club, Cardiff.

I knew that on our ball, Charlie would put me under pressure, and he didn't disappoint me. He went about his business in grim and determined silence. One of my tricks when I was under attack was to pack down with my left arm round the hooker as normal but with my right arm on my chest. When we went down, I would move my arm up inside the left arm of the loose head, and thus gain the more powerful inside position. I brought off this little subtlety on five or six occasions in succession, which stopped Charlie putting me under the sort of pressure he would have liked. He had no immediate answer, but you could almost hear his mind working. Right at the very end of the game, with millions of people watching and with none of them suspecting or even caring what we were up to, Charlie worked it out. As we went down for a scrum, he clenched his fist, really banged it down hard and clutched my shirt, absolutely refusing to let my arm inside his. He had done it: there was Charlie with blood coming from somewhere, who hadn't said a word all day, but now he had outwitted me. Suddenly, the whistle blew and we had to break up. An injury had to be attended to before the ball could be put in. Charlie stood up in disgust. 'Awww. Bloody 'ell Mike, I 'ad yew then, din'I?' When Wales won a Grand Slam, the television producer tried to snatch a quick word with each of the side after the match. Fourteen players stood before the camera; Charlie, the quiet man, went for a beer.

Ian McLauchlan was a good deal noisier than Charlie and a good deal more ferocious. He was a punishing scrummager, although a small man by the standards of international forwards – hence his nickname, the Mighty Mouse. He had repelled all those who wanted to do ill to the Lions scrum on the 1971 Lions tour of New Zealand and the subsequent trip to South Africa in 1974. He was an abrasive player and a quite ruthless competitor. Like me, he was never prepared to accept punishment without returning it with considerable compound interest. My most famous collision with the Mouse came in 1976 at Murrayfield, and it was a fairly nasty incident. But, once again, I should emphasise my respect for him and his attitude: he was good company.

The English and Scottish teams in 1976 were presented to Her Majesty The Queen before the match. Somehow she managed to get in the way of the Mouse and I and interrupt our glowering contest to shake hands. In fact, she showed considerable distaste for my great outstretched hand covered in mud and vaseline. The English props were myself and Fran Cotton, while Scotland fielded McLauchlan and Sandy Carmichael – the 1974 Lions pool of props. I was mentally prepared for a real afternoon out: the Mouse was almost as sharp on the field with his fists as he was with his tongue.

The match began well for England, because Cotton quickly gained the upper hand over Sandy Carmichael and, with a combination of different moves and some luck, we took two balls against the head. Now that was hardly likely to cause a broad smile to crease the face of the Mouse. Soon afterwards, something happened which made the man even more displeased. He was under a high ball, waiting for it to drop: 'my ball' he barked in his gruff Scots accent. As he caught it, I arrived simultaneously and hit him with a flurry of elbows and arms. I took the definition of a fair tackle well beyond its limits, and the Mouse was down. But he was a proud man and a proud Scot – he got up without complaint and without saying a word, and trotted upfield. A few minutes later, there was a line-out right in front of Her Majesty's seat in the stand. It was so close to her that she could have decoded the line-out signals, and even thrown the ball long herself for a line-out peel, given a following wind.

I glanced at McLauchlan as he arrived at the line-out. Like the old Western movies, things were quiet. Too quiet. I then made the mistake of sticking my head through the line-out, which Scotland were winning, to watch the ball's progress. I took a punch right between the eyes and it was good enough to put me down. I didn't spend much of the immediate future trying to work out who had thrown it, either. I never did find out if McLauchlan was a Scottish Nationalist, but he certainly didn't show much respect for Her Majesty's feelings. I shouldn't think she liked the blood and the wind from his punch must have nearly blown her hat off.

I always reckoned I did well enough against McLauchlan but few could ever say they mastered the Mouse that roared. He took everything anyone could dish out on either side of the laws, and captained Scotland from the front. He had the ability and technique to burrow in under the big tight heads of the world and lift them clean out of the scrum, from where they could contemplate the mightiest mouse in history.

Technically, the best prop I ever met was Ray McLoughlin of Ireland, whose influence on the forward play of Ireland and the 1971 Lions was immense. He was one of the very few people who were world-class players on either side of the scrum. He was a serious and brilliant man – and, with respect, he was often wasted in Irish rugby when they wanted to bustle around the field with footrushes and consume everything in their path. Prophets, after all, are usually appreciated more outside their own country.

It may come as a surprise to many people, and certainly to Phil Blakeway, that I would place him, the square fruit salesman from Gloucester, on that very short list of props like McLoughlin who could switch from one side of the scrum to the other and still absorb all the stick going. McLoughlin and Cotton could do so because they proved it time and again; they were at various times amongst the best tight heads and the best loose heads. Blakeway began life as a loose head and impressed me. Later on he moved back to loose head from his more favoured tight head side occasionally, though often under protest. He even switched in the 1981 Wales-England match at Cardiff, when he moved to loose head to take on Graham Price after Fran Cotton left the field with a hamstring injury and Austin Sheppard, another Gloucestershire prop, came on to win his first cap. But Blakeway survived and I knew he would: Price never got on top of him. Over the last few seasons Phil has had very few peers as a scrummager on the tight head side, but he has the ability to switch and I will try convincing him of that one day. One summary of his play is that he is Burton without the punches, but I have yet to work out whether that is a compliment to Blakeway or to myself.

I have discussed my high opinion of Steve Mills elsewhere in the book. I would like, during this discussion of the noble and the nutters I met in the front row, to answer a question which I have been asked many times. Which of England's two great hookers of recent times, John Pullin or Peter Wheeler, was the best? Pullin, as I have said, was a superb striker, and if any publisher is looking for an author for the complete encyclopaedia of hooking and general front row play, then all they have to do is tear John Pullin away from his farm and they will have their man. He has no place in the chapter as a puncher because he was a fair man. He knew all the tricks, but he preferred to use those which were inside the laws. He would always try to answer skulduggery and illegality by winning an endless stream of ball, despite provocation from the likes of me.

During one Gloucester-Bristol game on their ground, played under floodlights, I decided on a surprise move to put Pullin off, since he knew all my other moves backwards. As we went down in the first scrum, I bit him. I didn't try to take a chunk out of his ear, it was just a little warning nip. Morton Howells, the old Aberavon hooker, used to give me a bit of a chewing now and again – never anything too serious, but then perhaps my ear was a little rare for Morton's liking. Or, perhaps he only did it when he had missed his lunch. Anyway, I gave Pullin a quick reminder that I was around. He bit me straight back. I decided to end that little line of attack immediately, because when I turned round in the scrum I saw the floodlights glinting on the most magnificent pair of gnashers ever.

I tried another basic ploy later in the game when we were camped on our own line and desperately needed a scrum ball. I slipped my hand off the Gloucester hooker and over Pullin's eyes. We won the scrum and a ruck followed. I ended up on the floor and, through a hole in the pile of bodies on top of me, I saw Pullin's face framed by the glow of the lights and there was fury on it. He was pulling at arms and legs to get to me and muttering something about people having to resort to those sort of tricks. Needless to say, he came out of the game with his usual honours. He was a difficult man to take ball from and, quite apart from my admiration for him as a man and a captain, I thought he was a world-class hooker.

I was involved in Peter Wheeler's first game for the Leicester club – he appeared for their seconds at Kingsholm and I turned out for Gloucester United. He wasn't the rugged, all-round player he is today but he did have the same blond mop of hair and chorister's face. I couldn't believe Leicester were serious about sending him out on to Kingsholm. Neither could I believe the high number of occasions the choirboy hooked the ball! I made a few sporadic attempts to rearrange some of those cherubic features, and it was a measure of the man that he was undaunted.

Wheeler, along with his coach Chalky White, has made Leicester a magnificent club; and he has been all round the world as a robust and durable hooker. Like any front row man worth his place, he has met fire with fire. And yet he is one of the new style hookers – a big man who can scrummage and play in the loose. A certain abrasiveness and willingness to take on all comers, that inner steel, was in both Pullin and Wheeler although it manifested itself more in the Leicester man. I would conclude by saying three things. England are fortunate that they have been able to call upon two such world-class hookers. John Pullin took on the world and held his own; while Peter Wheeler has done exactly the same. And he still looks like a bloody choirboy.

That leaves two props and punchers left of the many who crossed my path. Readers will have noticed that Fran Cotton played a large part in my career in many ways. He was the man I most wanted to best in South Africa in 1972; we waged a continual battle for the prop position in the England side; he was on hand to dispense comfort in the dressing room at Ballymore, to where I had just been sent in 1975 in the international; he had toured the world with me. We were usually trying for the same position because the selectors rarely moved him to loose head. Yet Cotton became my closest friend, and I value his friendship highly. He is basically a shy man although he does fulfil some speaking engagements. I was always very flattered if he came up to me in the dressing room after a match in which he had been playing and which I had been watching. 'What did you think of the do this afternoon?' he would say. He didn't want to know what I thought of the game; it was his way of asking me how he did in the scrum – how straight was his back, how were his feet, was the other prop uncomfortable. There was never any bitterness in our rivalry.

Fran comes from a socialist background, and from a rugby league background; rugby league scouts were forever snapping at his heels like excited hounds throughout his career. He has a warm relationship with his father, Dave Cotton, who was a fine hooker and could recall in minute detail games he had played a generation before. I visited the Cottons on several occasions and they never seemed to realise or care that I was their son's rival. Mr Cotton used to shake my hand warmly and the whole family made a fuss of me. Just before a visit which I made with John Watkins to the Cotton household, I was given a stern warning by Fran's friend, Steve Smith, about the generosity of Mrs Cotton's cooking. 'You'll never get it all down you', he said admiringly. We arrived at the house and were greeted as usual like a combination of the prodigal son and the man bringing the cheque from the pools company, and we sat down. Mrs Cotton was in the kitchen preparing our meal. 'She's having a big pot-banging session out there', Fran said. When Mrs Cotton came in with the plates, we couldn't believe it. They were piled up so much that the table groaned underneath them. It was as big a challenge as taking on Cholley on the Parc des Princes. To our satisfaction and Mrs Cotton's delight, we won. No wonder Fran weighed in at around seventeen stone. If there is one thing I envy him, it is not his caps, his ability, his versatility, it is his happy family background and his relationship with his father. Those are things I never had.

He has now retired after a fabulous career, an injury-troubled one but still a memorable period. No one deserved success more than Cotton and I was delighted that he was part of England's recent Grand Slam. Even the Welsh boys loved him and respected him. They realised the stick he had taken during his career and begrudged him none of the good days. I know, because they told me so.

There was a worrying moment on the 1980 South African tour when it seemed that he had suffered a heart attack. But it was no surprise when he returned to full health and it was found that his heart was as big and sound as everyone had suspected. Now, rather than cashing in on his name and taking advantage of the many lines of business which would benefit him because of his name, he has decided to retain his amateur status so that he can coach. He even trains with some of the old fanaticism. Of all the England players I came across, Fran Cotton cannot be overrated.

Finally, I come nearer home. My rambling through props and punchers has taken me to New Zealand, South Africa and Australia as well as all over France and Britain. Now I return to Gloucestershire. One of the players I most admired was little known outside the county but that was not because he was not a top-class prop. Jack Fouke was a bull of a man, rather on the lines of Jean Iraçabal, the famous Frenchman. I was lucky to meet Jack in my teens during Gloucester trial matches when, rather than taking liberties with his inexperienced opponent, he was kind enough to offer some advice and thoughts on technique as the game went on. I used much of what he taught me throughout my career and rarely met a stronger man or a better prop wherever I played.

That leaves the Greek. The scene is the Memorial Ground, Bristol, or Kingsholm, Gloucester, where a prop called Mike Fry regularly used to lock horns with me. He was a Bristol and Somerset player, I was a Gloucester and Gloucestershire player: he was a loose head, I was a tight head. We met often – and, often, it wasn't pretty. Fry was nicknamed the Greek because of his dark complexion and his flashing eyes, which used to stand out and stare right through you. He was small by modern front row standards but was a fiery, competitive and unbending man and we had some tremendous, unforgettable, battles. Neither of us ever took a backward step and our names became linked in local circles like Ovett and Coe, Frazier and Ali. The crowds used to relish our meetings. I was the international and the Lion, but against the Greek reputation meant nothing. He was the man who buried his head in my broken jaw and who dogged me throughout my career, or so it seemed. I rarely shook him off.

Yet after the game, we would seek each other out. Fry would come over with his pint pot and we would pass the time of day. There was never any crowing about the game of the day. When we meet now, he always sticks out that big mitt of his and greets me warmly. He never played international rugby but I respected him more than many props who did.

After all this talk of the front row, people may be tempted to advise me that if I had ever lifted my nose out of the scrum and looked around, I might have seen a better game going on around me than the one I was playing. But mother nature ordained that I should be a prop, and my approach ordained that I would be a controversial one. But I always enjoyed my rugby, even on the occasions when fear was creeping over me. I won respect, and respected most of the opposition in return.

16

COME THE REVOLUTION

INTERNATIONAL rugby matches now represent big business for so many people that it is amazing that such commercial activity could surround a supposedly amateur sport. Everyone makes money and some people make fortunes. The host unions make thousands (international tickets at Twickenham now cost £12 per match for the best seats); the ticket touts make money, the hot-dog sellers, the people who cobble together scruffy cardboard rosettes – they all cash in. The travel agents ferrying people to the game make a lucrative killing due to the legions of supporters who follow their teams; trains running to stations near the main stadia are full for perhaps the only time in the year; hotels put up their prices. (For instance, certain Cardiff hotels produce temporary and vastly inflated tariffs for the weekends which just happen to coincide with an international at the Arms Park.) Businessmen entertain their clients at the game and provide seats in the stand for them; committeemen bring along their wives for expenses-paid weekends. There are benefits all round – everyone, absolutely everyone, makes money. Except the players.

The small group of men engaged in the rather important activity of actually playing the match everyone has come to watch and often to profit from, those players will be savouring the honour of playing for their country – indeed, it may be the highlight of their lives. But they will probably have paid a price. To bring themselves to a peak of fitness and the team to a peak of organisation, they will have pounded roads and attended squad sessions all over the country. They will have been engaged in some sort of rugby activity on average at least six nights out of seven. There will have been personal training, club training, county training, perhaps divisional training, international training, and a barrage of other engagements involving speaking at dinners and opening fêtes, the organisers of which may spread unpleasant rumours if such invitations are refused. As I said, the players will probably think it all worthwhile, if they can wear a red rose or the three feathers or a shamrock or a silver fern on their jerseys: but the cost is high.

Almost any other leading sportsman would be well rewarded for the work load that rugby players who reach the top have to undertake. For the same amount of sweat expended at the top level, a boxer would probably be a millionaire, a golfer likewise. If a snooker or a darts player put in the same hours, and endured seeing his family only about twice a week for an extended period, even he would be attracting relatively large rewards.

Not only are rugby players themselves not rewarded, but they actually lose in many cases. For example, all that time preparing and participating in top rugby means time off work. Happily, there are many generous employers to whom big names are good for business and who reciprocate by allowing their employees time off with pay. But there are also employers too hard up or unenlightened – who may never have even heard of Bill Beaumont or Andy Irvine – who will grant only unpaid leave, or no leave at all. Instances of players being unable to make major tours on commercial grounds are occurring more frequently, and often international tours are devalued as a result.

The lot of the leading sportsman has improved beyond recognition in recent years. Cricketers and athletes, especially, can now buy houses every bit as big, with just as many bathrooms, as pop stars, golfers and lip-service socialists. Rugby players, as they scrape together their mortgages, can reflect that although their talents help to produce commercial gain for many people, none of that gain benefits their own bank accounts.

For the moment, that argument should come to a dead stop while I partly contradict myself. Anyone who really knows the rugby scene at the moment will be well aware that certain financial benefits *are* available unofficially, yet sometimes extensively. And never having been slow off the mark when opportunities present themselves, I admit with enthusiasm that some of these came my way.

Direct cash payments together with huge inducements of jobs and housing are available in France from the leading clubs. Indeed, rugby union can offer so many more lucrative deals for players than rugby league that the ludicrous situation exists where the professional game (rugby league) is very much less rewarding than the amateur game (union) – which is why league in France is such a distant second to union. In Wales, nothing so overt occurs although extremely generous 'expenses' are paid. For instance, the only way in which one player of my acquaintance in Wales could have actually spent the expenses he was given for travelling to the ground, four hundred yards from his house, was if he had flown there by way of the Far East. To be fair, what happens in Wales is that players are looked after in almost the way that they should be. They never have to buy boots and other kit, rarely have to fork out for beer – and the expenses *are* generous!

Unless you count a voucher from Gloucester towards a new pair of boots, which was just enough to put down a deposit on the laces, I never received that sort of help. For me, it was much more subtle. I first noticed a phenomenon of international European rugby when I was training at the Lensbury club, near Kingston, for my early internationals in the seventies. The players would be congregating around car boots and inside would be items of kit, including the latest and most expensive boots, bearing the brand names and trademarks of various sportswear firms. I remember seeing Derek Ibbotson, the former athlete, and another Olympic runner, John Cooper, dispensing boots to the England players. The idea, apparently, was that leading sportsmen should be seen to be wearing the boots of a particular company. Each firm has its own distinctive boot, with flashes or stripes signifying the maker, and for a big name of the rugby world to be seen wearing them by thousands at a ground – and, more to the point, by millions on television – was good business and good promotion for the company. Ibbotson and Cooper represented different firms, and others as well tried a bit of gentle persuasion so that their companies' boots would be worn.

After I made a point of parading past the open car boots a few times during one training weekend, it was accepted by a firm's representatives that even a new prop might be an aid to promotion if his big feet were enclosed in a particular brand. I gratefully accepted a pair of boots, and in return I had to promise to wear them for the forthcoming international. Andy Ripley had his lines slightly crossed, or perhaps with typical charm and generosity he found himself unable to say no, and therefore was given two different pairs of boots and made two promises. The ingenious compromise was for Andy to take the field for an England match with the boot of one firm on one foot and that of his joint benefactor on the other. No money ever changed hands on these occasions. Not yet.

Of course, as the competition built up, the pressure on the various representatives to get the England side appropriately shod increased; and so did the inducements. It was a natural evolutionary process. Adidas were especially generous, dispensing tracksuits, T-shirts and boots bearing their distinctive striped emblem. A large part of their market strategy to this day seems to be that top sportsmen should be seen wearing their gear, and many do. The stakes were becoming higher as the 1974 season approached, and I held a regular England place.

The firm's recognition of this fact led to what was for me a startling incident in a hotel in Versailles, where the England side were staying in preparation for a match against France in 1974. By that time, the whole French side and many of the England players wore Adidas boots – there was only the odd English straggler to win over. John Cooper of Adidas was a very nice man. He was moving around the hotel dispensing kit of all sorts, when he walked into a room where some of the players were watching French television – not understanding a word but at least killing the nervous hours as the match day approached. I had a well-worn yet comfortable pair of Adidas boots with me; Cooper came over, and, noticing that they had seen better days, picked them up and regarded them sadly. He even wet his finger and began wiping the mud off the three distinctive yellow stripes so that they would show up better on the television next day, and I reflected that here was a man who was twice the athlete I would ever be almost literally licking my boots in his company's cause. Cooper gave up the boots as a bad job and left the room. When he returned he was carrying a pair of Adidas Cap boots of lovely soft calf leather, and he held them out to me.

I was wary of taking the field for an international with a brand new pair of boots on: new boots usually take some wearing in, and players always wear them for at least a couple of training sessions first. 'Try them on', said Cooper. I duly left the room and went into a toilet where I sat down and pulled on the first boot. However, I could hardly force my foot into the toe, and I held the boot up to try to discover what was hindering its progress. In the toe of the boot was a wad of packing paper and in amongst the paper were five £10 notes. 'How do they fit?' John asked as I emerged from the toilet. 'Perfect', I replied, and put them in my kitbag.

In fact, the boots were so good that I had not a single blister – and they had that fifth stud on the sole which was so useful for scrummaging. In fact, the recent ruling forbidding the extra front stud is yet another of the rule changes which has undermined the position of the tight head prop, because grip is much more difficult to come by without it. The notion that by outlawing the stud the game is made safer is largely ridiculous, since there are still four others on the sole to do damage. Anyone contemplating deliberate damage will only have to move his foot forward two inches. I took the money and wore the boots, as so many others have done at international level since. Don't think that I was an isolated case or that other players didn't 'earn' more.

That weekend in Paris, after a satisfying 12-12 draw against Jean Iraçabal and France, I joined John Cooper and others for a pleasant evening in Paris. Next day, Cooper was among those tragically killed on his return to England, when a DC10 crashed after take off. Many rugby people were among those who died, including *News of the World* journalist Lloyd Lewis, and many supporters. When the England team arrived unaware at Heathrow on a later flight, anxious officials of the Rugby Union urged us to phone our families to let them know that the crashed flight did not contain the England party – although it could so easily have done, and the rugby world would have had its own Munich. As it was, the loss was numbing enough.

Those five tenners represented the beginning for me, because I gradually learned to hold out my hand and, along with others in the international scene in Britain and France, I was rewarded for wearing Adidas kit. Other firms may have rewarded other individuals, but I was 'with' Adidas. For several seasons, I was paid per match to wear their boots, with much of the 'negotiating' being done by Robbie Brightwell, another former Olympic athlete. Robbie invited myself and two other England forwards to lunch at Poynton, near Manchester, which is the Adidas base in England, and he proved a fascinating man. He told us of his exploits in the athletics world, his belief that the power men of rugby, especially the props, would eventually take anabolic steroids. Eventually we were ushered into the 'cage', a kind of warehouse full of Adidas products, for us to stock up on all manner of sports goods – T-shirts for the children as well as all sorts of training tops and footwear. It was like Aladdin's cave.

This meeting took place early in the 1975-76 season and England were due to play five internationals – the normal four in the International Championship, and one against the Australian tourists. Brightwell gave me £250 to cover these five games and, in return, I was to wear Adidas boots during the games. One rather famous figure from across the Severn had earlier left Poynton with a good deal more than £250 cramming his wallet, but a prop was a prop and hardly a glamorous position on which to waste Adidas money. Actually, apart from the benefits of the cash, it was no hardship to wear the goods because I always felt that they were top quality and by far the best in any case.

So although earlier in this chapter I bemoaned the fact that players are treated shabbily and that remuneration for their efforts is not forthcoming – they receive nothing from unions or clubs, and are unable to enter into promotional contracts – some players do get round the rules courtesy of sportswear firms, and I was most assuredly one.

More important, I can see absolutely nothing wrong with the principle of Adidas's dealings with the players, nor any earthly reason why individuals should not negotiate sponsorship and promotional contracts with anyone at all. Why should everything have to take place in secret, under the counter, outside the laws? My only complaint regarding the Adidas approach is that technically, at the going rate of £50 per match which applied to me, they could buy the whole England side for £750. Following this theory, if they bought up the French side for the same amount, they could have eighty minutes live coverage, eighty minutes of prime television time, during which their kit would be easily distinguished and associated with the top players: and all this for £1,500, a tiny, tiny fraction of what a similar time would cost as paid advertising.

I suggest, therefore, that rugby could stop selling itself short and let any player openly negotiate promotional deals. As hands and eyebrows shoot up in horror, I am going to explain how players should be able to cash in on all their efforts, and on all that talent, and still leave the nature of the game untouched.

Players like Barry John, Andy Ripley, David Duckham and Gareth Edwards would probably today be almost millionaires if they had been able to endorse products and companies. My system to allow them to do so would be based at their clubs and in the hands of a club commercial manager. Each large club would have its own commercial manager, who reports directly to the club committee, and he would be responsible for making the most of the club's assets and promoting the club's image. He would be marketing the club to the local community; he would make the most of all club facilities and not have large stadia and first-class leisure facilities lying idle for six days per week. The commercial manager would also help the club's most precious commodities, the players. He could help individual players secure sponsorships and endorsement opportunities with a range of national and local firms.

For example, since leading international players are becoming household names, to have the products of car firms, oil companies, and others, associated with them would be vastly advantageous – why should other sportsmen be able to cash in, and not rugby players?

Each commercial deal would be recorded on a standard RFU sponsorship form revealing the parties to the agreement, the terms and the length of the agreement, and a copy filed at the RFU headquarters. The RFU, meanwhile, would keep all the money they receive from existing sponsorships, television and advertising contracts, and direct the money elsewhere than to the major clubs – towards any of a score of worthy causes. In time, each first team squad player would, I hope, secure one of an array of possible commercial deals for himself. And before I am accused of neglecting the lot of the smaller clubs, whose players would not be so appealing to major firms, there is absolutely no reason why their own commercial manager should not help them negotiate local sponsorships. There are thousands of small community businesses which would benefit from identifying with players in that community – providing cash, or a car, or even pullovers or pork chops, or freezers or televisions, in return for various types of promotional work. The commercial manager, a paid employee of the club by the way, would therefore be attending to the needs of his club and his players and making sure that as many players as possible are rewarded. There will be many opportunities for players at all levels. Lastly, any club unable to afford a full-time manager could employ sports management companies on a part-time basis.

If you think that all these moves would be revolutionary, then how many people in the days of Jeff Butterfield and Clem Thomas would have predicted that the stands at Twickenham would be covered in advertising hoardings; that a cigarette company would pay thousands of pounds to sponsor a keenly-contested knock-out cup competition; that even in conservative Scotland rugby a drinks firm would be sponsoring official leagues? But the real merit of allowing players to negotiate promotional deals and sponsorships would be that there would be no effect on their approach to the game itself. There would be none of the win-at-all-costs attitude which could occur if straight payments were introduced with win bonuses. Admittedly players would be more appealing to potential sponsors if they were successful but their appeal would not change overnight with a few defeats.

Rugby should bow to the natural evolutionary process I have been talking about; should follow soccer, cricket and now athletics. Players should not be treated like children, but as the precious commodity that most of them at all levels undoubtedly are. There is a law about restraint of trade, and no one with a real grasp on the business world will deny that even in a recession there are plenty of firms – and plenty of pounds – waiting to go into sport. I feel sure that they could do this without the essential fabric of the game suffering.

Of course, there is a much more basic way in which players could be compensated for the occasions when rugby intrudes into their earnings. It is ludicrous that players who often help make vast sums for unions have to lose money themselves. Broken-time payments must come, by which rugby authorities compensate the player who misses out on a shift, or a week or even three months wages should he become a Lion. The responsibility to make up pay packets should be with whichever representative body stages the match for which the player sacrifices his time – the RFU should pay players suffering because of England squad sessions or matches, the county committees should look after players losing money due to county games or practices. Strict rules could be laid down to prevent abuse and to ensure each claim is genuine. Broken-time payments are overdue. People who ignore the sacrifices made by players, who fail to appreciate the sacrifices made by firms, who ignore the rising trend for people to miss important games and tours because the financial sacrifice is just too great to bear; those who believe players are there for the amusement of committees and spectators and that they tamely melt away after each game; those who pay only lip-service to the needs and the pressures of the modern player – they are all doing so at their peril.

In fact, English rugby would quickly become stronger should some types of payment be introduced and, more important, if the sort of commercial agreements I have mentioned come into being. The financial rewards available in union would probably kill off rugby league, which would leave a vast reservoir of talent, usually creamed off to the league game, left in the union game. Welsh observers may well claim that they suffer the most grievously from the attentions of rugby league scouts, but it is not true. Wales lose a small number of leading players in moves which are always highly publicised: and sometimes the players have given good service to the union game before they decide to go north. In England, talented players just disappear by the score into the league game, before they become well known – in league areas, they turn to the league game as naturally as they go to the pub, and the union game loses them for ever.

Yet if the destiny of English rugby would be changed by the arrival of financial rewards in union, consider the case in Australia. Add to their successful sides of the early 1980s the players who have turned to rugby league recently, and you have the world champions, or at least, enough good backs to fill each of the four home international sides. The breach over broken-time payments which brought rugby league into being in the first place will be healed by broken-time payments being introduced in rugby union – surely one of the ironies of rugby history.

The third means by which players should be allowed to cash in on their talents involves the writing of books. Recently, a number of great players have been ruled right out of rugby because they have told the story of their careers and pocketed the proceeds. This makes them dirty professionals in administrative eyes, and they are banned from playing, even coaching or selecting, in rugby union again. David Duckham, Phil Bennett, Ian McLauchlan, Gareth Edwards, Mervyn Davies and Barry John have all bowed out of the amateur world in this way and what an utter tragedy that has been. The combined rugby knowledge and experience of those players will now never be passed on, either to school learners or full internationals. Think of the contribution which David Duckham could have made to back play coaching for any side; the wealth of knowledge on propping which Ian McLauchlan could have brought to the Scottish squad. Imagine the contribution any of them could have made to the higher echelons of the game's administration, the fresh air and enlightened thought they could have provided in stuffy corridors of power. But they are outcasts, and irreplaceable outcasts too. I too have been banned for life for writing this book, and accepting payment for doing so.

Now I am not suggesting that things should go the way of the Andy Haden case, for example. He has recently been writing newspaper columns on games in which he actually played – and surely not for just a free subscription to the paper. And there *are* anomalies in the laws which seem to have allowed certain players to retain both the money and their amateur status. For the rest, the law which makes a rugby writer a professional should be first for the chop at the next International Board meeting. Rugby's brain drain is becoming a real torrent.

So I have put forward three ways in which rugby players can be compensated for their efforts and their losses; none of them represents outright professionalism as one understands the term in soccer or cricket. No pay packets, no win incentives, no increase in pressure. Just a recognition that rugby is changing and evolving, and, in some areas, booming. Those thirty people out on the field are the kings of the game and everyone had better start recognising the fact.

APPENDIX: CAREER DETAILS

INTERNATIONAL, COUNTY AND CLUB APPEARANCES

Matches for the British Lions (all on the 1974 tour to South Africa):

Eastern Province 14, British Lions 28 (Port Elizabeth)
South-West Districts 0, British Lions 97 (Mossel Bay)
Proteas 6, British Lions 37 (Cape Town)
Quaggas 16, British Lions 20 (Johannesburg)
Griqualand West 16, British Lions 69 (Kimberley)
South African Leopards 10, British Lions 56 (East London)
Border 6, British Lions 26 (East London)
Eastern Transvaal 10, British Lions 23 (Springs)

Matches for England:

1972
Wales 12, England 3 (Twickenham)
Ireland 16, England 12 (Twickenham)
Scotland 23, England 9 (Murrayfield)
France 37, England 12 (Paris)
South Africa 9, England 18 (Johannesburg)

1974
France 12, England 12 (Paris)
Wales 12, England 16 (Twickenham)

1975
Scotland 6, England 7 (Twickenham)
Australia 16, England 9 (Sydney)
Australia 30, England 21 (Brisbane)

1976
Australia 6, England 25 (Twickenham)
Wales 21, England 9 (Twickenham)
Scotland 22, England 12 (Murrayfield)
Ireland 13, England 12 (Twickenham)
France 30, England 9 (Paris)

1978
France 15, England 6 (Paris)
Wales 9, England 6 (Twickenham)

Matches for the Barbarians:

1972
Cardiff 10, Barbarians 10 (Cardiff)
Swansea 27, Barbarians 15 (Swansea)

1973
Llanelli 33, Barbarians 17 (Llanelli)
East Midlands 15, Barbarians 32 (Northampton)
Penarth 6, Barbarians 24 (Penarth)
Newport 15, Barbarians 60 (Newport)

1974
Leicester 7, Barbarians 16 (Leicester)

Appearances for Gloucestershire – 40
County Championship final results:

1974
Gloucestershire 22, Lancashire 12 (Blundellsands)

1975
Gloucestershire 13, Eastern Counties 9 (Gloucester)

1976
Gloucestershire 24, Middlesex 9 (Richmond)

1978
North Midlands 10, Gloucestershire 7 (Moseley)

Appearances for Gloucester – 360
Knock-out Cup finals

1972
Gloucester 17, Moseley 6 (Twickenham)

1978 (John Player Cup)
Gloucester 6, Leicester 3 (Twickenham)